Lou Fisher

MILITARY JUSTICE
IN VIETNAM

MILITARY JUSTICE
IN VIETNAM
THE RULE OF LAW
IN AN AMERICAN WAR

William Thomas Allison

 University Press of Kansas

Chapter 7 is based on William Allison, "War for Sale: The Black Market, Currency Manipulation, and Corruption in the American War in Vietnam," *War and Society* 21, 2 (October 2003): 135–164. Used by permission.

Published by the University Press of Kansas (Lawrence, Kansas 66045), which was organized by the Kansas Board of Regents and is operated and funded by Emporia State University, Fort Hays State University, Kansas State University, Pittsburg State University, the University of Kansas, and Wichita State University

Library of Congress Cataloging-in-Publication Data
Allison, William Thomas.
Military justice in Vietnam : the rule of law in an American war / William Thomas Allison.
    p.   cm. — (Modern war studies)
Includes bibliographical references and index.
ISBN 0-7006-1460-5 (cloth : alk. paper)
1. Courts-martial and courts of inquiry—United States— History—20th century. 2. Military law—United States— History—20th century. 3. Vietnam War, 1961–1975—Law and legislation—United States. I. Title.
KF7620.A949 2006
343.73'0143—dc22   2006026526

British Library Cataloguing-in-Publication Data is available.

Printed in the United States of America
10 9 8 7 6 5 4 3 2 1

The paper used in this publication meets the minimum requirements of the American National Standard for Permanence of Paper for Printed Library Materials Z39.48-1984.

FOR MOM AND DAD

CONTENTS

Preface

ix

List of Acronyms

xv

ONE

A New Code for a Different Kind of War

1

TWO

Lawyers in the Vanguard

21

THREE

Jurisdiction for U.S. Military and Civilian Personnel

in Vietnam

50

FOUR

Discipline, Military Crimes, and Courts-Martial

67

FIVE

Violations of the Laws of War

90

SIX

The Drug Problem

117

SEVEN

The Black Market, Currency Manipulation,

and Corruption

140

EIGHT

Still in the Vanguard

168

Notes
187
Bibliography
211
Index
221

PREFACE

The U.S. military justice experience in Vietnam is important for several reasons. It came at an important evolutionary period for the Uniform Code of Military Justice, which underwent major revision in 1968, the midpoint of U.S. involvement in Vietnam. The memory of this experience has been tainted by the terrible tragedy of My Lai and the publicly perceived failure of military justice to effectively deal with this worst of war crimes. As I will explore in this book, however, military justice in Vietnam was much more than My Lai and war crimes. Designed to maintain discipline and help make the military machine run efficiently and effectively, military justice directly affected much of what is ingrained in the popular imagination of the war—things such as fragging, corruption, and drug use. The U.S. military suffered a nearly complete breakdown in Vietnam for a variety of reasons. In a limited war, military justice ran into limitations brought about by the unconventional military, economic, and political conditions of Vietnam, conditions that undermined the U.S. effort in Southeast Asia. Military justice, however, helped keep the machine running through these difficult periods.

Military justice and military lawyers were part of the broader objectives of U.S. nation-building in Vietnam: to instill democratic ideals and capitalist values, including respect for the rule of law, in a country threatened by communism. As a result of its history, Vietnam had developed a system of justice heavily influenced by village tradition, Chinese law, and the French Napoleonic Code. Vietnamese villages tended to deal with disputes and other legal issues through local custom and tradition as interpreted by village elders rather than any sort of national legal precedents or decrees. Under Chinese rule, Vietnam absorbed Confucian concepts of law and ethics. In addition to solidifying strict social stratification in Vietnam, the Confucian influence brought what by Western standards would be considered rather loose ideas toward legal settlement, including resolution of conflict by negotiation and less-than-binding agreements. Under French rule, attempts at implementing Napoleonic criminal and civil codes while trying to preserve some level of local autonomy met with mixed results. The French colonial government tailored codes according to region (Annam, Tonkin, and so on) and still further according to the groups to whom the codes applied. The resulting legal system was inconsistent, if not contradictory, by U.S. standards. For the United States, rule of law and respect for due process and civil rights formed the heart of a democratic society. In trying to establish such a society in Vietnam, U.S. military justice became the vanguard of the effort to show the Vietnamese that a legal system based on the rule of law could work in their culture and certainly be preferable to the apparent looming alternative of communist rule, under which the rule of law and individual civil rights would certainly suffer.[1]

According to prevailing Western counterinsurgency concepts espoused by academics and military thinkers of the early 1960s, an indigenous government facing insurgency "ought" to do three things: provide good government, provide security for its populace, and provide an atmosphere conducive to economic and material gain based upon the precepts of capitalism and respect for the rule of law, all to win the "hearts and minds" of the people. These "oughts" placed government administration at the very center of counterinsurgency success. In South Vietnam, a consistently corrupt and morally bankrupt government struggled to provide what the United States deemed "good government": effective administration, free from corruption, that could establish respect for the rule of law and make economic opportunity available to the broadest possible range of citizenry. In essence, bad governments promote support for insurgency; thus bad governments must become good governments to effectively combat insurgency. Establishing "good government" was the seminal struggle for the United States in its support of the South Vietnamese government, which never proved itself to be a legitimate client state. U.S. military justice was an essential component of this endeavor.[2]

Military justice is a part of the U.S. experience in Vietnam that is often overlooked but is an important aspect of the war. It was in many ways very successful and in other ways a miserable failure. The U.S. legal presence in Vietnam was widespread, touching several facets of the war, including discipline, drugs, the black market, claims for damages, and crimes and offenses committed against Vietnamese noncombatants. It also touched larger issues, such as diplomacy, politics, and economics. On both levels, U.S. military justice represented a point of almost daily contact with the Vietnamese people. In a war that has been portrayed repeatedly as a clash of cultures and characterized by the nearly catastrophic collapse of military and social structure, the U.S. legal experience provides an unusual window to shed light on what happened in Vietnam and perhaps offer some guidance for contemporary military operations and nation-building missions.

U.S. nation-building objectives in Vietnam, changes in military justice, and the nature and evolution of the war itself influenced U.S. military legal affairs in Vietnam and vice versa. My primary purpose is to explain the variety of military legal activities in Vietnam, evaluate them, and share the human side of those activities, all in the context of the war itself. The broader purpose is to expose readers to the complicated nature of military law and military justice in a democratic society as well as to show how difficult it is to include military justice and legal affairs in the vanguard of nation-building operations that include spreading U.S. values as a political objective. The role of military justice in democracy and in nation-building is an issue that haunts the U.S. public to some degree as nation-building continues in Iraq. It is hoped that recent work, this book included, on military justice in Vietnam will spur more research into this important area. The history of military justice needs to find its way into the broader mainstream of military history and legal studies, even social history. I hope that this book will contribute to that goal.

The broad conclusion is that U.S. military legal affairs in Vietnam had uneven success. Military justice may not have completely achieved its primary purpose, but the *practice* of military justice in this unique conflict proved adaptable and successful. Attempts to show the South Vietnamese the great benefits of the rule of law generally *failed* despite attempts to fight corruption and expose the Vietnamese people to Western-style rule of law. The claims and solatia program, run by military lawyers, was in part intended to show to the Vietnamese people the benevolent benefit of democracy and rule of law, but the program had mixed results. War crimes, atrocities, fragging, drugs, and so on provide excellent lenses through which to evaluate the purpose, practice, and impact of military justice and legal affairs in relation to the U.S. military effort as well as nation-building programs in Vietnam.

The book is organized to examine the U.S. military justice experience topically. First, a brief overview of the history of military justice in the United States up to the Vietnam War provides context and describes how military justice has struggled to coexist with a democratic society that values due process and dislikes arbitrary judgment. Next is a discussion of what it was like to be a lawyer in Vietnam, factors influencing military justice, and the role of military lawyers in nation-building through the claims and solatia program. Then follows a chapter on jurisdiction issues in Vietnam, a patently legal issue but also one that involved diplomacy and bureaucracy in the fragile political atmosphere of South Vietnam. With this background in hand, chapters follow on specific topics, such as disciplinary offenses, war crimes, illegal drugs, the black market, and currency manipulation. In each of these chapters, context and cases provide the framework for examining how the military justice system functioned both as a judicial system and also as part of broader issues stemming from the overall U.S. experience in Vietnam. The book concludes with a chapter on subsequent alterations to the military justice system, which continues to evolve, and the role of military lawyers in combat operations since Vietnam. Military justice and military lawyers are both still in the vanguard.

My interest in the U.S. military justice experience in Vietnam and the lawyers who administered it is in part historical. As a historian, I find the U.S. legal experience in Vietnam to be an intriguing story with some lessons to impart. In order to understand our experience in Vietnam, we must examine all aspects of the conflict. We can learn a great deal from history, all kinds of history. This subject is no different, and each reader will take away different things as lessons learned. As the insurgency against the U.S. occupation of Iraq continues and the U.S. public learns about prisoner abuse, unauthorized killings, corruption, and other unpleasant aspects of the darker and often misunderstood side of war, it is fitting and useful to reexamine similar conflicts. Vietnam, arguably, is one such conflict. Nation-building is an extremely difficult and halting task, as we learned in Vietnam and are learning again in Iraq and Afghanistan.

The other part of my interest is personal. My father served in Vietnam as a Marine Corps lawyer in 1968 and 1969. I was only two years old at the time and have no recollection of those years. I wish I did. I do not even remember when he returned home, when my mother, our poodle Mary Poppins, and I went to pick him up at the airport. Apparently, I hid behind my mother's skirts, somewhat frightened of the unfamiliar uniformed man. The dog, however, recalled its master fondly and immediately ran to greet him. It has only been since my years in graduate school at Bowling Green State University that my father and I have talked about Vietnam and his experience there. My being a historian and teaching a course on Vietnam helped, but I think most of our conversations arose from the simple fact that the time was right for him to talk and for me to appreciate his experience.

Like many lawyers who served in Vietnam, my father entered officer candidate school in the Marine Corps fresh out of law school from the University of Texas. After completing the military law course at the Naval Justice School at Newport, Rhode Island, he went to Vietnam in August 1968. Assigned at first to legal duties with the Third Marine Division in Quang Tri province, he soon found himself serving as executive officer for I Company, Third Battalion, Third Regiment of the Third Marine Division near the demilitarized zone. When the need for junior officers in the field arose after the Tet Offensive, my father—who, like all marines had been trained first and foremost as a rifleman—had to put aside his law books to do the marine's chief job. After a few months of combat operations near the fabled Rockpile, he was promoted to captain and advanced to company commander. As replacement officers began to fill the void from Tet, he was then pulled from the line and returned to legal duties.

He handled cases ranging from illegal drug use to murder and also processed and investigated claims. One rape case that stands out in his memory involved a young Vietnamese woman from a rural hamlet. It took some time to locate a witness, another young Vietnamese woman. When finally found, she could not identify the attacker in a lineup because to her all Americans looked alike. Such a comment from a Vietnamese is ironic considering the stereotype that U.S. forces thought all Vietnamese looked alike.

From his experience practicing military law in a combat zone, my father brought home a sense of confidence and thorough preparation for civilian practice. In Vietnam, a lawyer learned patience and pragmatism, two characteristics that have made my father, like so many others who cut their legal teeth in Vietnam, a successful civilian attorney.

Many institutions and people provided invaluable help, advice, and criticism for this project. I am a historian, not a lawyer, and colleagues in both professions helped tremendously. The fine staffs at the service historical branches, especially Lt. Col. Gary D. Solis (United States Marine Corps, retired) of the Marine Corps Historical Center and also of the Department of Law at the United States Military Academy at West Point and Archie Difante of the Air Force Historical Research Agency, were professional, helpful, and encouraging. Gary also graciously gave me access to his research files for the official Marine Corps history on military law in Vietnam, which have recently been deposited in the National Archives at College Park, Maryland. His comments on the manuscript were most constructive, helpful, and enlightening. Bob Boylan, military archive specialist at the National Archives at College Park, Maryland, pointed to invaluable documents, organized and less so. Many colleagues provided advice, criticism, and encouragement through conversation or reading parts of the manuscript, including: Professor Darrel Phillips, chief of international law at the Air Force Judge Advocate General School; Professor Gary R. Hess of Bowling Green State University; Professor Marc Jason Gilbert of

North Georgia College and State University; Ed Rodriguez of the Air Force Judge Advocate General Association; Jeffrey Grey of the Australian Defence Force Academy; Professor Thomas A. Hughes of the United States Air Force School for Advanced Air and Space Studies; Col. Gordon Hammock, United States Air Force Judge Advocate General's Corps; and Professor Oliver Griffin of Saint John Fisher College. Professor William G. Eckhardt, currently of the University of Missouri–Kansas School of Law and in 1970 and 1971 chief prosecutor in the My Lai cases at Fort McPherson; Professor Robert Buzzanco of the University of Houston; Professor Michal Belknap of the California Western School of Law; and Brig. Gen. Anthony E. Hartle (United States Army, retired) of the faculty of the United States Military Academy offered methodical comments and helpful suggestions on the entire manuscript.

As a visiting professor in the Department of Strategy and International Security at the United States Air Force Air War College in 2002 and 2003, I was assisted immensely by the library staff, in particular the interlibrary loan office, and was given time and encouragement to research and write. The faculty at the Air War College provided a wealth of knowledge, advice, and encouragement. My colleagues in the history department at Weber State University were, as always, a fount of encouragement.

Michael Briggs and the fine staff at the University Press of Kansas are professional, timely, and—most important—a pleasure to work with. Michael provided encouragement, criticism, and praise, all in appropriate doses and with marvelous timing.

Family, of course, offers the most encouragement yet sacrifices more with a historian among the brood. My sisters, Beth and Amy, and their wonderful families always ask, "How's it going?" and patiently listen to the often lengthy response. My wife, Jennifer, made sure I spent time writing rather than skiing, a most difficult of duties worthy of spouses spanning the ages. I could not do this without her. My parents, Kay and Tommy, never stopped believing in their son. To them, I am always and forever thankful.

—*William Thomas Allison*

ACRONYMS

AIDS	acquired immunodeficiency syndrome
ARVN	Army of the Republic of Vietnam
AWOL	absent without leave
CBS	Columbia Broadcasting System
CD-ROM	compact disk–read-only memory
CIA	Central Intelligence Agency
CID	Criminal Investigation Division
CIP	Commercial Import Program
DMZ	demilitarized zone
GED	general equivalency diploma
HQUSARI	Headquarters, U.S. Army Ryukyu Islands
IAC	Irregular Activities Committee
KP	kitchen patrol
LMDC	Lawyers' Military Defense Committee
LSD	lysergic acid diethylamide
MACV	Military Assistance Command, Vietnam
MPC	military payment certificate
NATO	North Atlantic Treaty Organization
NAVFORV	United States Naval Forces, Republic of Vietnam
NCO	noncommissioned officer
NLF	National Liberation Front
NVA	North Vietnamese Army
OSS	Office of Strategic Services
PX	Post Exchange
R and R	rest and relaxation
SJA	Staff Judge Advocate
III MAF	(III Marine Amphibious Force)
UPI	United Press International
USAID	U.S. Agency for International Development
USARV	United States Army, Republic of Vietnam
USASCV	United States Army Support Command, Vietnam
USOs	United Service Organizations
VC/NVA	Viet Cong/North Vietnamese Army

MILITARY JUSTICE
IN VIETNAM

CHAPTER ONE
A NEW CODE FOR A
DIFFERENT KIND OF WAR

By its very nature, the United States has had an interesting military justice history, characterized by reconciling military justice, with its goal of maintaining order and discipline, and civilian justice, which has a different purpose in a democratic society. The traditional and indeed popular concept of military justice—of a system that relies upon stern discipline at the expense of due process—is very much at odds with U.S. democratic judicial processes. U.S. military justice, which began as a traditional system copied from British articles of war, evolved into a codified structure that maintained the basic purposes of military justice while respecting individual rights. Still, the role of military justice in a democracy, which continues to develop, has been fraught with challenges.

The first military codes written in the United States came during the Revolutionary War. It should come as no surprise that the articles of war in the former British colonies were heavily influenced by George III's "Rules and Articles for the better Government of Our Horse and Foot Guards, and all other Forces in Our kingdoms of Great Britain, Ireland, Dominions beyond the Seas, and Foreign Parts," which went into effect in 1765.[1] With the outbreak of hostilities at Lexington and Concord in the spring of 1775, the Massachusetts assembly adopted articles of war for the state militia. For the most part these articles were copied directly from the British "Rules and Articles," and like them the Massachusetts articles of war were harsh and arbitrary but effective. Even more so than the king's army, colonial militias needed the strict discipline and order that the Massachusetts articles of war provided. Soldiers' rights and review of convictions basically did not exist.[2]

The Continental Congress adopted Articles of War for the new Continental army in June 1775, again using the British articles as the model. At the suggestion of Gen. George Washington and under the guidance of the keen legal mind of John Adams and the populist leanings of Thomas Jefferson, the Continental Congress addressed the review question in 1776, allowing for command review of court-martial convictions. Review could go either way—punishments could be commuted or made more severe. Still, military law in the young nation continued to follow precedents set by the mother country. Adams was also instrumental in creating the first "Rules for the Regulation of the Navy of the United Colonies of North America," which the Continental

Congress adopted in November 1775. The Continental Congress relied heavily upon the British Royal Navy's version and retained the traditional clause that "all other offenses" should be punishable by the "laws and customs of the sea."[3] It is significant that the Continental Congress established courts-martial several years before it created the federal judiciary, thus setting the precedent for involving the legislative branch in military justice reform.[4]

At this early point in the development of the United States, it is interesting to note the contribution of Washington, Adams, and Jefferson, three of the more revered revolutionary era patriots, in creating a judicial system based not on fairness or even justice but rather on harsh discipline and arbitrariness. Considering their position as leaders in the Revolution, however, their conservatism on military justice makes sense: victory depended upon military success, and military success depended partly upon discipline. Defeat would cost them their fortunes, if not their lives. Sacrificing due process for a well-disciplined army was not too high a price to pay.[5]

After the Revolutionary War, Congress substantially revised the military justice system. Enacted in 1786, this revision represented the first serious break from British tradition. In the new Articles of War, any officer could be appointed as a judge advocate, although a judge advocate was not necessary to try courts-martial. Commanders could now appoint courts of inquiry to investigate charges, much like a grand jury. Unlike a civilian grand jury, however, in the military inquiry the accused could question witnesses and view evidence. Legal historian Jonathan Lurie noted that this practice made military due process much more liberal than its contemporary civilian counterpart, and this before the Constitutional Convention had even met.

To be sure, Congress and the military held firm in the belief that military justice should be treated separately from civilian jurisprudence. The 1806 revision, for example, included strengthened articles against officers who used "traitorous or disrespectful words" against the United States, Congress, and most certainly the president as commander in chief. Arguments against these articles claimed that these were emotional sentiments still lingering from the Alien and Sedition Acts of 1798, which allowed for the deportation of any foreigner suspected of subversive activities and made illegal any severe criticism of Congress or the president. Should U.S. soldiers be held to a standard different from that for the civilian citizens of the new country? Congress thought so, as did President Jefferson. That Jefferson agreed to limit freedom of speech in the military shows the degree of separation between the military and civilian systems. Moreover, there was still no firm review process in the military justice system. [6]

The navy Rules underwent revision in 1800. As with the Articles of War, the new navy Rules, called "Articles for the Government of the Navy," basically copied the 1775 version and its British counterpart. Conduct of courts-martial remained vague, inconsistent, and open to abuse. Congress established two courts: a court of inquiry to establish fact and the traditional general court-martial to administer discipline on officers. The "captain's mast," punishments meted out at the discretion of a ship's commander, continued to be the disciplinary tool of choice for enlisted sailors. The role of judge advocates remained unclear for the most part, although the revision specified such duties as giving oaths and recording court proceedings.[7]

Although the Articles of War remained remarkably unchanged until the Civil War, the Navy Department fought a lengthy battle with Congress to revise and update the navy regulations during the 1840s and 1850s. The Navy Department offered detailed instructions for the conduct of courts-martial and a qualified right for the accused to be represented by counsel in a proposed revision of the navy Rules in 1841. Before the revision could leave the House Committee on Naval Affairs, Secretary of the Navy Abel Upshur withdrew the proposed regulations because of lack of civilian input into the revisions. He created a committee, which included civilian lawyers familiar with naval law, to reexamine the revisions. Upshur additionally wanted to have all navy courts-martial held in Washington, D.C., which would have caused a logistical nightmare for an ocean-going navy, to say the least. Opposition to the 1841 revisions from navy traditionalists and other officers kept Upshur from getting the package through Congress before he left office in 1843.

The revisions stayed on the table but failed to get through Congress for the rest of the decade. In 1850, Congress, in a separate act, outlawed the use of flogging as a disciplinary punishment.[8] Without the traditional punishment of the captain's mast, sea commanders suddenly lost their principal method of maintaining and enforcing discipline on their vessels. Complaints that discipline and order were breaking down caused President Millard Fillmore to issue an executive order establishing a set of naval articles, titled "Orders and Instructions for the Direction and Government of the Naval Service of the United States," in 1853. Written by a board of junior officers by authority of Secretary of the Navy George Bancroft, these Orders adopted much of the proposed 1841 revisions. Nonetheless, because the 1853 Orders were issued by authority of the president and not through Congress, the Justice Department ruled that they were invalid, once again leaving the navy with outdated naval regulations.

Congress finally came through in 1855, passing updated naval regulations but ignoring many of the 1841 proposals. As discipline problems and desertions increased, Congress could delay no more. The 1853 version did create a summary court-martial, similar to the modern special court-martial, with a range of punishments, including dishonorable discharge. Disciplinary regulations, however, remained consistent with the old 1800 rules, and meaningful review of courts-martial had yet to be addressed. Although outlined in the 1855 regulations, procedures and punishments remained governed by custom rather than law, as enforcing the new regulations on ships spread across the world proved nearly impossible.[9]

The Civil War gave Congress cause to again return to the navy regulations and modernize what still mainly resembled the old 1800 rules. The 1862 revision was Congress's best effort up to that time. In response to disputes arising from the capture of Confederate contraband vessels, the 1862 revision included improved prize procedures. Still, court-martial guidelines remained hazy, as did the duties of navy judge advocates. References to "customs of the sea" were removed, and the accused now had the right of representation at courts of inquiry and could also cross-examine witnesses at inquiries.[10]

Despite their vague status in navy regulations, naval judge advocates during this period wore many pragmatic hats. They recorded court proceedings, gave oaths, arraigned the accused, interrogated witnesses, advised courts on form and law, and simultaneously both prosecuted and tried to act as watchdogs for the few rights of the accused. The Civil War had also brought more civilian lawyers into naval service. As had been navy tradition, many judge advocates were civilian lawyers who also advised the Navy Department on other legal matters, such as contract disputes, prizes, and procurement irregularities, in addition to trying cases. In response to this increased need for legal specialists in the navy, Congress approved the creation of the navy judge advocate general's office in March 1865. Unlike the army, the navy at least let some civilian legal experience through the door, or rather the hatch.[11]

The notion of keeping military and civilian judicial systems separate held for the rest of the nineteenth century and through World War I. In fact, the tradition of holding military justice to a different standard became more entrenched as the decades passed. During the Civil War, the duties of the army judge advocate division increased to include giving advice on "national safety," enforcing laws and the Constitution, dealing with state prisoners, and assisting provost marshals in police duties. Each unit in the field now had a judge advocate officer. These were significant steps forward in the structural organization and scope of military justice activities.[12]

In 1874, the 1806 Articles of War were recodified.[13] For a small, professional, volunteer force, the old system seemed to work. In 1879, Gen. William Tecumseh Sherman testified before Congress that military and civilian judicial systems were as "wide apart as the poles" and should remain separate. Sherman believed that injecting civilian judicial ideas and practices would only weaken the system and hamper the military's ability to carry out its duties as charged by the president and Congress. He explained the difference between civilian and military law: "The object of civil law is to secure to every human being in a community all the liberty, security, and happiness possible, consistent with the safety of all. The object of military law is to govern armies composed of strong men, so as to be capable of exercising the largest measure of force at the will of the nation."[14]

The experience of the U.S. military in World War I began the rather dramatic change in attitudes such as Sherman's. In this time of progressive reform and professionalization, the seeds for civilizing military justice were at last sown in fertile ground. One of the most substantial revisions of the Articles of War occurred during and after the war. The 1916 revision, resulting in 121 codified articles, represented an important joint army-congressional effort to modernize and professionalize military law. For citizen soldiers, the revised code stepped into the realm of civilian jurisprudence. Common law felonies became military offenses, regardless of wartime or peacetime. Jurisdiction of civilian offenses committed during peacetime was turned over to civilian authorities through formal procedures. Murder and rape committed by soldiers in the continental United States would not be tried by court-martial but rather by civilian courts.

The 1916 code also formalized what are now the three categories of courts-martial: general, special, and summary. Previously there had been only general and summary courts-martial. General courts-martial dealt with serious crimes and breaches of discipline that could result in lengthy confinement, dishonorable discharge, or execution. Summary courts-martial usually handled minor infractions resulting in light punishment but not discharge. Special courts-martial were meant to fill the void between general and summary trials—for instance, special courts-martial could pass harsher punishments than summary courts but could not grant dishonorable discharges as general courts-martial could. Capital offenses were limited to wartime, except for sedition, rape, and assault and disobedience toward a superior officer. Also, as part of the 1916 re-visions, the accused could be represented in trial by counsel of his own choos-ing, as opposed to counsel being assigned by the convening commander. These new codified articles were published in the first functional *Manual for Courts-Martial* in 1916, theoretically making military justice consistent across army commands.[15] The manual specifically prohibited outdated punishments, such as wearing leg irons and being forced to march with overloaded packs. The 1916 *Manual* faced its test in combat as the Yanks headed "over there" to France in 1917.[16]

The navy followed a similar path to World War I. The navy judge advocate general's office produced a manual for courts-martial, investigations, and boards in 1896.[17] Although earlier versions had appeared since the Civil War, this was the most ambitious attempt to provide a precise judicial guide for line officers. The 1896 revision of navy regulations expanded the duties of the judge advocate general, charging him with reviewing contracts, patents, land sales and purchases, even advertisements, in addition to overseeing courts-martial and other disciplinary matters. In 1909, the navy judge advocate general's office began requiring its officers to have legal training. Many at-tended law school through the navy's law postgraduate program. The navy hoped that by sending these officers to law school, the judge advocate general's office would be more professional, following the trend of professionalization in the early-twentieth-century United States, and more legally proficient than the navy solicitor general's office (which in 1921 was deemed redundant and abolished), which had been staffed by civilian lawyers. The judge advocate general's office struggled during this period to gain control of civil legal affairs in addition to military legal matters involving the navy. Some reformers advo-cated establishing a permanent navy Judge Advocate General's Corps.[18]

The entry of the United States into World War I and the subsequent expan-sion of the armed forces brought more civilians and civilian lawyers into ser-vice. The army Judge Advocate General Department increased from seventeen to 436 officers in just eight months in 1917. Among the civilian advocates now in uniform were future secretary of war Henry L. Stimson and future Supreme Court justice Felix Frankfurter. These "realist" lawyers from Northeastern law schools brought to the military their civilian experience and progressive atti-tudes toward the administration of justice. Their impact was soon felt.[19]

With the war, too, came an expanded role for military lawyers. As in the Civil War, military lawyers found themselves dealing with more than enforcing the Articles of War. Industrialized warfare and mobilization required legal counsel on contracts, claims, patents, and other issues. Much as they had advised their civilian clients, lawyers in uniform now advised soldiers on personal legal matters, such as divorce, finances, and wills. Moreover, these lawyers had a major impact on the system itself. As civilian lawyers in uniform, they noticed the lack of due process, the continued arbitrariness, and the absence in many circumstances of constitutional rights that were guaranteed to U.S. citizens but not U.S. soldiers.

The soldiers noticed as well. As volunteers and draftees, these citizen soldiers knew their legal rights as U.S. citizens but suddenly found those rights stripped away as soldiers. The great dilemma of military justice in a constitutional democracy finally hit home: How could military justice in a democracy represent the rights of that democracy while it ignored those rights in the name of order and discipline so that the military could defend democracy?

In World War I, 88 percent of army trials resulted in conviction; the fact that nearly 75 percent of sentences were later reduced by convening authority showed that they were excessive. Even though a table of maximum punishments now existed, the range of sentence for the same offense was extreme. With a shortage of qualified defense counsel, accused were often left with inadequate representation.[20] Civilian influence and disenchanted soldiers combined with two high-profile incidents—the Fort Bliss "mutiny" and the Fort Sam Houston race riot—to bring the shortcomings of military justice to public light. At Fort Bliss, a group of noncommissioned officers under arrest for minor infractions refused to attend drill as ordered because they were under arrest. The commanding officer charged them with mutiny under the Articles of War. The entire group was dishonorably discharged and sentenced from ten to twenty years imprisonment. At Fort Sam Houston, black soldiers rioted against discriminatory treatment by local townspeople, destroying property and killing or injuring several people. Subsequent courts-martial sentenced thirteen of the black soldiers to be executed. Because of the vague review process, no higher authority was able to review the sentences before the executions were carried out. The cry went out to reform the system and make it more akin to its civilian counterpart. The American Bar Association, among other groups, concluded that military justice was indeed grotesquely inadequate and ill suited for a democratic society that valued due process and civil rights.[21]

The call for reform came from within the military as well. The acting judge advocate general of the army, Gen. Samuel Tilden Ansell, led the charge. Ansell set out to reverse the traditional attitude, such as that held by Sherman in

1879, toward military justice. The disparity between the military justice system and U.S. ideals of justice, Ansell argued, jeopardized the effectiveness of the nation's armed forces. Hoping to change the U.S. public's perception, he openly called for a revolution in military justice. Ansell's plan for reform would truly civilianize the military justice system. He wanted to specifically codify crimes with clear definitions and exact maximum punishments. Ansell proposed that independent military judges and courts chosen by judges, not commanders, would try courts-martial, thus lessening the convening authority of commanders and overcoming the serious problem of command influence, in which a commander could arrange for the verdict that suited his command needs. For these courts, Ansell wanted members selected in part from the same rank as that of the accused. He further proposed binding pretrial investigations and real legal representation for the accused—a legally certified attorney of the accused's own choosing.

Each of these reforms would have helped the military justice system conform more closely to civilian courts. Courts-martial would have become courts in the commonly accepted sense of the term. Ansell's reforms would have alleviated much of the tradition of separation between the military and civilian justice systems. His biggest wish, though, was an independent civilian court of military appeals. Such a court would assuredly make military justice more palatable for its "citizen soldiers."[22]

Gen. Enoch Crowder, the provost marshal, who had been judge advocate general before Ansell, vehemently disagreed with Ansell's radical proposals. An army traditionalist resistant to change, Crowder claimed that Ansell's plan, if enacted, would destroy military discipline and the military's purpose. The congressional hearings that followed fueled what came to be known as the "Ansell-Crowder dispute." Crowder took issue with Ansell's suggestion that military justice was too far removed from the civilian judicial mainstream. Moreover, suggested Crowder, giving more rights to soldiers was not consistent with military discipline. In Crowder's view, taking away command control and allowing an appeals process attacked the very nature of military order.

Ansell enlisted the help of progressive senator George Chamberlain of Oregon to get his reforms through Congress. Early in the hearings, public attention to military justice reform was as high as it had ever been. But the hearings dragged on, and with the war over for several months and attention now directed toward the treaty fight, public support and attention faded. The military and the war had exhausted the public's patience. Ansell's testimony grew more desperate as congressional enthusiasm followed the public's lead. He resigned his commission in frustration, hoping he could speak more freely and critically without insignia. But it was not enough. By late 1919, Ansell's reform movement had run out of steam. Nonetheless, it had been the best effort yet to bring the military justice system more in line with U.S. judicial practice. Ansell's reforms died in committee, but not in principal.[23]

A "revision," if it could be called that, did come to pass in 1920, although it in no way resembled Ansell's original proposals. The 1920 revision addressed procedural issues to some degree but left command influence intact and did not include Ansell's dream of an independent civilian court of military appeals. Judge advocates could review courts-martial, but commanders were not obligated to follow their advice. The most significant revision was the creation of a three-member board of review appointed by the judge advocate general. Made up of officers, the board could review only those sentences requiring presidential approval. The board's review would be sent to the judge advocate general, who would then add his comments and forward the case to the president for final action.[24]

The navy escaped such a tumultuous conflict over its administration of naval justice. Its Articles for the Government of the Navy, passed by Congress in 1916, broadened the convening authority for courts-martial, especially in time of war. Marine Corps commanders were even given the power to convene trials. For the first time, the navy judge advocate general's office would review all courts-martial for legal accuracy. Anticipation of entering the Great War motivated the change in order to make naval justice a bit more efficient once hostilities commenced. The expansion of convening authority showed during the war. In 1917, 17,768 cases were tried, equaling 18.60 percent of total navy and Marine Corps enlistment. The next year brought 34,853 trials, representing 8.45 percent of total enlistment. The number of cases tried in the following two years increased even more, with 46,639 in 1919 (10.43 percent) and 41,259 (24.64 percent) in 1920. The subsequent high number of court-martial reviews strained the resources of the navy judge advocate general's office. Navy judge advocate general George Ramsay Clark recommended in future assigning each court-martial to an officer "trained in the law," to make sure trials were conducted properly, thus cutting down the number of substantive reviews. Inconsistency in procedures and varying quality of prosecution and defense counsel also made review burdensome. In response, Clark recommended establishing a Judge Advocate General Corps for the navy. His proposal failed in Congress in 1920.[25]

Part of the reason the navy did not experience such a critical public outcry against wartime justice may have involved the navy's reluctance to upset established customs and social patterns of civilians coming into naval service, compared to the situation in the army. The navy had no Ansell-Crowder dispute, and the reason may have been as simple as the naval custom of keeping social classes separate. Unlike the army, which selected officers based on merit during wartime, the navy relied upon college graduates to fill out its officer corps. Whereas in the army enlisted men represented a mixed bag of social and economic class, the navy maintained a degree of separation. In other words, in the navy, those who most likely experienced court-martial were the ones who most likely had experienced civilian justice. They were accustomed to wrongdoing and subsequent punishment. In the army, the friction, malcontent, and grumbling, partially caused by class conflict within the ranks, exposed a larger range of people to military justice, thus the bitter complaints against the army system after the war. For the navy little change came from World War I, and much remained the same up to World War II.[26]

Throughout this turbulent period, the scope of judge advocate duties continued to expand. As the war ended and the military returned to peacetime duty, discipline problems and public attention to the Articles of War subsided. Still, other legal issues required attention: issuing and carrying out contracts, giving legal advice to the secretary of war on financial and property matters, and processing claims by soldiers, civilians, and businesses. Patents from military research and development fell under the purview of military legal affairs.[27]

World War II increased the scope of these legal duties to an unprecedented scale in U.S. military history, and the issues and reforms supported by Ansell and citizen soldiers returned with a vengeance. With over 16 million Americans serving from 1941 to 1945, military justice and judge advocates of the army and navy were spread thin and in high demand. In addition to dealing with claims, contracts, international law issues, prisoner of war conventions, and the legal needs of soldiers, the army tried over 1.7 million courts-martial of all varieties. One hundred members of the armed forces were executed by court-martial sentencing, and another 45,000 were in prison at the end of the war. Eighty percent of the convictions were for crimes unique to the military, such as absence without leave and desertion. Between the two services, an average of sixty court-martial convictions of the highest military court took place each day, and for all types of military courts there were over 2 million convictions.[28] Some of these same sailors and troops who were on the receiving end of military justice during the war returned home to write their members of Congress, urging reform.

The War Department responded. In March 1946, after receiving reports critical of military justice during the war from the American Bar Association and veterans groups, the War Department created the Advisory Committee on Military Justice. Chaired by Arthur T. Vanderbilt, dean of New York University Law School and later chief justice of the New Jersey Supreme Court, this committee of fifteen military and civilian lawyers held regional hearings across the country, hearing testimony from hundreds of veterans, legal advocacy groups, and active-duty service members, then submitted a 400-page report in December 1947. Not surprisingly, the Vanderbilt committee's report concluded that there had been a breakdown of military justice during the war. Two major problems hurt the system. First, command control continued to influence verdicts and investigations, and courts-martial did not follow the guidelines in the *Manual for Courts-Martial*. Second, inconsistent and excessive sentencing remained a critical problem. In many incidents, the convening authority revised the sentence to get across the point that discipline had been enforced while being able to show some latitude in punishment. In other words, the system remained fixed to suit the needs of the commander, which proponents claimed was the primary purpose of military justice in the first place. Court-martial members were not independent of command influence and often received administrative punishments for daring to exercise their own judgment. The committee also found that officers who were "volunteered" as defense counsels had neither the experience nor the knowledge to adequately defend accused and that pretrial investigations were often disorganized and sometimes even rigged. These criticisms all too closely mirrored Ansell's concerns from the previous war.[29]

The navy had its fair share of criticism as well. Among several reports on naval justice during the war, two stand out. The Ballantine Report, prepared by the committee chaired by Arthur Ballantine, a former undersecretary of the Treasury, concluded that judge advocates in the navy had little training in the law and that even less effort was made to provide it. Although the navy "required" its judge advocates to be trained in law and to advise courts on matters of law and procedure, they also often simultaneously acted as prosecutors, thus creating a crippling ethical conflict in navy court procedure. The report also noted sentence rigging similar to that that had plagued the army. Command influence and lack of independence of navy judge advocates from command gravely undermined justice. The report further found that the navy often penalized lawyers in promotion and assignments.[30]

In 1945, the McGuire committee report, named for the committee chaired by Matthew F. McGuire, a federal judge in the District of Columbia and member of the Ballantine committee, found even harsher criticisms of naval justice. The McGuire committee concluded that naval justice was based upon archaic traditions and blatantly ignored sailors' rights. Reiterating the Ballantine committee's findings, the McGuire committee criticized the predominant use of naval judge advocates as line officers rather than legal officers. As such, legal duties for navy judge advocates tended to be incidental to their purpose. The McGuire committee also heavily criticized command influence, which still littered the system with inconsistency, arbitrariness, and other abuses.[31]

Both the Ballantine and McGuire committees recommended a radical and sweeping overhaul of the system. The McGuire committee suggested a complete revision of the Articles for the Government of the Navy. It wanted to reduce the number of articles from seventy to eleven, require courts-martial to adhere to the "law of evidence" used by federal courts, and establish a review board made up of at least one civilian. The Ballantine committee proposed increasing the punishment authority of summary courts-martial, since general courts-martial dealt with too broad a range of offenses. It also recommended that the articles remain intact save for a few minor changes. Both committees urged the establishment of a real, independent Judge Advocate General Corps whose only duty would be that of military justice and legal issues. This would be the only way naval justice could avoid command influence and maintain more than a thin appearance of rights for accused.[32]

Not surprisingly, these critical reports drew a heated reaction from both the army and navy. Fearful that reforms might take away commanders' ability to enforce discipline among their own troops, army and navy senior officers tried to preserve their traditions of justice. Congress, however, moved forward. Talk along the halls of the Capitol discussed unifying the armed forces. Hearings by the new House and Senate Armed Forces Committees, which had replaced separate Army and Navy Committees, threatened to establish an independent air force and reorganize the War Department. The more the committees delved into the military justice issue, the more they became convinced that the only viable alternative to reforming each code was to establish a unified code equally applicable to all branches of the armed forces.

Before reaching uniformity, however, Congress, sensing that bringing the army and navy judicial systems together would be a Herculean task, passed a revision of the Articles of War in 1948 and also established for the army a Judge Advocate General's Corps, replacing the old Judge Advocate General Department. The 1948 revision allowed enlisted personnel to sit as members of general and special courts-martial of an accused enlisted person if requested by the accused. A qualified lawyer was now required to be one of the members for general courts-martial, and if the trial judge advocate in general courts-martial was a lawyer, the defense counsel also had to be a lawyer. Accused could request representation at pretrial investigations, and command coercion of trial members was specifically forbidden.[33]

By the time Congress got to the navy, the tide had definitely changed toward a uniform code as opposed to revising the navy articles. The navy did establish a separate cadre of "law specialist officers," many of whom would serve in the navy judge advocate general's office. These law specialists could not hold sea commands and were assigned exclusively to legal duties. It was not a "corps," but it was near enough to make a difference. The navy judge advocate general's office also began publishing the *JAG Journal* to inform legal specialists throughout the navy of the latest military justice developments and military legal issues, again reacting to the prevailing currents of reform.[34]

With the creation of the Department of Defense in 1947, Secretary of Defense James Forrestal moved to unify military justice. In 1948, Forrestal appointed a committee to draft a uniform code of military justice for the army, navy, Marine Corps, and the new air force. The committee was headed by Harvard law professor Edmund M. Morgan, a protégé of Ansell in the judge advocate general's office during World War I. Several civilian legal groups, including the American Bar Association, the New York Lawyers' Association, and the War Veterans' Bar Association, petitioned the committee to include certain revisions in the new code, including the removal of command control, the adoption of formalized appellate and judicial review systems, and the requirement that both trial and defense counsels be lawyers in all courts-martial. The draft uniform code went to the House for hearings in March 1949. The principal point of contention from the military was the provision for a civilian appellate review board. Despite testimony against such a board, the House Armed Services Committee sent the draft to the full House, where it passed on May 5, 1949.[35]

Passage in the Senate proved more challenging, and hearings and debate were not completed until April 1950. Much of the testimony dealt with command control and the whole concept of giving a soldier civilian status in law. That, according to the critics, would defeat the purpose of military justice as a disciplinary deterrent. Detractors from the code won a partial victory in the final version. Article 37 technically made command influence in courts-martial illegal and punishable by a general court-martial. In reality, however, this article had no teeth. In order for a commander to be court-martialed under Article 37, the proof would have to be considerable, and another commander would have to convene a trial of a fellow commander for exercising authority to discipline troops. This was a nearly impossible scenario, as the only way command influence could be eradicated was to place charges under the jurisdiction of a federal district court. Despite this weakness, the final version included an all-civilian court of military appeals as the court of last resort. This alone was revolutionary.[36]

President Harry Truman signed the Uniform Code of Military Justice into law on May 5, 1950, and the new code became effective May 31, 1951.[37] The 1951 *Manual for Courts Martial, United States,* which incorporated and applied the new code to each service as well as the coast guard, received its first test in combat in Korea without benefit of any time to work out the kinks.[38] The Uniform Code of Military Justice provided civilianized justice while maintaining order and discipline in the armed forces. It outlined traditional military crimes, including sedition and conduct unbecoming an officer. Civilian crimes, including extortion and perjury, were defined in separate articles. It allowed the president to set a table of maximum punishments, which appeared in the 1951 *Manual.*

The most important changes came in new protections for members of the armed services. Now any soldier or sailor subject to the code could prefer charges against another, whereas under the old system, only officers could lay charges. General courts-martial required a pretrial investigation and hearing, outlined in Article 32. The accused had representation and could cross-examine witnesses and bring evidence in the pretrial investigation. The accused also had the right either to free government counsel or to civilian defense at his or her own expense and could have counsel present at interrogations. Additionally, members of the armed services had the right against self-incrimination.

Commanders still had the ultimate say in bringing a case to trial. Command influence was punishable, but it was still difficult to prove under the new code. Commanders could not censure, reprimand, or admonish any court member or counsel for failure to pass judgment according to their own wishes. Coercion and attempts to influence the court or any court member were specifically illegal. An accused enlisted man or woman could request at least one-third of the court be made up of enlisted members. The convening authority reserved the power to make such appointments based upon experience, knowledge, and length of service. This is as close to being tried by a jury of one's peers as the military would come after more than fifty years of reform effort.

The "judicialization" and civilianization of military justice in the code came in many forms. All general courts-martial required a law officer, appointed by the convening authority, who acted in all respects as a civilian judge. The law officer had to be a member of the bar or highest court of a state and be legally certified by the judge advocate general. The law officer would instruct the court on points of law, burden of proof, and the presumption of innocence. The senior officer of the court continued to be the administrator of the court, setting trial dates, administering oaths, and running the courtroom. The rise of the law officer as a required aspect of a military court planted the seed for what would grow into an independent military judiciary.

The new code created what would quickly become its most important feature: the Court of Military Appeals. Three civilian judges, appointed by the president and confirmed by the Senate, served fifteen-year terms. Before a case reached the Court of Military Appeals, it would pass through review from the convening authority and boards of review established by the judge advocate general of each service. As the court of last resort, the Court of Military Appeals not only ruled on appeals but also interpreted the Uniform Code of Military Justice.[39]

The new Uniform Code of Military Justice hit the Korean War midstream. The most significant hitch in the new system's wartime test came in specifying punishments for offenses critical during war, such as desertion, absence without leave, and misbehavior of sentinels. Under the Uniform Code of Military Justice, these offenses and others had limited punishments in peacetime and much harsher punishments in time of war. The judge advocates general of the three armed services concluded that although Congress had not passed a formal declaration of war, war did indeed exist. With their help, President Truman signed Executive Order 10149, on August 8, 1950, expanding punishments for wartime offenses in the Far East command only.

Enabling commanders to enforce wartime articles greatly improved their ability to maintain discipline and deterrence in combat conditions. The problem, however, arose in the disparity of sentences for the same offense, given the latitude available to courts under wartime regulations. A harsh sentence for an offense in one unit might be a light slap on the wrist for the same offense in another. Such disparities affected morale and discipline across the many units serving in Korea. To resolve the inconsistencies, the army judge advocate general used certain cases as standards to level punishments for like offenses.[40]

The new review system under the Uniform Code of Military Justice received a great deal of business during the Korean War. By January 1952, seven three-member review boards were busy reviewing sentences for army cases. Seventy-six percent of those convicted used their new privilege to request a review. For every 1,000 convicted, 181 requested appeal to the Court of Military Appeals; of these, 28 received review and 14 were reversed. Korea proved a fair test of the new code under combat conditions, showing that although the system was not perfect, it could function and achieve its purpose.

Korea also brought increased judge advocate activity for lawyers of each of the services. Prisoner of war exchanges required delicate legal negotiations in addition to diplomatic talks. Claims and procurement kept lawyers busy. Military patents during the war increased by 25 percent, again requiring the services of military lawyers. Contracts, taxes, and legislative matters filled out legal duties during and after the war.[41]

Changes in the code for the rest of the decade would come more through the courts than legislation. Trying civilians in peacetime was successfully challenged, as was the code's generous statute of limitations on persons already discharged from being convicted of crimes committed while in service.[42] The system had some kinks to be worked out, but as the United States approached the edge of the Vietnam abyss in the early 1960s, the Uniform Code of Military Justice had demonstrated a great improvement over its predecessors and seemed ready to accept another combat challenge.

Legal education for judge advocate staffs of the services also received much needed attention during the 1950s and 1960s. Having traditionally relied upon reserve officers with law degrees to fill duty rosters, the military now made "military" lawyers. In the army, the old Judge Advocate General's School at the University of Michigan law school had been shut down after World War II. The new code and the Korean War, however, demanded intensive military law training. A new, permanent army Judge Advocate General's School at the University of Virginia in Charlottesville opened in 1951. The Naval Justice School at Newport, Rhode Island, opened in 1950 to train navy law specialists and Marine Corps legal officers. The air force Judge Advocate General's School first opened at Maxwell Air Force Base in 1950 but closed there after the Korean War. From 1954 to 1969, military law training for air force judge advocates operated through the Air Force Chaplain's School at Lackland Air Force Base.

The navy suffered through a service-dividing schism in the early 1950s with its postgraduate legal program. Traditionally, line officers had been sent through the program to become naval lawyers. With the new code, however, and legal training at Newport, the navy's law specialists took over. Congress cut the postgraduate program for line officers for one simple reason—funding. It seemed a waste to send a cadet through Annapolis to make him a line officer, then send him through law school and not have him return to a line command. If the navy needed lawyers, then the navy should either recruit lawyers or make lawyers to serve as lawyers. The navy responded, upgrading its Naval Reserve Law Program to meet the challenge.[43]

Marine Corps lawyers found themselves in a difficult spot, which lasted well into the Vietnam War. For the Marine Corps, legal services were not a priority as such. An officer who happened to be a lawyer would find himself in the Marine Corps' legal services and a dead-end career. Although marines technically belonged to the navy, Marine Corps lawyers focused mainly on military justice matters, leaving contracts, claims, and the like to navy law specialists. Like the navy, the Marine Corps had a postgraduate law program aimed at line officers to provide legal training to enhance their knowledge of military justice; following the program, they were put back into the line. No cadre of Marine Corps lawyers seemed necessary, thus pursuing law in the Marine Corps was, again, a dead-end track. The Marine Corps resisted a separate legal division because it believed, under the institutional limitations of what a military lawyer did in the Marine Corps, that a Marine Corps officer could be both field officer and legal specialist. The Marine Corps also opposed a separate navy Judge Advocate General's Corps because such a branch might take disciplinary law out of the Marine Corps' hands, thus robbing what little legal independence the Marine Corps had. As a consequence, of all the services, the Marine Corps had the worst retention rate for lawyers.[44]

The code went through minor revision in 1962. With all of the focus on civilianizing military justice over the previous four decades, some remembered the purpose of military justice—discipline. Under the Uniform Code of Military Justice, Article 15 provided for nonjudicial punishment for minor offenses. The 1962 revision gave commanders thirty days of "correctional custody" to deal with lesser offenses. This gave the commander latitude for deterrence to maintain discipline, a procedure that could also cut down on the number of summary and special courts-martial. The other addition to the Code in 1962 was the bad check article. Under Article 123a, a service member passing a bad check with intent to deceive could be court-martialed. Additions to the code such as this were meant to cover any loopholes in status-of-forces agreements with nations where U.S. forces were stationed. These revisions also sent a signal to the public, both U.S. and otherwise, that the military was indeed civilianizing its judicial code.[45]

As U.S. forces became more active in southeast Asia, thus stood the Uniform Code of Military Justice and the military lawyers charged with enforcing it and the numerous other duties they had inherited because of their growing expertise in legal matters. Vietnam would challenge their abilities, resources, and manpower. The military justice system had evolved from a purely military tool to a quasi-military judicial system.

Other legal changes in U.S. society triggered further revision. The Miranda warning, mandated in *Miranda v. Arizona* by the Supreme Court, and new rules forbidding the admissibility of improperly seized evidence, as directed by *Mapp v. Ohio*, applied to military just as to civilian courts.[46] Command influence remained a serious issue. The Uniform Code of Military Justice was already complicated, perhaps too much so for the regular officer to fully understand and use. Only trained military lawyers and court judges could ensure the fair and impartial administration of military law. Congress received complaints from service members and their families about the inadequacies of the system. To remedy these problems, Congress, led by Senator Sam Ervin of North Carolina, continued debating revision of the Uniform Code of Military Justice following the 1962 changes. It would take almost six years of investigations, hearings, and compromise to come up with an improved, more efficient, and even more civilianized military code.[47]

The very idea of revising a military judicial code during a major conflict is indeed extraordinary. The 1968 revision of the Uniform Code of Military Justice occurred at the height of the Vietnam War, and the significant changes it brought to the system had a direct impact on the way military justice was administered in Vietnam. The trend of civilianization continued, as rights of accused and procedural consistency highlighted the revised Uniform Code of Military Justice. The revision process was also extraordinary, in that suggestions came from each of the services, the Court of Military Appeals, citizens and veterans groups, and bar associations. Military justice interested a broad spectrum of organizations and people, and their input through testimony in Congress influenced the 1968 revision. None got all that they wanted, but many got at least some of their recommendations into the revised Uniform Code of Military Justice.

From the services and the Court of Military Appeals came recommendations to make court-martial procedures more efficient and fair. The so-called Code Committee, made up of the judge advocates general of all the services and the judges on the Court of Military Appeals, formalized these recommendations in several draft legislative bills throughout the 1950s and 1960s. The

committee wanted to expand the use of the single-officer court, give law officers more authority, establish pretrial sessions in front of law officers in special
and general courts-martial, and extend the time limit for petitions for new
trials from one to two years. In addition, the committee recommended that a
special court-martial have the authority to give a bad conduct discharge only if
the accused had the opportunity to be represented by a qualified lawyer. These
proposals passed in the House in June 1968.

Veterans' groups and bar associations had their say as well. The American Legion deeply criticized the current system and strongly urged Congress to completely remove command influence from courts-martial and make military justice more closely resemble its civilian counterpart, but neither of these ideas
could be wholly carried out. The American Legion also wanted all lawyers appearing before courts-martial of any type to be rated and under the command of
the respective judge advocate general and further wanted all law officers of
courts-martial to be given status equal to that of a federal judge. The services and
the Secretary of Defense vigorously resisted these extreme measures. Alternatively, the Bar Association of New York City found little wrong with the system as
it existed and recommended only minor procedural alterations. University of
Texas Law School professor Joseph M. Snee recommended that the Uniform
Code of Military Justice adopt single-officer courts, that law officers be renamed
military judges, and that boards of review become courts of military review.
These suggestions would bring process and nomenclature more in line with the
civilian judicial system. Many of Professor Snee's recommendations would find
their way into the final version of the 1968 Military Justice Act.[48]

Senator Ervin's proposals in 1968 mirrored much of the above. Although he
did not disagree with the spirit of the House bill, he found the House version
lacking and proposed additional revisions. In a perfect world, Senator Ervin
would have changed the title of law officer to military judge for general courts-
martial, established an independent judiciary for each service to remove command influence, established a Judge Advocate General's Corps for the navy, replaced boards of review with courts of military review, given accused the right
to be represented by a lawyer when facing any sentence involving a bad conduct discharge and the right to waive trial by summary court-martial without
command consent, created single officer general and special courts-martial,
and abolished summary courts-martial.

The military complained that many of these measures were impractical. The
navy, for example, could not guarantee lawyers in its widespread courts-martial
jurisdictions. Allowing accused to waive trial by summary court-martial would

hinder efficient due process. The logistical demand of an independent field judiciary for all courts-martial would catch the services short-handed on qualified military lawyers and judges. The services countered that such a requirement might be feasible for general courts-martial, but not special courts-martial, which made up the majority of court-martial actions in the military justice system.[49]

Ervin compromised but still got much of what he wanted in the final version of the Senate bill that became the Military Justice Act of 1968. For special courts-martial, qualified legal counsel was required to represent the accused when a bad conduct discharge was involved; for all other special courts-martial, the accused had to be represented by a lawyer unless impractical because of military conditions. The act created an independent judiciary for each of the armed services. These judges would not be under line command and thus avoided command influence. They would also have powers and functions in trial similar to those of federal judges and could now rule on pretrial motions as well as on points of law. The old law officer concept disappeared. Under the act, the accused now had the right to request trial by a military judge instead of a full court and could also object to trial by a summary court-martial for trial in a higher court. The appellate boards of review became more formal-sounding courts of military review staffed by independent judges.[50]

These were indeed significant changes to the military justice system. Command influence, that age-old scar on the face of military justice, had now apparently been wiped away for good. Substantive due process had finally evolved from virtual nonexistence at the beginning of the twentieth century to a full-fledged reality with the Military Justice Act of 1968. Critics feared that the 1968 changes, combined with the sweeping reforms the Uniform Code of Military Justice had brought to military justice since 1950, had undercut traditional military order and ruined the commander-soldier relationship. Yet, according to Edward F. Sherman (an assistant professor of law at Indiana University School of Law and an expert on and vocal critic of military justice throughout the Uniform Code of Military Justice debates of the 1960s), the Uniform Code of Military Justice, with its 1968 revision, although not perfect, promised "a more equitable system of justice which will strengthen the morale of servicemen and restore the confidence of the public in the quality of military justice."[51] The Military Justice Act of 1968 went into effect August 1, 1969. U.S. military justice had indeed come a long way since King George's "Articles of War."

CHAPTER TWO
LAWYERS IN THE VANGUARD

In July 1963, air force captain H. Harrison Braxton Jr. arrived in Vietnam to take up duties as one of three judge advocates assigned to the Second Air Division.[1] Headquartered at Tan Son Nhut airfield, Braxton embarked on a legal adventure that in the end gave him the confidence to "handle law practice anywhere." Braxton's arrival coincided with one of the pivotal years of U.S. involvement in Vietnam. In January 1963, an outnumbered and outgunned Viet Cong force had inflicted an embarrassing defeat at Ap Bac upon troops of the Army of the Republic of Vietnam (ARVN), which was advised by Americans. In June, Buddhist monk Thich Quang Duc had immolated himself in an ultimate act of protest against the South Vietnamese government of Ngo Dinh Diem, producing one of the most recognizable and haunting images of the Vietnam era. By July, students and Buddhist monks had paralyzed Saigon and surrounding areas with riots.

Braxton and his colleagues in the Second Air Division were among the growing number of U.S. "advisers" in South Vietnam, aiding and guiding the struggling postcolonial society against so-called Viet Cong insurgents and North Vietnamese communist forces under the leadership of the dynamic Ho Chi Minh. American advisers did just about everything, from training troops in the field to assisting the Vietnamese government in running its day-to-day operations. The U.S. Military Assistance Command, Vietnam (MACV), in conjunction with the American Embassy in Saigon, supervised this expanding effort. With 15,000 U.S. military personnel in South Vietnam, a few lawyers were necessary to deal with the legal needs of U.S. soldiers and to help negotiate contracts between U.S. companies and the Vietnamese government and, in a broader context, to continue the nation-building process begun in the late 1950s. Braxton's job had no exact description, he soon discovered, as he was called upon to do anything and everything a military lawyer might be asked to do. He quickly became a "general practitioner" in every sense of the word.

Before arriving in Vietnam, Braxton had undergone a brief training program at Clark Air Base in the Philippines to prepare him for what he might encounter. Of course, once he arrived in Vietnam, he concluded that few at Clark had the "foggiest idea" of what was going on in Vietnam. Although a young lawyer, Braxton had some experience. A 1961 law graduate of the University of

Virginia, Braxton had accepted a direct commission into the air force. At that time, the air force had no Judge Advocate General School, as it does today, so Braxton attended the thirty-day crash course at Lackland Air Base in San Antonio, where Legal Division training was part of the United States Air Force Chaplain's School. There, he and his fellow advocates studied the Uniform Code of Military Justice, the Koran, the Torah, and the Ten Commandments. He stayed at the Lackland Base Legal Office for two years, trying courts-martial and sharing his experience with other newly arrived lawyers at the Chaplain's School.

The assignment to Vietnam, however, was unlike anything he had experienced stateside. The people, the language, the culture were all truly foreign, and the Staff Judge Advocate (SJA) office at Tan Son Nhut Air Base fell far below standards in the United States. The Second Air Division had taken over the old dilapidated French barracks, mostly metal buildings of various shades of yellow and green with sealed windows and a few air-conditioning units that worked only sporadically and then only at night. After 0800, the electric generator could not provide enough power to the buildings to run lights and air conditioners at the same time. Electric service in general functioned only sporadically. The buildings, with their sealed windows and metal roofs, steamed in the tropical heat.

Work actually revolved around electric service: when the electricity flickered on, the clerks would rush to their typewriters to complete at least part of a form before the electricity shut off again. Braxton had no secretary; a single Saigon Post, Telephone, and Telegraph phone line, which rarely worked; and few other amenities of legal practice. The combination of tropical heat and outdated chemicals made the Kodak wet-process copier "hopeless." The Second Air Division law library consisted of two books: the *Manual for Courts-Martial* and volume four of the 1963 Martindale-Hubbell *Digest*. The only forms he had were ones he had had the "wits" to bring with him from Lackland. Other than that, he and his colleagues were on their own, enjoying the odd fluctuation of frustration and success that comes with "on-the-job training."

Braxton was billeted in an apartment in Saigon and took a navy bus to and from Tan Son Nhut. Wire mesh covered the bus's windows to keep out grenades. Braxton recalled many interesting characters on his bus trips, including journalist David Halberstam, then of the *New York Times*. Braxton learned more about what was going on in Vietnam from Halberstam in one thirty-minute bus ride than in his first three months of being in the country. He and his colleagues enjoyed the facilities of the Cercle Sportif and played golf at the

Golf Club du Saigon. Some discreetly carried weapons, though it was against regulations to do so. That would change by the end of the year.

Getting to other South Vietnamese airfields and bases, such as Bien Hoa, Nha Trang, or Pleiku, or to bases in Thailand required creative air transport and in Braxton's case rides on thirty-four different types of aircraft during his tour. When traveling by air, he always carried a .38 pistol in his briefcase, just in case. The only time he did not take the pistol, on a trip to Thailand, the Army Caribou aircraft lost an engine over the Mekong Delta, forcing a dicey trip back to Saigon. Coming so close to being grounded in the delta convinced Braxton to take his pistol on all flights, no matter what the destination.

Braxton spent much of his tour handling claims and giving legal assistance to U.S. air force and army troops. In addition to needing representation for discipline infractions and other violations of the Uniform Code of Military Justice, U.S. soldiers had the same legal needs as other Americans: help with taxes, wills, powers of attorney, and other day-to-day legal matters. Military justice matters also occupied his time, although at this early stage of the war the drugs and related activities that are often associated with Americans in Vietnam were not wide-scale problems. There were so few U.S. military lawyers in Vietnam during this period that they often handled matters for services other than their own. Braxton was involved in at least one navy and nine army Article 32 investigations, similar to a grand jury hearing, either as investigator or defense counsel.

Dealing with claims for damaged property, from both U.S. service members and Vietnamese, took up an increasing amount of time, especially as the air force became more active in providing air support for ARVN forces. Cultural barriers often complicated claims involving Vietnamese; simply applying common sense did not seem to be adequate. For instance, in one case, Braxton spent several hours trying to convince a Vietnamese witness that the U.S. judicial system, represented by the Uniform Code of Military Justice, was just and fair and that the procedure of cross-examination was an important part of that process. The witness, however, refused to be cross-examined because of "face." It was beneath his dignity to speak to the defendant or to anyone representing the defendant.

Notable experiences of Braxton's tour included being in Saigon during the November 1963 coup that overthrew the Diem regime and resulted in the murder of Ngo Dinh Diem and his brother Ngo Dinh Nhu. Braxton also narrowly escaped injury when a satchel charge (a small explosive device often concealed in an abandoned briefcase or bag) exploded some 70 feet away from him as he approached the entrance to a movie theater in Saigon. A Marine Corps captain who recognized the danger shouted for all to get down, saving several lives, but sadly he died in the explosion. Capt. Charles Baldree, an army judge advocate and friend of Braxton, was injured. Shaken by the close call, Braxton enjoyed his first martini later that day.

Braxton recalled his legal experience in Vietnam as one of personal growth and confidence, learning to overcome obstacles that in normal circumstances might seem impossible. The conditions in Vietnam, even for lawyers, required adjustment and adaptation, and Braxton learned to be flexible and patient and to appreciate the proper context of particular circumstances. Military lawyers prosecuted one day, defended the next, and then investigated the day after that. Some were in offices, some in tents; most traveled all over South Vietnam dealing with case after case, seven days a week, twelve to fourteen hours a day. Some judge advocates saw combat, either by command or bad fortune.

Braxton was among the earliest military lawyers to serve in Vietnam. The organization of U.S. military legal services in Vietnam more or less resembled that of any other U.S. command in the world. In fact, for much of the war, the Pentagon tended to statistically and judicially manage military justice matters in Vietnam just as in any another command, even though Vietnam was an unconventional combat zone in a limited war. Often Pentagon data do not distinguish between Vietnam and other parts of the world where U.S. forces were stationed. Although the number of U.S. troops sent to Vietnam escalated from 1965 to 1969 and then decreased with Vietnamization and the gradual U.S. withdrawal, military justice organization changed very little.

In 1962, the Department of Defense created MACV to coordinate U.S. advisory efforts in Vietnam. As troop numbers escalated and the United States began to take over the bulk of the war effort from the South Vietnamese, MACV became the operational headquarters for all U.S. forces in Vietnam. In addition to planning and coordinating combat operations and military advisory efforts, MACV also managed legal services. Within the MACV command structure was a staff judge advocate, usually a colonel. The MACV Staff Judge Advocate's Division's main mission was to serve as the chief legal adviser to the MACV commander, but it also helped coordinate military justice activities with the United States Army, Republic of Vietnam (USARV); Seventh Air Force; United States Naval Forces, Republic of Vietnam (NAVFORV); and the III Marine Amphibious Force (III MAF). The MACV Staff Judge Advocate's Division included six subdivisions: criminal and military law, claims, administration, international law, advisory, and civil and military affairs.

The MACV Staff Judge Advocate's Division's criminal and military law branch handled traditional military justice supervision and monitored discipline, making sure the military justice system functioned efficiently. Much of its work was advisory in nature, helping commanders and staff judge advocates in subordinate commands deal with disciplinary and criminal violations of the Uniform Code of Military Justice and ensuring that there were enough judges and lawyers to cover court-martial jurisdictions for all units in Vietnam. The Claims Division processed claims made by Vietnamese for the entire MACV command in Vietnam. Although air force, Marine Corps, or navy activity might cause a claim for damages to be filed, the claims division processed all claims. The administration branch kept records and handled the normal range of administrative duties for the Staff Judge Advocate's Division.

The international law division had interesting work. In addition to drafting and reviewing agreements between the United States military and the South Vietnamese military forces, the international law division also advised on questions concerning international law of war and the Geneva Conventions of 1949 regulating prisoner of war treatment and the protection of noncombatants. Because the war in Vietnam was not a declared war of the United States in the strict sense of the term, questions did arise as to the level of applicability of the international war conventions. The advisory division played an important role in the nation-building process and counterinsurgency effort in South Vietnam. As the main liaison of MACV to the South Vietnamese civil and military justice systems, the advisory division helped the effort to establish a Western-style respect for law and order in what the United States hoped would become a free society. This work was particularly important in the Vietnamese military, whose justice system did not work well and was riddled with corruption. The advisory division assisted the Vietnamese Directorate of Military Justice in improving due process and consistency by helping to analyze court-martial and other data and to draft proposals to improve the system. Advisory division staff worked closely with Vietnamese military judge advocates and civilian lawyers to improve court structure, jails and prisons, and legal education. The advisory division also translated and kept on file copies of Vietnamese decrees and court decisions and advised MACV on Vietnamese legal matters.

The civil and military affairs division dealt with some of the more troublesome problems in Vietnam. This division had the unenviable task of managing currency and coping with the extensive black market. It also recommended and enforced disciplinary action against civilian contractors, both Vietnamese and U.S., for black-market activities, currency fraud, and other corruption. Last, the civil law and military affairs division handled more mundane matters, such as making sure U.S. military and civilian contract holders maintained their exemptions from Vietnamese government taxes, customs duties, and inspections, and it advised on other regulatory questions.

The command structures of USARV, Seventh Air Force, NAVFORV, and III MAF all had similar subdivisions, and each corps, division, and other command had its own staff judge advocates or legal officers. Coordination and cooperation among these judge advocates from each service and the MACV Staff Judge Advocate's Division were vital to the effective working of the system in Vietnam. The multipurpose mission of military justice kept judge advocates very busy. This mission and the basic organization and structure stayed fairly continuous throughout the U.S. involvement in the war in Vietnam.[2]

The judge advocates who would perform these duties came from three main sources. Some were career officers whom the military sent to law school to become judge advocates. Many were reserve officers who had graduated from law school, had varying degrees of military and civilian legal experience, and had been called into service. Others volunteered for officer training after law school and were assigned to legal services. Thus, military lawyers in Vietnam had somewhat diverse backgrounds and experience. For some, their first legal practice took place in Vietnam. Their tools were the *Manual for Courts Martial*, MACV directives, and whatever legal reference books they thought to bring with them.

In characteristic military fashion, military lawyers in Vietnam made do with what they found and improvised to make up for what they lacked.[3] Quonset huts provided living quarters, called hooches, for most lawyers, and some were altered to become quite lavish, at least by the standards of the Vietnamese living in the nearby villages. It was not uncommon for lawyers to locate their hooches near the mess hall or the officers' club. First Marine Division lawyers had hooches that had been remodeled extensively to include a bar, movie room, and a small kitchen and launderette with running water. The grandest luxury, however, was a flush toilet. Usually, a few Vietnamese women worked as housemaids and cooks. In order to combat the constant problem of humidity and mold, innovative "hot boxes"—boxes rigged with a couple of light bulbs for heat—helped dry out shoes and clothing.

In one hooch, a lawyer built his own personal bunker, to avoid the risk of running during a rocket attack for the larger bunker located just up the hill. He cut an opening in the floor beneath his bunk, dug a nice hole complete with sandbagged sides, and installed a trap door, giving the minibunker an attractive, finished effect. Proud of his new bunker, the lawyer gathered fellow marines to demonstrate its effectiveness. It proved to be a short demonstration: upon leaping down into the hole, the man discovered it was already occupied by a snake of unspecified size. The bunker was subsequently permanently sealed; weeks of colorful commentary by his colleagues followed.

Given the busy workload, recreation was valued but not often available, thus leaving the lawyers again to seek improvised solutions. Makeshift tennis courts, bars, and other homemade amenities could be found at many legal offices and hooches. Movies such as *The Green Berets* and *The Sound of Music* arrived in such a reduced and patched state after making the rounds all over South Vietnam that they were barely viewable. Parties offered rare opportunities to relax. Holidays or the completion of a tour and a return to "the World" provided welcome excuses to celebrate. As with just about all U.S. military personnel in Vietnam, any distraction was welcome.

A military lawyer in Vietnam often spent a great deal of time traveling, which required great improvisational "hitch-hiking" skills. The nature of the South Vietnam combat zone required lawyers to hitch rides to all corners of the country. Defendants were normally confined at Long Binh, the Marine Corps brig at Da Nang, or the air force facility at Tan Son Nhut, but witnesses and convening authorities could be spread across a large area, often in hostile zones. Lawyers hitched rides on trucks, Jeeps, half-tracks, C-130s, all sorts of helicopters—anything that could get them where they needed to go. One Marine Corps lawyer caught a lucky ride in a Special Services helicopter, scoring a seat next to Gypsy Rose Lee.

Sometimes, though, the rides elicited a different kind of excitement. Marine Corps lawyers Clarke Barnes, Clark Halderson, and Tommy Allison took a thrilling Jeep ride from Quang Tri to Con Thien in November 1968. Going to arrange pretrial agreements for court-martial with a battalion commander at Con Thien, the three plus a driver armed themselves with .45 pistols, an M-16, and a shotgun for the trip. Traveling the dirt and gravel highway through small hamlets and villages and successfully talking their way through several checkpoints, they arrived at Con Thien to see marines with recoilless rifles only a few hundred yards from the road firing at North Vietnamese troops. The commander asked how they had arrived, and when informed "by Jeep," he "came unglued." Apparently and unbeknownst to the lawyers, the highway had been closed to all traffic except for convoys protected by tanks and trucks with .50 caliber machine guns. A convoy had been ambushed earlier in the day along the same stretch of road. If caught in such a situation, the meager arsenal of the Jeep would have proved of little use. Later, the marines discovered the shotgun had a faulty firing pin. For the trip back to Quang Tri, the group made sure they had a more proper escort. According to Barnes, "guardian angels" had protected the young lieutenants, who were not "smart enough to be prudent, cautious or scared" when traveling in "Indian country."

Army, navy, Marine Corps, and air force judge advocates and legal officers faced a difficult task in dealing with the thousands of courts-martial and other disciplinary actions occurring yearly in Vietnam. Although special and summary courts-martial could be handled without too much hassle, general courts-martial required an Article 32 investigating officer in addition to prosecuting and defending attorneys, court members, a military judge, and many hours to conduct. All courts-martial involved bringing many people together, yet the participants tended to be spread out across South Vietnam, if not the United States. Witnesses had to be located and transported to the trial site. Schedules had to be rearranged for judges, lawyers, and members. Security personnel were often needed to staff courtrooms and escort prisoners and witnesses. The twelve-month tour of duty (thirteen months for marines) frequently resulted in a witness having been rotated back to the United States or even already discharged out of the service. The length of their tour of duty also affected the judge advocates themselves, who might be ordered home in the middle of a case. If the case involved Vietnamese witnesses, they had to be located and brought to the trial site or have depositions taken by a judge advocate. All of these obstacles made patience and perseverance desirable and practical virtues. At the height of the military buildup in Vietnam, the army only had 135 judge advocates serving the legal needs of 365,300 troops, and the Marine Corps rotated close to 400 lawyers to Vietnam from 1965 to 1971.

Other practical matters made the judge advocates' jobs a challenge. Equipment constantly failed. Recording devices broke down because of the humidity and the ever-present red dust from the rust-colored earth common across Vietnam. Mimeograph machines succumbed to the damp heat. Telephones worked sporadically, and the electricity could be on or off at any given moment. Clerical personnel often had little training for the legal processing they were doing, despite efforts to provide it. On occasion, the Viet Cong interrupted proceedings with rocket attacks. Once, a rocket struck a Quonset hut next door to a Marine Corps courtroom, destroying the hut and doing serious damage to the chambers, including blowing the blindfolded head off a statue of *Justice with Scales*. The scheduled trial began the next day amid the rubble.[4]

All of these challenges forced judge advocates to be patient, creative, and dedicated, characteristics that obviously would serve a military lawyer well later for a career in the military or as a civilian attorney. The delays caused by these problems could be long and frustrating to all involved, but the system nevertheless lumbered along effectively.[5]

Military justice helped keep the U.S. military machine running in Vietnam, even through the critical years toward the end of the conflict when the machine seemed to be breaking down. Maintaining discipline and punishing those who broke the rules kept judge advocates quite busy. A military lawyer might prosecute one day, conduct an Article 32 investigation on another day, then defend on the next. In a war that is remembered for the breakdown of discipline during its latter years, enforcing the Uniform Code of Military Justice was crucial to averting a complete disintegration of military order. As one might expect, during the early years of the conflict, discipline and order were not considerable problems. Military personnel sent to Vietnam through 1966 came from selected units made up of screened volunteers along with career officers and noncommissioned officers. The rapid escalation of the number of U.S. forces, however, brought draftees, other volunteers, noncommissioned officers, and officers who lacked experience, extensive training, and the motivation to deal with the unique circumstances of Vietnam.[6]

Many soldiers sent to Vietnam were arguably set up to fail, even under the comparatively rigid disciplinary rules of the Uniform Code of Military Justice. Eighty percent had little better than a high school education. High school dropouts sent to Vietnam were three times more likely than college graduates to be in combat. U.S. soldiers in Vietnam averaged nineteen years of age, compared to twenty-six in World War II. Christian Appy's extensive study of U.S. soldiers in Vietnam found that 25 percent came from poor families, 55 percent from working-class homes, and 20 percent from middle-class backgrounds. Only a handful could be classified as "well off."[7]

To add to this large group of young, barely high-school-educated, working-class soldiers, the military began lowering its standards for enlistment. Beginning in 1965, the military began accepting more applicants who scored in the two lowest categories of the mental examination required for enlistment. Many of these enlistees, who had intelligence quotient scores of less than 85 and came from poor and broken homes, were readily accepted into service. Adding to this problem was the infamous Project 100,000, the brainchild of Assistant Secretary of Labor Daniel P. Moynihan and Secretary of Defense Robert McNamara. Designed to give young men with extremely low examination scores from inner cities and rural areas a chance to grow and develop skills through military service, Project 100,000 had quite the opposite result. From 1966 through 1968, Project 100,000 accepted 240,000 inductees. The additional training that promised to better educate these young men with basic skills never materialized: a mere 6 percent went through some sort of technical training, mostly in getting their reading skills up to a fifth-grade level. Although the military trained 25 percent of all enlistees for combat, 40 percent of Project 100,000 enlistees received training for combat duty. One-half of all Project 100,000 participants were sent to Vietnam. The death rate among these troops was twice that of the overall rate for U.S. forces. Prewar mental standards had eliminated 3 million draft-eligible males from military service, but lower standards during the war reduced the rejection figure to 1.36 million. The military itself arguably created conditions where discipline would be a problem.[8]

Project 100,000 participants required high maintenance for disciplinary infractions. In the 1968–1969 period, for example, Project 100,000 sailors made up 32.5 percent of all navy general and special courts-martial although they made up only 11.4 percent of the navy as a whole. In the Marine Corps during the same period, 39 percent of Project 100,000 participants received nonjudicial punishments, compared to 19 percent for regular marines of similar rank and tenure. Project 100,000 participants in the army in Vietnam had a court-martial conviction rate twice that of regular troops. According to Lt. Gen. Walter T. Kerwin, the army deputy chief of staff for personnel in the early 1970s, in the army alone, Project 100,000 soldiers even as late as 1970 had a disciplinary rate double that of the rest of the army as well as higher courts-martial and Article 15 (nonjudicial punishment) rates.[9]

Military justice also had to contend with race. Racial tension spilled over from U.S. society into the military in Vietnam. Even though many soldiers reported few racial problems in combat units, racial incidents frequently did occur in rear areas. From October 1968 to September 1969, 19 percent of all murders, 50 percent of attempted murders, 43 percent of aggravated assaults, and 71 percent of robberies in the army in Vietnam involved a black assailant and a white victim. It is impossible to tell from these figures how many cases were distinctly racially motivated. Blacks made up 58 percent of the stockade population in Southeast Asia, even though they only represented 9 percent of the army in Vietnam.[10]

The military often downplayed racial incidents by narrowly defining what actually constituted an "incident." In testimony before Congress in 1971,

Lt. Gen. Bruce Palmer, army vice chief of staff, stated that based on a standard of clearly racially motivated intent to do bodily harm during the first three months of 1972, only eighteen racial "incidents," including five in Vietnam, occurred in army forces worldwide. For comparison, Palmer noted that similar numbers of incidents occurred in major U.S. cities each night and that what many considered racial incidents were in reality drug related as opposed to race related. Sweeping one problem under the rug of another did not, of course, lessen the overall disciplinary problem in the U.S. armed forces either in Vietnam or elsewhere.[11]

Another major factor in the military justice experience in Vietnam was the 1968 revision of the Uniform Code of Military Justice. In Vietnam, the first court-martial tried under the revisions commenced the morning of the day before the Military Justice Act went into effect, because of Vietnam's location west of the international date line. There were not enough judge advocates in Vietnam to give instruction to all units, regardless of service, on the changes and how they affected U.S. forces in Vietnam. Each of the services had to ultimately send more military lawyers to Vietnam to meet the new standards set by the Military Justice Act. Judges had to be trained. Judicial circuits had to be organized. Now, all general and special courts-martial required the presence of three legally qualified lawyers—a judge, defense counsel, and trial counsel. This, of course, was in addition to the Article 32 investigating officer, who was also a military lawyer.

The army Judge Advocate General's Corps alone had to add 405 lawyers service-wide beginning in 1969 to meet the demands of the 1968 Uniform Code of Military Justice revision. The USARV staff judge advocate asked for and received an additional seventy-seven judge advocates by December 1969, almost doubling the number of army judge advocates in Vietnam (between judge advocates and nonjudge advocate lawyers, the army had approximately 150 lawyers in Vietnam by the end of 1969). The army anticipated an increase in special courts-martial from 600 to 800 per month, with one judge advocate defending fifteen cases and another prosecuting as many as twenty per month, each taking about four days to try, including travel time. The army also instituted a crash two-week course to qualify military judges according to the 1968 revision. To make better use of its legal personnel and military judges, USARV consolidated its thirteen general court-martial jurisdictions into six and created a system of trial teams within each jurisdiction. Special court-martial jurisdictions were similarly combined. For example, at Qui Nhon the army consolidated ten special court-martial jurisdictions into three, using two judge advocates and several nonjudge advocate lawyers in four trial teams that processed about seventy special courts-martial per month. Retention was always a long-term issue under these circumstances, and to minimize burnout, army lawyers in Vietnam were rotated between trying courts-martial to working the myriad of other legal jobs in Vietnam, such as claims, contracts, and advisory positions.[12]

In response to the 1968 revision, the navy created Law Centers to act as clearinghouses or headquarters to "pool together all judge advocates under one roof" while keeping the traditional staff judge advocates with large commands. These Law Centers provided legal assistance to area naval commands, helping prepare for trials and providing trial teams for special courts-martial and Article 32 investigations. Claims, admiralty issues, and "routine items of legal interest" also fell under the purview of the Law Center. In Vietnam, the navy had Law Centers at Saigon and Quang Tri.[13] The air force had anticipated the demands for more lawyers and already had in place enough judge advocates to ensure that all air force general and special courts-martial in Vietnam had qualified legal counsels and a military judge. The major problem affecting air force courts was the lack of trained court reporters.[14]

One advantage for all of the services in Vietnam was that the withdrawal of U.S. forces beginning at the end of 1969 gradually eased the legal personnel problem. In other words, by 1971, the army did not need 150 lawyers in Vietnam. The Marine Corps had only one division in the country in 1970, and it left Vietnam in 1971; the air force and navy had scaled back as well. Fortunately for all of the services, Vietnamization and the U.S. withdrawal perhaps helped avoid a potential personnel crisis that quite possibly could have seriously hindered the military justice system in Vietnam.

It is important to understand that military lawyers were not the only U.S. attorneys in Vietnam. Dozens of civilian lawyers from the United States represented military personnel and civilians during the war. Still, because of cost, few members of the armed services could afford a civilian lawyer. In conjunction with the accused's new right to an attorney as stipulated in the Military Justice Act of 1968, a movement gained momentum among civilian jurists in the United States who believed that the military justice system was overworked and approaching a breaking point. Under such circumstances, these lawyers worried, defense by military lawyers could not be equal or consistent. To rectify this situation, civilian lawyers offered their services to accused servicemen in Vietnam. Many of these groups formed as antimilitary, antiwar advocates for dissident soldiers, whereas some others were solely interested in ensuring justice.[15]

One of the most successful and least militant groups was the Lawyers' Military Defense Committee (LMDC) of Cambridge, Massachusetts. Among its sponsors were Ramsay Clark, former attorney general; Abraham S. Goldstein, dean of Yale University Law School; and Burke Marshall, former assistant attorney general. The LMDC began offering free legal representation from an office in Saigon in 1970. Directed by a group of law professors, including Edward Sherman of Indiana University and John Mansfield of Harvard University, the LMDC kept a small number of civilian lawyers in Saigon who worked on salary instead of a case-by-case basis. The LMDC worked out cooperative details with MACV, including use of military transport and post billets when available and free access to the USARV law library. Gen. Creighton Abrams, MACV commander, knew that accused had the right to civilian counsel if they could afford it under Article 38 of the Uniform Code of Military Justice, so he encouraged the LMDC to set up shop in Vietnam. Up to this point, soldiers had largely been devoid of the opportunity to have civilian counsel because of high fees and transportation costs. The LMDC offered a viable alternative by giving free on-the-spot representation.

The LMDC was not out to show the shortcomings of military justice or expose corruptive command influence; rather, it was in Vietnam to offer soldiers the opportunity to use civilian counsel if they wished to do so. Lead attorney William P. Homans Jr. assured General Abrams that LMDC lawyers would not accept fees from U.S. military personnel and would defend only U.S. military personnel in courts-martial. Homans stressed the need to assure the U.S. public that service members were getting fair and equal treatment in light of news stories about command influence and cover-ups (the Peers inquiry into the My Lai massacre was pointing to a cover-up at this time) and that as the military justice system became more like its civilian counterpart, contact between the two would benefit both and would "further the orderly procedural and substantive development of the law." The civilian legal community still tended to look upon military justice as arbitrary and archaic, not seeing the amazing reforms that had modernized the system since the early 1900s. Homans suggested that LMDC connections with major law schools in the United States could enhance and balance civilian understanding of military justice. Nothing but good, according to Homans, would come of LMDC–military justice cooperation in Vietnam.[16]

Although the MACV Staff Judge Advocate's office and General Abrams welcomed the LMDC for all the benefits discussed above, there was some understandable hesitation. Their experience with civilian attorneys coming to Vietnam to make more publicity out of already high-profile cases gave good reason for pause. Moreover, the military understandably resented the insinuation that accused were not getting proper defense. They had a point, as the judge advocates and military lawyers on the whole were of high quality, hard working, and fair. Consequently, MACV assured the LMDC that although it would cooperate as best it could with transportation and access, it would stop short of giving LMDC lawyers Post Exchange (PX) or mess privileges and access to military payment certificates (MPCs).[17] There was enough trouble with civilians abusing those privileges as it was, so MACV was probably wise to close the door of temptation. Always taking every opportunity to avoid litigation, MACV stipulated that LMDC lawyers would have to sign releases when using military transport.[18] The LMDC defended dozens of soldiers through the end of 1972, including a fairly high-profile case involving ten black soldiers who allegedly conspired to murder their commanding officer.[19]

There was plenty of work to go around under less than ideal circumstances, whether it was done by LMDC attorneys or military lawyers. Thousands of courts-martial, economic chaos fed by the black market, hundreds of claims investigations, increasing drug use, the breakdown of discipline, and other issues demanded the participation and attention of U.S. military justice and military lawyers in Vietnam.

Although military justice activities occupied much of a judge advocate's day, other lawyers were involved in civil affairs–type programs to support the U.S. nation-building effort in Vietnam and to "win the hearts and minds" of the Vietnamese in several ways. One of the least known is the claims and solatia program. The U.S. government paid Vietnamese people and businesses for personal and property damages resulting from military accidents and, in some cases, combat. This effort also included solatia, payments of condolence fundamentally different from claims. Prompt and just payment for both personal and property damages was seen as one of several ways to convince the Vietnamese people that formalized civil law was useful, fair, and—perhaps most important—not corrupt. The claims program also represented an effort on the part of the Americans to build a sense of community with the Vietnamese by recognizing local customs, and on a more practical level, an effective claims process avoided lengthy suits in court. The United States paid out millions of dollars over the course of the war in claims and solatia. According to George S. Prugh, staff judge advocate for MACV from 1964 to 1966, the payments were as "liberal . . . as the law would allow" to support nation-building.[20]

The payment of claims and solatia was a significant program, considering the insurgency situation in Vietnam. With part of the population in active insurgency against the South Vietnamese government and U.S. involvement in the war and with perhaps an even larger segment of the population "apathetic" toward its government, building confidence in government to overcome insurgency and establish democratic order was imperative. Making government compensation in a just and appropriate manner for damages and injuries would theoretically show the unaligned population that government cared about the people. Because the communist insurgents could not provide similar restitution, this segment of the population might be persuaded to side with the government rather than the insurgents. Thus, the program would help establish respect for law and procedure and fight insurgency at the same time. There is little evidence of its impact other than the fact that the U.S. military carried out the program with vigor and sincerity under difficult conditions.[21]

The army adjudicated noncombat claims under the Foreign Claims Act and the Military Claims Act for each service in Vietnam. Each service, in turn, investigated and helped process claims, particularly those in which its own service was involved. Combat-related claims were processed through the Vietnamese government via the Military Civic Action Program. As the U.S. military presence increased in number and activity, the total dollar amount for foreign claims rose accordingly. In 1965, claims obligations totaled a mere $10,000. By 1966, the figure had increased dramatically to $102,000. The year 1967 brought a total of $650,181 in payouts. In 1968, as the troop level approached its highest point, the United States paid out more than one million dollars in foreign claims. The following year, the annual total increased to $1,236,000.[22]

The number of incidents and approved disbursements give these dollar amounts some meaning. For example, during the third quarter of 1967, 1,205 foreign claims were filed. The Claims Division approved 968, paying out a total of $395,545, or an average of $408 per claim. This was a significant increase from the previous quarter in 1967, when 656 claims of 775 filed were approved for a total of $197,684, or about $300 per claim.[23] The gradual withdrawal of U.S. troops and subsequent decrease in U.S. military activity at first did not dramatically decrease the number or amount of claims, partially because claims were often filed six months after the incident occurred. The number of claims filed remained constant with levels in 1968 and 1969 until late 1971.[24] By 1972, however, the number of claims filed had begun to decline. In December 1971, the Saigon three-member claims commission had only 95 claims in the works, compared to 402 the previous December. Fourteen of the December 1971 claims had been open for more than sixty days, whereas in December 1970 ninety had been active for more than sixty days.[25]

The claims process remained more or less unchanged during the war. From 1965 to 1968, claims supervision rested with the commanding general, United States Army, in Okinawa. From there, claims commissions were appointed in Vietnam as needed. The increased number of claims, however, convinced the Department of Defense to shift appointing authority in 1968 to the commanding general, USARV. Processing claims kept approximately forty officers, enlisted men, and Vietnamese clerks in the Claims Division very busy. Maj. Leonard G. Crowly, for example, directed the Claims Division from March 1969 to April 1970 and handled claims by Vietnamese against U.S. forces during his year-long tour. Crowly had four captains in the Tax Department Store building plus one other in Da Nang to help process claims with the assistance of thirty-five Vietnamese and U.S. military clerks. In addition, two three-member foreign claims commissions, based in Saigon, handled claims from $1,000 to $15,000, and twelve single-member commissions dealing with claims up to $1,000 operated out of the Claims Division to adjudicate claims. The single-member commissions were scattered across South Vietnam, usually attached to a district or area headquarters. It is interesting to note that the number of claims the different commissions handled sometimes fluctuated with the exchange rate between Vietnamese piastres and U.S. dollars, suggesting that more claims may have been filed when the exchange rate favored the claimant.[26]

A wide range of incidents resulted in claims for property damage. Homes, places of business, carts and motor scooters, and particularly boats were all occasionally struck by errant artillery rounds and bombs, a two-and-a-half-ton army truck, or other objects. Claims could also be made for noncombat injuries and deaths resulting from accidents involving the U.S. military. Anyone who was in Vietnam during the war or has been there more recently will not be surprised to learn that up to 1970, traffic accidents made up 80 percent of all filed claims (roads and streets crowded with animals, bicycles, motor scooters, and larger vehicles, all traveling without any apparent regard for traffic laws, create conditions that for the uninitiated are ripe for accidents). For the month of February 1967, for example, thirty-one traffic fatalities involving Vietnamese and U.S. military vehicles were recorded across South Vietnam. The month before, twenty-nine accidents resulted in thirty-three Vietnamese fatalities. Considering the increase in traffic congestion caused by convoys and other military vehicles in urban and rural areas where drivers were more accustomed to scooters and bicycles, the numbers are perhaps not so high.[27]

As the U.S. withdrawal reduced traffic driven by U.S. soldiers as opposed to that driven by Vietnamese accustomed to local traffic eccentricities, real estate claims overtook traffic incidents as the main source of claims. As U.S. forces abandoned firebases, outposts, and buildings used for offices in major cities and towns, claims for assumed back rent and damages began to pour into claims offices across the country. What property owners did not realize was that agreements between the United States and South Vietnam gave U.S. forces use of most land and buildings rent free. In many cases, Vietnamese property owners lost the use of their property for years. The South Vietnamese government was responsible for claims dealing with property used by the Americans and was subsequently left to deal with angry property owners. In the end, U.S. aid to the South Vietnamese government probably paid some of these claims.[28]

Filing a claim was not complex in and of itself. The frustration came in the length of time it took to adjudicate the claim. It could take as little as a few weeks, but most likely it would be as long as six months or sometimes even years. After an incident, the person wishing compensation would either contact the local district chief or the nearest U.S. command to file a claim. A claims officer, usually a judge advocate, would assist the person in filling out the proper forms and conduct an interview about the incident in question. An investigation would follow. If the incident had occurred recently, the more likely it was that the investigation would go smoothly and relatively quickly. Claims could be filed, however, up to two years from the date of the incident. Investigating an incident that had taken place so long before presented all kinds of problems, not the least of which were missing paperwork and other records, fuzzy memories, and, not surprisingly, fraud. After the completion of the investigation, the nearest appropriate foreign claims commission would recommend payment or denial, then send the judgment to the USARV Claims Division, headquartered in the Tax Department Store building in downtown Saigon, for approval. Upon approval, a check would be made out to the claimant. Paying by check proved to be a problem for many Vietnamese, as few banks outside Saigon would cash a check. Judge advocates often cashed the check on the claimant's behalf and delivered cash (Vietnamese piastres) to the claimant.

There are many good illustrations of incidents resulting in claims that show how the process worked. Many incidents involved damaged or lost fishing boats, or junks. One such claim was denied because of lack of evidence.[29] Huynh Thi Thi, a widow with three sons, sought damages when the fishing

junk she had leased was lost in an incident involving a United States Navy patrol boat. On the night of December 4–5, 1968, her three sons and a nephew
had the junk out of Hon Mot near Nha Trang, several hundred yards from
shore. A navy patrol boat, identified by the boys as PT 72, stopped the junk to
check identification and cargo. The boys were ordered onto the patrol boat,
which then attempted to tow the junk to shore. Somehow, the junk sank while
under tow. According to the boys, the "GIs laughed at us and they seemed to be
satisfied" as the boat sank. The boys were brought to shore and released.

Huynh Thi Thi was understandably upset upon learning the fate of the
leased junk. She had rented the boat so the boys could make money for the
family. In addition to the lease, she had used all of her savings to buy nets and
other fishing equipment to outfit the junk. The owner of the boat, understandably, wanted payment for his lost boat. Damages filed included the boat
(VN$20,000), engine (VN$50,000), fishing nets (VN$30,000), and other items
that went down with the junk.

The widow filed a claim with the navy at Tay Ket in Nha Trang but had heard
nothing by February 1969. She sent letters inquiring about the status of her
claim to her district chief, the area commander of the U.S. forces, and the
American Embassy in Saigon but received no reply. By October, Huynh Thi
Thi's family was in dire circumstances. The claim had not been processed, and
she did not know why. Having lost her savings because of the "heartless Americans" aboard the patrol boat and with no way to make a living through fishing,
her concern and frustration grew. She estimated that her boys brought in
VN$1,000 per night fishing and calculated the loss of a year's income, adding
VN$365,000 to the original claim.

The investigation ran into difficulties from the start. PT 72 proved difficult
to locate, much like a stolen car whose thief had changed the license plates. Although the boat itself could not be located, a record of it in area operational
logs showed that the boat in question had not been involved in any such incident on the night of December 4–5, 1968. The log did report that the boat had
been fired upon early in the morning of December 5, sustaining heavy damage. The incident occurred on the Song Ong Doc River, some distance away
from where the boys had been picked up. A rocket had demolished the patrol
boat's cabin, taking the boat out of commission for repairs. Moreover, Shore
Undersea Unit Warfare Group One, West Pacific Detachment Unit 4, which
operated in the area under investigation, had no patrol boats numbered 72.

The boys had been delivered to a checkpoint near Nha Trang; that much was
for certain. Exactly who delivered them, however, remained a mystery. The

boys described the Americans who detained them as "GIs." This made investigators suspect that they were looking for the wrong type of boat, although navy personnel operating patrol boats wore the standard issue combat fatigues common across Vietnam. This hole in the story persuaded investigators to recommend rejecting the claim. They did not directly accuse the boys of making up the story, but that is certainly a possibility.

Mai Ban's junk met a similar fate, but a better claim result.[30] On January 24, 1969, the crew sailed the junk out of the Nha Trang estuary after midnight, properly lighted for night travel. About three hours later, Navy PCF 97, on a mission and thus not lighted, struck the port side of the junk just less than two miles from Hon Bac, sinking the junk along with all its equipment and fishing nets. The three fishermen onboard, slightly bewildered but unhurt, found themselves in the water, yelling for help. The patrol boat quickly turned about and let the three men hold on to the side while the crew signaled another nearby junk to pick up the fishermen. The men asked the navy crew to take them to Cau Da, but since the boat was on patrol, they refused. The other junk picked up the wet fishermen and took them to Nha Trang. The patrol boat then left the scene, but not without its crew first informing the fishermen that they should file a claim for damages.

Early on the morning of the same day, Mai Ban filed a claim at the local harbor defense unit. Damages included one 3,806-ton junk at VN$303,000, two engines totaling VN$160,000, one fishing net at VN$70,000, plus other miscellaneous items. Mai Ban had receipts and other documents verifying the value of the lost property. With all forms filled and filed, Mai Ban awaited his payment. Weeks passed, as was to be expected. By June, however, no word had arrived. Mai Ban filed another claim for lost income, amounting to over VN$1,100,000. He politely requested payment for his "unlucky boat" so that he could "save the economic situation" of his family. The file on the incident does not indicate exactly when Mai Ban received his claim, but it confirms that the claim was indeed paid.

An example of a claim involving personal injury caused by non-combat-related gunfire occurred on June 12, 1967, when an M-79 grenade exploded near Van Long in Van Dinh district, Kanh Hoa province.[31] Again, a navy patrol boat was involved; its crew fired several rounds at a partially sunken barge near the shore for gunnery practice as it returned from patrol. The commander of the craft, Lt. James Pugsley, allowed the crew to exercise its guns despite a standing order prohibiting such fire without authorization. Lieutenant Pugsley had no such authorization. After firing forty-two M-79 rounds and 140

AR-15 rounds, Pugsley's PT 48 left the barge and made its way back to base. At least five of the M-79 grenades fired did not explode. A short time later, six youngsters and an elderly man from Van Long were in the vicinity collecting firewood. They had heard the firing, and after the patrol boat had gone, let their curiosity get the best of them and approached the barge. Exploring the freshly damaged barge, the boys found a dud M-79 round, about the size of a tennis ball. The unexploded M-79 round proved their undoing, as one of the boys picked it up and threw it, causing it to explode.

Twelve-year-old Nguyen Lan, the boy who threw the yellow grenade round, suffered shrapnel wounds in his chest, stomach, cheek, and mouth. Pham Long, age seven, was hit by shrapnel in the left thigh. Le Eh, also seven, caught shrapnel in his chest. Sixty-two-year-old Nguyen Tuy had a fragment of the grenade in his upper left arm. Ha Van An, another seven-year-old, was killed. One of the injured boys was able to make it back to the village to get help. A junk took the injured boys to a hospital a short distance down the coast. One boy was taken by helicopter to a better-equipped trauma center.

Claims were subsequently filed for injuries and the death, ranging from VN$10,000 to VN$100,000, including VN$100,000 for the death. Solatia payments, ranging from VN$200 to VN$4,000, were made to the families commensurate with the extent of injuries. The investigator, Lt. Cdr. Isaac Wiltse, took almost a year to investigate and process the claims and pay the families. Wiltse's investigation also recommended a charge of negligence against Lieutenant Pugsley for indirectly causing the death of Ha Van An. PT 48's log and crew testified to the activities of the day in question. On the afternoon of June 12, PT 48 had already been on station for several hours. At a shore village, two crew members went ashore to give first aid to the local people as part of the boat's civic action duties. After a couple of hours, the boat left the village and went southward down the coast another mile, where it found the partially sunk barge, providing a perfect target for gunnery practice. Crew members testified as to the number of rounds fired and stated that some rounds did not explode. All testified that Lieutenant Pugsley had lectured the crew several times about weapons safety, rules of engagement, and unauthorized firing of weapons. Wiltse, however, recommended disciplinary action against Lieutenant Pugsley. A letter reprimanding Pugsley for disregarding a standing order and being negligent in failing to report unexploded ordinance in an area inhabited by Vietnamese civilians was issued by his commanding officer and placed in Pugsley's permanent record.[32]

Other incidents offer a glimpse of the hundreds of claims filed each year. In October 1971, an oil leak at the port of Qui Nhon caught fire, destroying boats and buildings along the harbor. One hundred and thirty claims were processed and paid. In April 1968 the ammunition dump at Da Nang exploded, causing many injuries and widespread destruction of property. More than 5,000 claims were paid, but not without long delays. Paperwork was "lost in transit" and not recovered until after the two-year filing period had expired. At first, the claimants were denied because of the statutory limitation. An investigation found the missing paperwork, revealed that the claims had indeed been filed within the time limit, and urged that claimants not be penalized because the military had lost the files. In August 1971, the claims were paid, more than three years after the incident had occurred. The sudden flood of cash into Da Nang because of the payouts caused more than 14,000 additional claims to be filed. Preliminary investigations found most of the new claims fraudulent and well past the two-year filing period. The Claims Division rejected all of the new claims.[33]

An earlier incident gives an example of how claims could result from protests and riots in Saigon. In May 1966, a ricocheting bullet fired by a U.S. guard on a gas truck killed a South Vietnamese military dispatch carrier. The guard had fired his weapon in the air to keep Buddhist demonstrators away from his truck, which had been separated from a convoy by a demonstration near the Vien Hoa Dao pagoda. Somehow, a bullet ricocheted, striking and killing the Vietnamese carrier. The unfortunate dispatch carrier's widow was given a claim payment for lost wages along with letters of condolence from the U.S. ambassador and the U.S. commander of the Saigon area. The payment was processed in two weeks, greatly reducing the tension caused in the local neighborhood by the death. It was a politically adept move to process the claim quickly in this case.[34]

There are, of course, countless other examples, but those described here are representative of what the Claims Division and claims investigators across Vietnam dealt with on a daily basis. Again, the total amount expended on claims by the U.S. government was nominal compared to the broader U.S. financial commitment in Vietnam. The greater benefit, in theory, fostered better relations with the Vietnamese people and helped fight the insurgency.

U.S. military personnel could also file claims for lost or damaged property, arising from accidents, attacks on U.S. military posts, and other incidents, under the Personnel Claims Act of 1964. The Claims Division processed these claims as well, and area judge advocates investigated these claims in addition to foreign claims. For example, during the early years of U.S. involvement, terrorist bombs and Viet Cong attacks occupied the Claims Division and judge advocate investigators. The Christmas 1964 bombing of the Brinks Hotel in Saigon found claims investigators on the scene almost before the smoke had cleared, and claims were paid out in only a few weeks.

The Viet Cong attack on Pleiku in February 1965 also resulted in several claims for damaged property. U.S. soldiers quickly had money to replace their belongings and government property. Claims arising from the Qui Nhon hotel bombing, also in February 1965, in which twenty-two American soldiers were killed and several more wounded, were quickly processed as well. In this case, survivors were flown to Saigon, given their money, and taken to the Saigon PX so that they could purchase replacement items. Obviously, these early examples were processed quickly compared to the processing time in later years. More Americans in the country and increased military activity resulted in more claims, which along with the increase in foreign claims lengthened the claims process. Taking care of the U.S. military as quickly and efficiently as possible, though, was seen as a way to help maintain troop morale.[35]

Among the more interesting claims cases involving U.S. military personnel was that of a U.S. soldier who found $150,000 in U.S. currency in a cave while on patrol. The owner or the origin of the money was unknown, but investigators guessed that Vietnamese civilians or military personnel had hid the cash and planned to recover it later. Donald W. Morrison, the soldier who found the money, turned it over to his company commander as regulations stipulated. Morrison asked if he would get to keep the money but was told he had no claim to it. Not long after, Morrison completed his tour and returned to the United States. He filed a claim for the money with the Defense Department, which promptly rejected the request. Morrison then sued the Defense Department in a U.S. district court for the money. The United States District Court for the Middle District of Georgia heard the case and ruled against Morrison. Under the Federal Tort Claims Act (28 U.S. Code, Sections 2671–2680), the U.S. district court had no jurisdiction because the claim was for more than $10,000. More important, however, was the fact that because the claim originated in a foreign country, the court could not provide relief under the law. Morrison countered that his claim was filed in the United States, but the court ruled that he was really attempting to "*enforce* a claim which *arose* in a foreign country."

The Federal Tort Claims Act prohibited claiming property found in time of war, thus Morrison had no right to it to begin with. Morrison's lawyers tried to argue that military operations in Vietnam were not commensurate to a declared war. The court ruled that declared or not, a "war is no less a war." Additionally, the Uniform Code of Military Justice in Article 103 clearly stated that all property captured or taken from the enemy had to be turned over to the proper authorities without delay. The finder had no claim even if fleeing civilians had left behind the money. U.S. courts had ruled that the same regulations applied. The case was dismissed, and Morrison did not get to enjoy the treasure he had found.36

The Vietnamese government also paid out claims for damages from accidents involving the Vietnamese military. Through a process roughly modeled on the procedures and policies used by the U.S. military, the United States helped the South Vietnamese government create a claims program. Doing so was not easy considering the insurgency conditions. Vietnamese courts and civil authorities functioned only in the cities. In the countryside, where much of the population resided, authorities and courts operated at the pleasure of whoever militarily controlled the area. Moreover, officials in the country tended to be poorly trained, if at all, in claims procedures. The principal obstacle, however, was the reluctance of the Vietnamese to turn to their courts to resolve civil matters such as claims. There was an old Vietnamese saying: "Better to go to hell than go to court." The South Vietnamese government set up a claims administration for combat claims (through the Directorate of Psychological War), noncombat claims (through the Directorate of Finance and Budget), and defoliation claims (through the Ministry of Interior). It is interesting to note that the Vietnamese government was given authority to process all combat-related claims caused by "Free World Forces," including the United States. The same applied for the defoliation program. According to a United States Army study, the "inescapable conclusion" was that these programs fostered "a popular respect for the rule of law."37

In 1972, with comparatively few U.S. forces remaining in Vietnam, claims against the United States began to decline. Claims Division headquarters kept its doors open into 1973 despite the peace accord. Toward the end, MACV established an assistance-in-kind fund to pay combat-related claims by Vietnamese, including indirect combat damage, such as might be caused by such reckless conduct as indiscriminate fire. Although the Foreign Claims Act prohibited appropriated funds from being used to pay combat-related claims, some military lawyers in Vietnam felt this was unfair to the Vietnamese, especially since the Vietnamese government claims program offered so little in restitution for combat-related losses. With the entire country of South Vietnam a combat zone and considering the intense guerilla nature of much of the fighting, Vietnamese loss of property seemed to warrant a just compensation program. Although the establishment of the assistance-in-kind fund was too little, too late, this policy change was an effort to show the Vietnamese that the United States would take responsibility for uncalled-for destruction and unwarranted behavior, thus fostering confidence in government and the rule of law. Ironically, the motivation for altering the MACV claims policy only further undermined trust in the Vietnamese government. If one's own government could not adequately handle combat-related claims and one had to rely upon another government to conduct that function, how does this build confidence in one's government?[38]

Solatia were processed in much the same fashion as property and injury claims and, as far as counterinsurgency was concerned, served much the same purpose. This program also represented a genuine effort to respect and abide by Vietnamese custom and was modeled after a similar program used in the Korean War. Unlike claims, which ultimately were an admission of fault, solatia were simply a means to express condolence to the bereaved, which is a Vietnamese custom as it is in similar societies, such as Korea, Japan, and Thailand. Claims could be filed if applicable, but accepting a solatia payment did not exclude filing a claim. In accordance with local tradition, a U.S. representative, usually a judge advocate or other officer, would offer sympathy in the form of a small gift of money. This gesture of sympathy, as perceived by the U.S. military, was a meaningful attempt to maintain, or achieve, as the case may have been, "good community relations." Solatia were given to any Vietnamese or surviving family member for loss of life, injury, and in some cases damage to personal property, caused "in whole or in part by members of the U.S. Armed Forces, DOD [Department of Defense] civilians, employees of U.S. government contractors, third-country national employees of the U.S., or local nationals in performance of their duties for the U.S."[39] There were some limitations. For example, payment would not be granted if the victim had criminally conspired to obtain a solatia payment, if the circumstances of the incident were deemed "acts of God," or if the person was "identified as VC/NVA [Viet Cong/North Vietnamese Army]."[40]

The authority to grant solatia rested primarily with area commanders through their staff judge advocates and claims officers. The Claims Division at the MACV Staff Judge Advocate's office was responsible for keeping records, but less so for administration. USARV, III MAF, NAVFORV, and Seventh Air Force each had single-service responsibility for solatia and paid solatia from their own funds. The yearly amounts were relatively small. USARV, for example, had a budget allocation of $65,000 for solatia for fiscal year 1968 (although by the end of February 1969 USARV had already expended $44,500). Payment procedures for 1968 outlined amounts ranging from VN$200 to VN$4,000 for injury, VN$200 to VN$1,000 for property damage, and VN$3,000 to VN$4,000 for death. In 1972, with the change in exchange rates, the tables were adjusted to VN$2,000 to VN$10,000 for injury, VN$500 to VN$2,000 for property damage, and VN$10,000 to VN$30,000 for death. The U.S. military placed great emphasis on solatia as gifts of condolence, not admissions of fault. Even so, some U.S. judge advocates felt as if they had placed a price on life. The strict procedures and instructions concerning solatia show how important this program was to the "community building" process. As an important element of civic action programs, monthly solatia amounts were supposed to be included in civic ac-[reports] for all U.S. commands in Vietnam.[41]

[In] addition to outlining qualifications for solatia, guidelines offered several [sug]gestions on how to actually give the payment to the victim or victim's family. [Sol]atia procedures paid close attention to protocol and avoided offending local [tra]dition, and guiding directives often included sample letters of condolence to [ac]company the sympathy payment. Solatia were to be paid within twenty-four hours of the incident, and in the case of death, before the funeral. Even the payment itself was specified—"unused paper currency placed unfolded in a plain white envelope with an appropriate condolence message." Written in Vietnamese, the message read, "This gift is an expression of friendship, sympathy, and condolence of your American friends." In addition, in the case of death, the senior commander of the unit involved should attend the funeral "as a further expression of sympathy." To avoid insulting or offending the family or victim, judge advocates and officers delivering solatia were not to request a receipt for the payment and were to avoid any sort of public display if possible.

Although victims or the victims' families could file a claim for damages, the condolence visit "must avoid soliciting claims against the United States." In other words, offer sympathy but do not open the door to further financial obligation. This policy changed in 1972, when solatia procedures were amended to have the officer presenting the payment also include information on filing a claim. There is no clear indication as to why the policy changed, but speculation suggests that those receiving the payment more often than not asked about claims, and the United States did not want to be seen as avoiding further responsibility. The ceremony of presentation was to be sincere and in keeping with local customs as much as possible.[42]

Of course, as with claims, actually carrying out solatia procedures often could be more difficult than the straightforward process outlined in the guidelines. Sometimes the size and scope of an incident warranted more practical procedures, which occasionally compromised local customs. Consider the experience of Air Force captain Joseph A. Bohrer.[43] As assistant staff judge advocate for the 337th Combat Support Group at Tan Son Nhut from 1966 to 1967, Bohrer often handled solatia resulting from accidents involving air force activity. In the spring of 1967, a flight of F-100s from Ben Hoa dropped a bomb load several miles short of target, destroying a small village in the Mekong Delta. Several civilians were killed and much property and livestock destroyed. Bohrer and an assistant were dispatched to the village, located in an unsecured area, to offer solatia to the survivors.

In battle dress, complete with flak jackets and M-16s, the air force men arrived by helicopter. An army squad took them into the ruined village, the[ ] of which caused Bohrer to take his M-16 off safety, "the only time I did [ ] thing during my tour." After investigating the area and taking an accou[ ] dead and wounded, Bohrer returned to Tan Son Nhut to arrange the sola[ ] money, leaving his assistant behind ("he rather liked being out in the countr[ ] side, perhaps he had seen too many war movies"). The next day, survivo[ ] from the destroyed village gathered in an assembly hall at a neighboring hamlet (so much for avoiding public display) to begin receiving solatia. Word spread that the Americans had cash to pass out, so a crowd of other villagers gathered outside the hall, hoping to get in on the money. A Vietnamese official called out the names of the next of kin and property owners, who came forward to receive the solatia, "along with an expression of sympathy." Bohrer remembered the scene where even the best intentions of the solatia program could not in the end lessen the loss:

> I recall, even after thirty-two years, one little Vietnamese man (Gim Po by name), who had lost his wife, two children, his house, and assorted livestock. He had tears in his eyes while I counted out $250 as evidence of our sympathy. I rather doubt he was at all political, and our expression of condolences in this manner probably did not mean a thing to him. I surely felt like an "Ugly American," and I expect that in his eyes, I was. Certainly, the Air Force had done nothing worse than the VC would have done at their best. I suspect that others in the assembly hall felt similarly (although no one turned down the money to my knowledge).

A situation that occurred during the Tet Offensive provides a good example of problems arising from confusing the foreign claims program and the solatia program. The incident, which took place during the period of February 1 through May 1968 but was not finally closed until mid-1972, involved the death of the children of Nguyen Van Hon and the loss of property. From February 1 to 3, 1968, Camp Red Ball, a United States Army post located some three miles northeast of Tan Son Nhut airbase, received approximately 120 artillery rounds during the confusing and widespread attacks of the Tet Offensive.[44] The artillery fire peppering Camp Red Ball apparently came from U.S. artillery batteries around Tan Son Nhut. Capt. John Felix, temporary commander of Camp Red Ball, could hear the voice of an American on his radio set, using the call sign "Vindicator Six Nine," directing fire onto the northern perimeter of his post. Twenty-five U.S. soldiers were wounded in this friendly fire incident. One was killed.

Amid these attacks was the modest home of Nguyen Van Hon, who lived with his family and livestock just off the northern perimeter of Camp Red Ball. His home and outbuildings were heavily damaged by the incoming shells, and according to Nguyen Van Hon, two U.S. helicopters fired rockets into his home, wounding himself, his wife, and four of his eight children. Tragically, his other four children, ages 18, 15, 11, and 8, were killed.

Nguyen Van Hon buried his children and took his surviving family to Camp Red Ball for shelter and attention to their wounds. On February 5, his house and outbuildings were burned by a U.S. patrol from Camp Red Ball to prevent Viet Cong units from using the wrecked buildings as cover to fire on the post. Lt. Lowell R. Gomsrud, the executive officer at Camp Red Ball, was with the patrol. Over the next few weeks, the post received enemy fire from Nguyen Van Hon's property. Captain Felix told Lieutenant Gomsrud to bulldoze the blackened remnants of the property and leave no shelter for the Viet Cong. Gomsrud carried out the order. Later, the property was mined to keep Viet Cong units out of the area. Nguyen Van Hon had lost four of his children and his home.

After the incident, Nguyen Van Hon contacted staff at Camp Red Ball about compensation for his losses. He was erroneously told he could file a claim under the Foreign Claims Act and be reimbursed. Apparently out of ignorance, Captain Felix and Lieutenant Gomsrud did not offer solatia condolence for the death of his children. Both were unaware of the solatia policy. A few weeks later, Nguyen Van Hon appeared in person at the Claims Division office in the Tax Department Store building in Saigon to inquire about filing a claim.

His trip proved a disappointment, as he was told that even though what had happened to his family and property was regrettable, the incident was the result of combat activity and thus not eligible for compensation under the Foreign Claims Act. Ignorance of the policy had led the poor man to Saigon, and harsh reality sent him back home. There was one ray of hope, however. The Claims Division suggested he inquire at Vietnamese claims agencies, which could make disbursements for combat-related damages. Nguyen Van Hon remained adamant that the Americans had caused his problem and they should pay for his loss, but he also pursued what the Vietnamese government could offer him.

Meanwhile, Lieutenant Gomsrud rotated out of the army and returned to the United States, but not before becoming aware of the solatia program and convincing himself that Nguyen Van Hon deserved a solatia payment of condolence. Gomsrud had inquired of the army several times to find out if a solatia had been paid but had not received a reply. In March 1971, he finally decided to contact his congressman from the Eleventh District of Minnesota, Donald Fraser. Fraser took up the cause, even directly contacting Secretary of Defense Melvin Laird to find out the status of the case and what could be done to ensure a solatia payment would be made. Not wanting to ignore a congressional inquiry, the army investigated the case. The findings were that Nguyen Van Hon had pressed his case against the United States while collecting claims from the Vietnamese government. Through the Vietnamese claims program, Nguyen Van Hon had received in May 1968 VN$4,000 for the death of the oldest daughter, who had worked at Camp Red Ball as a secretary. Also in May 1968, he was paid VN$19,000 for the deaths of his other children and an additional VN$8,000 for the loss of his house. He also received ten sheets of tin and ten bags of cement to help rebuild. The report did not indicate what he was supposed to do about the mines around his home.

Nguyen Van Hon's claim against the United States ran much higher. In July 1968, after being told verbally and in writing that he was not eligible for a claim under the Foreign Claims Act, Nguyen Van Hon requested through his district chief a claim of VN$4.5 million for the death of his children (lost wages) and VN$3 million for property damage. In early 1972, four years after the incident and having no reply to his claim request, he filed another letter, adding this time VN$2.16 million for four years back rent from the United States Army for the use of his land as part of the Camp Red Ball perimeter. Agreements between the United States and the South Vietnamese government were very clear that claims for combat-related damages were the responsibility of the South Vietnamese government and that the United States could use land and facilities rent-free.

Nguyen Van Hon apparently had not been aware of these policies and would not take "no" for an answer. He cannot be faulted for trying. Through his claim requests with the Vietnamese claims program, he had received a rather insulting $80 for the death of four of his children and the complete loss of his home and outbuildings. From the United States he sought $32,000. His claim with the United States was, of course, repeatedly denied.

This still left the matter of the solatia payment. Congressman Fraser's inquiry into the matter produced some interesting, yet predictable, results. The staff judge advocate for USARV, Col. William E. Donovan, replied that, unfortunately, nothing could be done. First, because the inquiry was three years after the fact, making a solatia payment now would "not conform with local tradition, and [might] establish an unfavorable precedent." Second, Gomsrud's account of events in his letter to Congressman Fraser could not be substantiated because of incomplete records (a common problem with administrative records from Vietnam). Third, the Tet Offensive had made doing anything about claims and solatia at the time impractical. Moreover, according to Donovan, opening the door three years later to claims and solatia from Tet would result in a deluge of filings, which the already overworked claims commissions and judge advocates could not handle. Too much time had passed. Besides, Nguyen Van Hon had never inquired about the solatia payment and had never mentioned being insulted at not receiving such. The intervention of Gomsrud and Congressman Fraser, although well intentioned, failed.

The U.S. effort to offer solatia and claims for damages to Vietnamese was well intended and indicated a tacit recognition of cultural traditions. Designed to assist in part in the struggle against insurgency, the claims and solatia program occasionally fell short for practical and logistical reasons. Processing claims and delivering solatia required a great deal of tact and some adaptability. Still, this aspect of military justice activity kept dozens of judge advocates and other soldiers busy and was seen as an important part of the nation-building effort in Vietnam. Otherwise, the United States might well not have bothered.

CHAPTER THREE
JURISDICTION FOR U.S. MILITARY AND CIVILIAN PERSONNEL IN VIETNAM

Establishing a clear and workable policy for jurisdiction over U.S. military personnel and civilians in Vietnam was important for many reasons, not the least of which included judicial process, maintenance of discipline, and sovereignty. The diplomatic, political, and judicial challenges to finding a feasible policy make this an intriguing piece of the U.S. military justice experience in the Vietnam War. The jurisdiction question shows how policy can bring together bureaucratic entities that are usually feuding—in this case Department of Defense and Department of State personnel in Vietnam and Washington—to find a solution to a problem. In the broader context of the cold war and the U.S. war in Vietnam, the jurisdictional question represented one of several efforts to demonstrate to the Vietnamese the benefits of the rule of law and judicial process, which communism allegedly could not offer.

Two issues in particular offer good examples of this problem. First, the decision to hold courts-martial in Vietnam because of logistical and disciplinary concerns created jurisdictional problems for the United States. Second, the related policy question of military jurisdiction over civilians attached to U.S. forces in Vietnam further complicated diplomatic problems and aggravated the already tense relationship between the Departments of Defense and State. In resolving both of these issues, policymakers and military lawyers had to always be mindful of the intended purpose of military justice and the rule of law.

Under normal circumstances, jurisdiction over U.S. forces serving in foreign countries is formalized by status-of-forces agreements. These agreements generally apply in times of peace, such as status-of-forces agreements between the United States and South Korea, Japan, and North Atlantic Treaty Organization (NATO) countries. In general, the United States holds jurisdiction over offenses committed by U.S. troops against other Americans or in the performance of duty. U.S. personnel committing offenses against citizens of the particular country often fall under local jurisdiction, though not always. In times of war, the jurisdiction of the Uniform Code of Military Justice is enforced and takes precedence unless precluded by such agreements. These largely diplomatic arrangements are sometimes arranged at some cost to jurisprudence.

Such was the case for U.S. forces in Vietnam. The United States and South Vietnam never concluded a status-of-forces agreement throughout the entire course of U.S. involvement. Instead, the two countries tried to resolve jurisdictional issues through political delicacy, diplomatic flexibility, and pragmatic cooperation, even though jurisdictional questions often presented more headaches to Americans than to the Vietnamese. The U.S. government tended to be concerned with the occasionally conflicting goals of establishing respect for rule of law and maintaining diplomatic hegemony in Vietnam, whereas the South Vietnamese remained content to pursue solutions that solved problems while limiting infringements on Vietnamese sovereignty. Justice, it seemed at some points in this development, became a secondary concern.

The origin and evolution of U.S. jurisdiction over soldiers and civilians serving in Vietnam follows the evolution of the overall U.S. military experience in this extraordinary conflict. Jurisdictional issues did not arise during the early years of U.S. involvement in South Vietnam. Escalation of troop numbers, however, brought a similar increase in crime, black-market activities, currency fraud, and other legal problems, which brought jurisdictional issues to the surface. As historians have occasionally debated whether the U.S. experience in Vietnam should be called a *war,* so too did judge advocates and U.S. courts discuss the same issue during the height of U.S. involvement. The "war" question would ultimately decide the issue of jurisdiction in Vietnam.[1]

To add to the complexity of jurisdictional questions, Vietnamese cultural attitudes toward law and justice differed dramatically from those of their U.S. allies. Vietnam was a country in which the legal system, which was based upon Chinese law, French Napoleonic code, and local tradition, was administered by a few lawyers and trained judges; this situation did not fit the U.S. ideal of justice. It was within the context of this patchwork system that the United States tried to show the Vietnamese the benefits of a working, effective judicial system based upon the rule of law and the protection of individual rights. The difficulty was that the very foundations of judicial process differed between the two countries. Unlike the U.S. system, which emphasized protecting the rights of the accused, Vietnamese courts followed the French model of finding truth, even at the expense of the rights of the accused. The Vietnamese showed little interest in adapting the U.S. model in place of their own.[2]

Even though U.S. counterinsurgency and pacification programs tried to instill democratic concepts of ethics and capitalistic ideals to help maintain South Vietnamese independence, corruption in Vietnam often undermined the goals and objectives of these U.S. policies.[3] This was certainly the case for legal matters. Corruption diluted Vietnamese civil and military courts and thinned the Vietnamese people's faith in justice and judicial procedures. Ironically, the U.S.

presence did not help alleviate this feeling. As the Vietnamese economy became dependent on the influx of U.S. goods and currency, crime and corruption, mainly through the black market, increased. Both Americans and Vietnamese became involved in illegal activities, which in turn forced the resolution of jurisdictional questions.[4] Vietnamese courts found the potential political consequences of bringing Americans to trial too great, even when Vietnamese sovereignty appeared neglected. Although solutions to these problems, such as trying U.S. personnel in U.S. military courts, often worked in Vietnam, they often failed before appellate courts back in the United States.

The United States concluded a multilateral mutual defense assistance agreement, known as the Pentalateral Agreement, with the French Union (France, Laos, Cambodia, and Vietnam) in 1950 to formalize U.S. support of the French war to reclaim Indochina. In addition to guidelines for military and civilian aid, the treaty provided for the jurisdictional status of military personnel serving in Indochina. Annex B of the agreement declared that military personnel, including those temporarily assigned, would be considered part of their respective diplomatic mission and enjoy diplomatic immunity according to rank. The agreement specified three categories. Category A included senior officers, who would receive full diplomatic immunity and privileges. Category B provided for junior grade officers, who would enjoy several benefits of diplomatic privilege, including exemption from local criminal and civil jurisdiction. Category C covered noncommissioned officers and enlisted personnel, who would have limited immunities equivalent to mission clerical staffs. No provision was made for civilians attached to military forces versus those associated with the American Embassy. The Pentalateral Agreement originally applied to a U.S. presence of only a few hundred troops; at the height of the U.S. war in Vietnam in 1969, more than 600,000 U.S. military personnel and civilians in Vietnam were technically under the aegis of the Pentalateral Agreement.[5] Because no updated status-of-forces agreement could be agreed upon, the Pentalateral Agreement maintained a sort of flexible inertia and would loosely guide jurisdictional issues for the United States in Vietnam until the final U.S. withdrawal in 1975.

The agreement worked well as long as the U.S. military mission remained relatively small. In 1950, U.S. military personnel numbered only in the hundreds. By the beginning of 1965, however, U.S. troop strength had increased to 20,000. By the end of the year, it had pushed past 180,000.[6] Larger numbers brought an increase in crime.[7] Because the military and political situation had changed dramatically since 1950, U.S. officials worried that the jurisdiction policy in the Pentalateral Agreement might encroach upon Vietnamese sovereignty. By 1965, both the U.S. and the South Vietnamese governments formally considered Vietnam a combat zone, and as such, the United States hoped to exercise customary military judicial authority as provided in the Uniform Code of Military Justice.

Increased U.S. involvement brought into play other issues, including legal logistical issues and disciplinary problems as well as concerns about judicial process involving U.S. personnel. For example, because MACV was attached to the Pacific command, general courts-martial were conducted at Headquarters, U.S. Army Ryukyu Islands (HQUSARI). Navy and air force general courts-martial took place at bases in the Philippines. At first, this was not a problem because only a few general courts-martial were tried involving U.S. forces in Vietnam. By the end of 1964, the number of crimes had grown with the increase in personnel. Only three general courts-martial were tried or considered for trial in 1963. There were twenty-two in 1964.[8] Lack of judicial personnel and inadequate detention and court facilities made holding trials in Vietnam problematic. Military justice support did not keep pace with escalation.[9]

Trial logistics caused headaches. Court members, the accused, and witnesses had to be transported to Okinawa or the Philippines at government expense. The Court of Military Appeals ruled in 1964 that the military had to make available witnesses if so requested by the accused, thus increasing the transportation burden.[10] Transport difficulties delayed trials. The delays concerned the MACV Staff Judge Advocate office more than the expense. If military justice is supposed to be "swift, certain, and severe" in order to maintain discipline and act as a deterrent, then delays in administering military justice hindered the deterrent effect.[11] In the opinion of one commander, delays in trials and the fact that trials took place in Okinawa rather than Vietnam "dimmed memories," caused discipline to "deteriorate," and also increased the possibility of "miscarriages" of justice.[12]

In the 1964 cases tried in Okinawa, the processing time from date of arrest or charge to action by convening authority ranged from 123 to 285 days, with an average of 177 days, almost six months. The MACV Staff Judge Advocate office claimed it could cut processing time in half by holding these trials in Vietnam and primarily for disciplinary purposes requested its own convening authority. Because general court-martial authority was vested in HQUSARI, commanders in Vietnam had increasingly turned to special courts-martial for a charge of a lesser offense instead of charging more serious offenses that normally fell under general courts-martial. As a result, some troops assumed that they were immune from general courts-martial and would thus only receive the maximum punishment of six months as stipulated for special courts-martial in the Uniform Code of Military Justice.[13]

Not all were convinced by the argument for holding trials in Vietnam. Gen. Ben Sternberg, the army vice chief of staff, claimed that focusing on expense and delay missed the crux of the problem. Sternberg without doubt believed that those in enough "serious trouble" to warrant general court-martial needed to be removed from Vietnam "without delay," regardless of cost. Getting troublemakers away from disciplined troops—"out of sight, out of mind"—was paramount in order to maintain order and discipline. Sternberg also worried that potentially negative coverage of general courts-martial by the "large and hungry" Saigon press corps could tarnish the U.S. mission and arouse bad publicity at home. He had no sympathy for the transportation problem, especially since regular military personnel could be moved in and out of Vietnam "by the first available transport" while "hooligans" were inexplicably held for weeks awaiting trial. He argued for maintaining the current system: "As long as Okinawa is willing to take care of Army dirty laundry, . . . we should be thankful and keep it that way."[14]

Granting convening authority in Vietnam would require extra personnel, namely judge advocates and clerks, to be transferred to Vietnam in order to handle trial duties in-country. MACV alone would need another four judge advocates and as many clerks. With this additional staff, the army estimate predicted that it would save 5.31 staff-years of work time for the projected number of general courts-martial (38.4 per year for a force of 20,000) as opposed to the extra time necessary for holding trials in Okinawa.[15] The same argument was made to augment MACV and the United States Army Support Command, Vietnam (USASCV) administrative discharge authority (which mainly dealt with hardship-related discharges).[16]

Yet, moving general court-martial convening authority to Vietnam involved more than practical solutions to delays, discipline, and personnel problems. Jurisdictional and diplomatic issues also had to be considered. The State Department and the American Embassy in Saigon wanted to avoid violating Vietnamese sovereignty and any other diplomatic difficulties caused by convening general courts-martial in Vietnam. The South Vietnamese government understandably wanted to present itself to the Vietnamese people as well as to neighboring countries as a sovereign state rather than a puppet of the United States. For its part, the United States also wanted to present South Vietnam as sovereign. Maintaining the thin veneer of Vietnamese sovereignty had always been crucial to U.S. policy in South Vietnam. Even more so, the State Department did not want to discuss the status of U.S. forces in Vietnam with the South Vietnamese government as the number of U.S. military personnel in Vietnam escalated. Drawing unnecessary attention to troop increases by asking permission of the South Vietnamese government to hold general courts-martial in Vietnam might have led to just such discussions.[17]

The MACV Staff Judge Advocate office, however, argued that concerns about Vietnamese sovereignty were "hollow." International law and tradition held that "jurisdiction over a nation's forces visiting in the territory of another nation remains in the visiting forces."[18] The government of South Vietnam, for its part, had to this point cooperated on both a practical and a legal level and accepted this principle. With its own military and civilian court systems overburdened, the South Vietnamese government was all too happy to continue allowing the U.S. military to take care of its own "dirty laundry." To gain State Department support for granting convening authority in Vietnam, MACV at first agreed to allow the State Department to approve individual trials in order to avoid any diplomatic incidents or unnecessary political tension.[19] It was indeed extraordinary for the military to even hint at allowing another federal department to have any say over its judicial jurisdiction.

Despite State Department concerns, the secretary of the army granted court-martial convening authority to USASCV in March 1965, the same month the first U.S. ground combat troops were introduced into Vietnam and the Rolling Thunder bombing campaign began. The navy, with the Marine Corps in tow, and the air force soon followed. MACV did not receive general court-martial authority because its size did not approach that of USASCV, which included army support and combat units that quickly surpassed 100,000 by the end of 1965. Any situations requiring a general court-martial in MACV were deferred to USASCV. The MACV Staff Judge Advocate office, however, did assist the new convening authorities in jurisdictional issues and other legal policy matters.[20]

The only attempt to modify this arrangement came in 1967, when the South Vietnamese military proposed a draft status-of-forces agreement to replace what it perceived as an outdated 1950 Pentalateral Agreement. With more than 300,000 U.S. troops in-country, the Vietnamese government and military sensed that sheer numbers had nullified the seventeen-year-old arrangement. From the U.S. standpoint, pressure on Saigon to adopt a new constitution and legal reforms, part of the nation-building program, spurred efforts to update the agreement. Concerning jurisdiction, the draft status-of-forces agreement from the Vietnamese Joint General Staff reiterated that "the laws of Vietnam applied throughout the territory of Vietnam must be observed by the servicemen, civilian personnel, and the dependents serving in the Military Forces of Signatory Nations." [21]

In the draft, minor offenses against the military and civilian laws of a signatory nation would come under the jurisdiction of that nation. Offenses against Vietnamese law, however, would be tried by the Vietnamese judicial system. Signatory nations could have "sole jurisdiction" over their own military personnel and civilians when offenses were punishable under the laws of the signatory nation and not "accused" by the Vietnamese government. Likewise, the Vietnamese government could exercise jurisdiction when the offenses violated Vietnamese law and were not punishable under the laws of the signatory nation. Actually, criminal violations under Vietnamese law and laws of signatory nations, that is, the U.S. Uniform Code of Military Justice, did not differ to any great degree. The proposed document attempted to provide for similar offenses by allowing signatory nations to exercise jurisdiction in cases involving the "security and property of the signatory nation concerned," the "lives and property" of other signatory members, and offenses "resulting from the delay in the execution of missions." The South Vietnamese government would hold jurisdiction over "all other violations." Signatory nations could "concede" jurisdiction to another signatory nation or the Vietnamese government with proper notification. Similarly, a signatory nation could request jurisdictional priority if the need arose.[22]

According to the draft, the South Vietnamese government could also arrest and detain signatory nation personnel in both Vietnamese and signatory nation jurisdictions. Either one or the other could try the accused, but not both. Sentences could be carried out under the auspices of either Vietnamese or signatory nation control. The draft status-of-forces agreement attempted to formalize what had been informal practice and to give the Vietnamese government the appearance of a more prominent role in judicial matters. It would give the South Vietnamese government a hint of sovereign power, which at this point in the conflict the United States had all but assumed.[23]

After reviewing the document, MACV "orally" replied to the Vietnamese Joint General Staff that replacing the 1950 Pentalateral Agreement with a formal status-of-forces agreement was a "highly sensitive" matter and that MACV was not "authorized" to consider it. The State Department ignored the draft since it came from the Vietnamese military, not the Vietnamese government. The draft died, largely owing to the hesitancy of the United States to enter into a more formal status-of-forces agreement and the South Vietnamese government's reluctance to annoy the United States when the war seemed to be going well. Had the draft been adopted as policy, the Vietnamese judicial system probably would have collapsed under the burden of the investigative and trial caseloads. Moreover, the lack of respect for the rule of law, in the U.S. sense of the term, raised serious concerns for due process and procedural fairness in the Vietnamese legal system.[24]

The draft status-of-forces agreement was the last effort on the part of either side to formally resolve the jurisdiction situation by diplomatic agreement. From 1968 on, the Vietnamese government was content to let the Americans take care of their own problems and not burden Vietnamese courts any more than necessary. Jurisdiction over civilians, on the other hand, proved more complex.

The policy of jurisdiction over U.S. civilians attached to military and government programs in accordance with the Uniform Code of Military Justice (Article 2 [10]) should have been a cut-and-dried case in Vietnam. As with jurisdiction over military personnel, court-martial authority over U.S. civilians "serving with" or "accompanying" U.S. military forces in Vietnam involved issues of discipline, maintaining cordial working relations with the Vietnamese government, and the already institutionally sensitive relationship between the Department of Defense and the Department of State. At stake was jurisdiction over U.S. civilians directly employed by the U.S. military and those who worked for U.S. government contractors. Those Americans not attached to the U.S. military mission, such as journalists, could not be tried by court-martial and remained under the jurisdiction of the Vietnamese government.

Much like the situation with military personnel, the Department of State wanted to review each case to avoid the appearance of threatening Vietnamese sovereignty. The first case to challenge the question arose in 1966, when a U.S. merchant seaman was tried by an army summary court-martial at Cam Ranh Bay. The army claimed jurisdiction under Article 2 (10) of the Uniform Code of Military Justice.[25] This caught the State Department off guard, as the political ramifications of such a trial had not heretofore been considered. Ambassador Henry Cabot Lodge told the State Department that although the mission counsel had not been involved in the decision to invoke convening authority and try the summary court-martial, he had now ordered the embassy counsel to consider the use of Article 2 (10) and how trying U.S. civilians might politically impact U.S.-Vietnamese relations.[26]

The judge advocates general of the army, navy, and air force weighed in on the discussions with the embassy counsel through their respective command staff judge advocates in Saigon. They concluded that exercising court-martial jurisdiction over civilians "serving with or accompanying" U.S. military forces in Vietnam was appropriate and, more important, legal under Article 2 (10). The keys to enforcing Article 2 (10) were the "in the field" and "in time of war" clauses. During peacetime, civilians could not be tried by court-martial, but wartime was another matter.[27] The "principal and largely political" question was not only whether a "time of war" existed in Vietnam but also whether the military should, "as a matter of policy," claim that a state of war indeed existed.[28]

Because Congress had not formally declared war and no president had asked for a declaration of war in Vietnam, proponents of establishing clear jurisdiction needed documentation and precedent to establish that a "time of war" existed. Col. Waldemar Solf, of the army Military Justice Division, cited cases that established the "time of war" standard. Salvage courts during the undeclared naval war with France in 1798 had ruled that salvage payments must be made in instances when a vessel had been retaken by a "public ship of war," thus inferring that a "time of war" existed without formal declaration of such. During this "Quasi-War" with France, one ruling declared, "every contention by force between two nations, in external matters, under the authority of their respective governments is not only war, but public war."[29] Throughout the Boxer Rebellion of 1900, the "time of war" clause in Article of War 58, which limited jurisdiction over murder and civil felonies, was upheld.[30] The conflict in Korea, where war was not declared, was judicially held to be a "time of war" nonetheless.[31] Vietnam apparently "met all the tests" established by these precedents.

More recent evidence further supported the existence of a "time of war" in Vietnam. On June 24, 1965, the South Vietnamese government issued a public proclamation declaring that a "state of war" existed throughout Vietnam.[32] In addition, President Lyndon Johnson used an executive order to declare that Vietnam (both North and South) and its surrounding waters were a combat zone, pursuant to section 112 of the Internal Revenue Code of 1954, effective January 1, 1964.[33]

Based on what was taken as overwhelming evidence and precedent, in January 1967 the MACV staff judge advocate, Col. Edward H. Haugney, advised judge advocates and legal officers in Vietnam that "all persons serving with or accompanying" U.S. military forces in Vietnam were subject to court-martial jurisdiction under Article 2 (10) of the Uniform Code of Military Justice. Haugney also declared that prior approval to seek jurisdiction waivers from the South Vietnamese government would not be required for trials involving

U.S. civilians who fell under Article 2 (10).[34] This decision opened the bout between the State Department and the Defense Department over which would exercise more influence on deciding jurisdiction in Vietnam.

Despite this finding, the South Vietnamese government held primary concurrent jurisdiction over U.S. civilians who committed offenses that violated both the Uniform Code of Military Justice and Vietnamese law, because civilians "accompanying" and "serving with" did not fall under the rubric of the 1950 Pentalateral Agreement. The judge advocates general of the army, navy, and air force asserted that court-martial jurisdiction under the Uniform Code of Military Justice should only be invoked when the South Vietnamese government had waived jurisdiction or when the Vietnamese legal system was not "available."

"Accompanying" and "serving with" also needed clarification. The judge advocates general maintained that civilians "accompanying" included persons who moved with military operations or "whose presence in Vietnam is not merely incidental, but is connected with or dependent on Armed Forces activities." These included contract employees and merchant seamen on ships transporting military supplies. "Serving with" referred to civilians directly employed by the military in-country.[35]

In March 1967, a joint Defense Department and State Department statement issued by the American Embassy in Saigon announced that U.S. civilians "serving with or accompanying" U.S. military forces in Vietnam would be under the jurisdiction of the Uniform Code of Military Justice, Article 2 (10). The problem came in implementing this policy. The State Department predicted that trying U.S. civilians under Article 2 (10) would "rarely be necessary." Thus, requesting a waiver of jurisdiction from the Vietnamese government on a case-by-case basis would be practicable. Seeking a waiver, however, was not so simple. Upon determining that a court-martial was necessary, U.S. military authorities would then have to apply to the State Department in Washington for a final decision on whether or not to ask for a waiver.[36] Both MACV and ultimately the American Embassy in Saigon disagreed with this requirement. The requests were cumbersome and could take weeks, thus delaying trials and hindering the "swift, certain, and severe" standard of military justice.

This issue proved divisive enough for Congress to offer its input on the matter. Hearings in June 1967 straddled the fence separating the military judge advocates general and the State Department positions. The Special Subcommittee on the Application of the Uniform Code of Military Justice to American

Civilians in the Republic of Vietnam found that Article 2 (10) did indeed apply to Americans in Vietnam. Because of the absence of a status-of-forces agreement, the subcommittee saw no other alternative for the trial of U.S. civilians attached to the military. The report did, however, suggest that the "executive branch" look into seeking waivers of jurisdiction from the Vietnamese government. Ultimately, the subcommittee's finding had no bearing on the issue, but congressional attention to the issue highlights its significance.[37]

In November 1967, MACV and the Saigon embassy filed a joint cable to the State Department and the Defense Department requesting that the waiver-request policy be revoked. U.S. authorities in Vietnam disagreed with the idea that trying civilians would be a rare occurrence. A special investigative group created by the American Embassy, called the Irregular Activities Committee, had concluded that U.S. civilians in Vietnam were heavily involved in the black market and currency fraud. As it stood, U.S. officials were powerless to do anything about these violations. The Vietnamese government rarely prosecuted U.S. civilians and often confiscated black-market goods or illegal currency, and that was the end of it. With this lack of deterrent, MACV wanted meaningful punishment through courts-martial. The increase in these illegal activities made lengthy waiver requests through the State Department impractical. The situation offered no good result. U.S. civilians had grown accustomed to the low risk and high return of black-market activities and currency fraud. This growing problem tarnished the respect for rule of law the United States wanted to present in Vietnam. The apparent "freedom from prosecution" brought Vietnamese "bitterness and resentment" against Americans, who the Vietnamese people came to believe were "getting away with it" while they suffered the consequences under the Vietnamese judicial system.[38]

MACV and the American Embassy jointly argued that Vietnamese government authorities would indeed support "measures that would hopefully suppress and control American lawlessness." In their opinion, sovereignty had become less of an issue for the Vietnamese government. With its courts overburdened and often corrupt, and prisons full, the Vietnamese government understandably "encouraged" the United States to take care of its own criminal problems. The cable further argued that simply by letting the word get out that court-martial jurisdiction would be enforced without protracted waiver requests, illegal activities involving U.S. civilians and military personnel would decline.[39]

Together, MACV and the embassy requested that the requirement for State Department review of potential court-martial cases involving U.S. civilians be removed and vested instead in the U.S. ambassador in Saigon. This "expedited" process would ensure swift justice to maintain discipline and curb illegal activities while also making certain that "pertinent political and legal factors" received due consideration. The Vietnamese minister of justice, Nguyen Duc Bu, agreed that the joint proposal's arrangement would speed up the process. He did, however, want to make sure that the emphasis on U.S. prosecution of U.S. civilians falling under Article 2 (10) did not give the Vietnamese public the idea that Americans were immune from Vietnamese justice (the sovereignty issue was not dead after all). In principle, he thought the new process would work. Ambassador Ellsworth Bunker and MACV commander general William Westmoreland concurred.[40]

The Department of Defense general counsel's office prepared a memorandum discussing the waiver request issue for the deputy secretary of defense and the Joint Chiefs of Staff. The State Department had ordered the American Embassy in Saigon to send requests for waivers to Washington, but the Department of Defense had told MACV that no such request was necessary. Discussions with the State Department had not resolved the issue. Even though relatively few courts-martial of civilians took place, more investigations than originally anticipated clogged the system, and having to request a waiver through Washington resulted in what the Defense Department saw as unnecessarily lengthy delays. More important, because of delays in pursuing civilian cases, U.S. officials now "channeled" their investigations toward military as opposed to civilian offenders. Civilians involved in black-market activities and currency fraud now went largely unpunished. For example, Vietnamese police exposed a black-market ring involving more than 116 American contractor employees, all of whom fell under Article 2 (10). No punitive action came from either U.S. or Vietnamese authorities because of administrative delays.[41]

Defense and State Department discussions began to make some progress. Leonard Meeker, Department of State legal adviser, forwarded a draft cable for approval to Paul Warnke, assistant secretary of defense, addressing the jurisdiction waiver issue. Meeker concluded that allowing more court-martial trials of civilians without review for waiver of jurisdiction would cause more problems for both the U.S. and the Vietnamese governments. The draft did not specify these possible problems, but they could certainly have included State Department concerns about sovereignty, the fragile political situation in Vietnam, and the negative impact that criminal activities (the black market) had on the war. Even though recognizing the problem of increased illegal activities of U.S. civilians in Vietnam, the State Department remained reluctant to open the door to more trials. The State Department promised to expedite waiver requests and encouraged MACV and the American Embassy to complete investigations to determine if trial was even necessary before requesting a waiver, a process that would in reality delay matters even more and potentially waste hundreds of valuable staff-hours.

The State Department wanted to put the problem back on the Vietnamese government: "Are there not ways in which we can encourage [Vietnamese] courts to impose fines adequate to be an effective deterrent?" Yet the draft also admitted that the Vietnamese judicial system was "strained" and lacked "resources" to deal with its own problems, much less U.S. offenses. The one helpful idea the State Department suggested involved exploring administrative penalties, such as deportation and fines, against U.S. government contractors and their employees. Such a policy could serve as a deterrent against criminal activity in place of prison sentences.[42]

The Department of Defense could not concur with the State Department draft cable. The problem remained: the State Department still wanted to review waiver requests in Washington. The Defense Department general counsel's office accused the State Department of trying to "freeze" consideration of the present policy. State Department arguments did not hold up. Nothing in the draft indicated the problems that might arise with more trials of U.S. civilians by courts-martial. No viable solution to the delay in bringing cases to trial caused by the waiver request through the State Department was presented. To the Defense Department, the State Department's attitude suggested that this issue was not a real problem but rather a turf tussle with the Defense Department.[43]

Warnke passed along these concerns to Meeker at the State Department. Warnke again suggested that the resolution to the problem involved three central solutions. First, delegate to the American Embassy the decision about the cases on which to request a waiver of jurisdiction, making certain that the embassy did not determine if the case should indeed go to trial. Second, allow the embassy and MACV to decide at what point in an investigation to request a waiver, which government level should offer the request, and what form the request should take. The Defense Department wanted to invest authority on this matter in the U.S. military/diplomatic establishment in Vietnam. Third, require "full conformity" with the Uniform Code of Military Justice. If the State Department would agree to this policy, dealing with the growing civilian crime problem in Vietnam would be made much easier while avoiding further jurisdictional problems with the South Vietnamese government.[44] The State

Department held firm, notifying the American Embassy in Saigon that the basic policy outlined in March 1967 should stand.[45]

Ironically, rather suddenly the decision was no longer one for the Department of Defense or the Department of State to make. Two general court-martial trials of U.S. civilians under Article 2 (10) made all of this wrangling obsolete and resolved the jurisdiction policy question. The first case involved James H. Latney, a merchant seaman onboard a fuel tanker under contract to the Military Sea Transportation Service. In August 1967, Marine Corps military police arrested Latney after he allegedly killed a fellow shipmate in a Da Nang bar fight. The timing of the case fell in perfectly with the waiver struggle between the Defense Department and the State Department. Although Latney was clearly guilty, the court-martial proved to be more about establishing jurisdiction under Article 2 (10) in Vietnam than about establishing guilt.[46] The burden of the prosecution was to show that Latney was "serving with or accompanying" U.S. military forces in the field. The State Department granted the waiver request and Vietnamese authorities willingly approved, wanting to avoid the case altogether. Two other cases involving U.S. civilians were already about to go to trial in Vietnamese courts.

Latney's court-martial did not convene until February 1968, some four months after his arrest. Part of the delay involved Latney's petition for writ of habeas corpus to the Court of Military Appeals, then to the United States District Court of the District of Columbia. Both petitions were denied, and on February 25, 1968, a general court-martial in Vietnam convicted Latney of unpremeditated murder and sentenced him to fifteen years confinement at hard labor. The conviction should have set the policy and precedent for trying U.S. civilians in a combat zone under Article 2 (10).[47]

The conviction and the precedent, however, did not last. Latney's lawyers appealed the conviction to the United States Court of Appeals in the District of Columbia. The court overturned the conviction, holding that Article 2 (10) did not apply because the Uniform Code of Military Justice could not have jurisdiction over a civilian seaman on his ship nor over a civilian who had not "assimilated" with the military. Latney's lawyers cited the recent landmark *O'Callahan v. Parker* decision, in which the Supreme Court had removed courts-martial jurisdiction from offenses that were not "service-connected."[48] Since Latney was just passing through and not in a permanent work situation with U.S. military forces in Vietnam, he was not "serving with or accompanying" the military "in the field." His presence was incidental. In June 1969, Latney was ordered released. U.S. attorneys did not appeal, believing, in error as it turned out, that the original conviction would be enough of a deterrent to get the point across to other civilians in Vietnam.[49] Yet Article 2 (10) had been only partially clarified while the departments of State and Defense wrestled for territorial control of jurisdiction over civilians.

The other case closely followed the *Latney* decision. Although *Latney* narrowed the question of "serving with or accompanying in the field," *U.S. v. Averette* dealt an even more severe blow to the ability of MACV and the American Embassy in Saigon to deal with crime committed by U.S. civilians attached to the military mission under Article 2 (10). Raymond Averette was a civilian employee of an army contractor who was convicted by an army court-martial of attempted theft involving a large stock of batteries. His sentence was one year at hard labor and a $500 fine. The Court of Military Appeals, however, ruled that although Averette was, unlike Latney, "serving with" a force "in the field," Averette's conviction should be overturned because it failed to meet the "time of war" requirement of Article 2. Congress had not formally declared war; therefore, Averette's offense was not committed in "time of war" and could not be tried by court-martial under Article 2 (10) of the Uniform Code of Military Justice.[50] The Court of Military Appeals had ruled in the 1967 case *U.S. v. Anderson* that the Article 43 statute of limitations for "time of war" did apply to servicemen in Vietnam, but "time of war" did not now apply to civilians.[51] Through *Latney* and *Averette*, the courts had made it very difficult to try U.S. civilians in Vietnam attached to the U.S. military mission by courts-martial.

How were MACV and the American Embassy supposed to control U.S. civilians under contract to the military mission in Vietnam when jurisdiction had been thrown back into the ineffective and overcrowded Vietnamese judicial system? The MACV Staff Judge Advocate office had fortunately foreseen the *Averette* decision and planned ahead by making a strategic change in its policy toward U.S. civilians. In July 1969, MACV directives informed contractor employees and other U.S. civilians attached to the military that administrative punishments (as the Department of State had earlier suggested) would be enforced to curb black-market involvement, currency fraud, and other criminal activities. Punishments included surrender of military privileges, loss of employment, and deportation. Companies with excessive violations among their workers could ultimately lose their contracts and be sent home and could also be barred from future government business. Americans involved in U.S. government aid programs were subject to similar reprimands.[52] Thus, U.S. soldiers were prosecuted and punished under the Uniform Code of Military Justice, whereas U.S. civilians suspected of similar criminal activity escaped trial, avoided Vietnamese courts, and might only lose their privileges or their jobs. In the absence of a viable alternative, however, this may have been the only workable policy option.

Up to the time of the *Averette* decision, sixteen cases involving U.S. civilians had been investigated. Ten resulted in no charge being filed, two had charges dropped, and four were tried by courts-martial, including *Latney* and *Averette*. A general court-martial of a U.S. civilian took place in the midst of these decisions on court-martial jurisdiction over civilians in Vietnam. In July 1969, a helicopter mechanic, Anthony Simonaro, under contract by the army from the Dynalectron Corporation, was arrested and charged with wrongful possession and the illegal sale of marijuana and opium at Ban Me Thuot. Simonaro pleaded not guilty to all three counts but was convicted of the two counts of possession under Article 134. He was sentenced to pay a fine of $1,000 and to serve hard labor up to six months until the fine was paid. Simonaro apparently paid the fine and did not appeal his sentence. There is no indication that he lost his job.

Simonaro's defense lawyer moved to dismiss the charges at the beginning of the trial, arguing that the army had no jurisdiction under Article 2 (10). Support for the motion to dismiss was rather weak. Simonaro had limited PX privileges, had never been allowed free military mail, and supplied his own tools. He was not issued or permitted to carry a weapon, and even though he lived on base, he was not required to do so according to his contract. Moreover, Simonaro's supervisor with the Dynalectron Corporation had disciplinary control over him according to Simonaro's contract arrangement with Dynalectron. Thus, defense counsel claimed that Simonaro was neither "serving with" nor "accompanying" an armed force in the field.

The prosecuting attorney easily rebutted this claim and firmly showed that Simonaro was under the jurisdiction of Article 2 (10). The request to try Simonaro had been approved by MACV. Simonaro had worked with the 155th Assault Helicopter Company for several months at Ban Me Thuot, which was in a combat zone and had been attacked several times, averaging about forty enemy contacts per month. Simonaro received hazardous duty pay from Dynalectron, used the PX, had a military ration card, lived in enlisted quarters, and was required to obey all post regulations. Testimony was even entered to the effect that sandbags protected buildings in which the accused worked and lived from rocket attacks and that numerous personnel protection bunkers scattered about the post were frequently used during attacks and alarms by both military and civilian personnel. Simonaro worked for, was commanded by, and had his work inspected by military personnel. The judge as well as the reviewing staff judge advocate easily concluded that Simonaro was indeed "serving with" and "accompanying" a force in the field and was thus under the jurisdiction of Article 2 (10). Although it is not entirely clear, it appears that the court's sentence held and was carried out despite rulings that civilians were not under court-martial jurisdiction.[53]

After losing court-martial jurisdiction over civilians and with Vietnamese courts unwilling to do the job, MACV and the American Embassy in Saigon did the best they could by utilizing the administrative punishment policy. A file maintained by the embassy listed so-called debarred U.S. civilians. By 1973, the end of the U.S. war in Vietnam, 943 U.S. civilians had been debarred. A movement to try civilians and service members who had been discharged from the military for crimes allegedly committed while in military service in Vietnam sputtered out in 1970. The proposal suggested military commissions established under international law as an alternative to courts-martial. The problem, however, centered on the fact that under the Uniform Code of Military Justice, military commissions and courts-martial have concurrent jurisdiction, and since courts had limited the jurisdiction of courts-martial over civilians and former members of the armed services, the idea quickly faded.[54]

The impact of these restrictive rulings on the military justice system was profound. They came just as the 1968 revision of the Uniform Code of Military Justice went into effect, which, as previously discussed, put great pressure on already overworked judge advocates in each of the services. The additional burden placed on military lawyers to meet an "uncertain standard" of whether or not the offense or the offender was service-connected meant that even though there might be fewer cases to try, more time would be necessary for each case. Moreover, appellate courts now faced a backlog of appeals based upon service-connection. At least one law professor, Robinson O. Everett of Duke University School of Law, who was also a reserve lieutenant colonel in the air force Judge Advocate General's Corps, strongly urged the Supreme Court to overturn cases such as *O'Callahan v. Parker* in order to restore jurisdiction and integrity to military justice.[55]

CHAPTER FOUR
DISCIPLINE, MILITARY
CRIMES, AND COURTS-MARTIAL

Courts-martial and nonjudicial punishments numbered in the tens of thousands over the course of the Vietnam War. Statistics are spotty and records are incomplete, but from what is available, a broad review of this experience can be constructed. Assault, murder, and fragging (the murder or attempted murder of a superior officer) rank among the more serious crimes that occurred in Vietnam, but other problems, such as drug use and lack of basic discipline, also had an impact on maintaining order among the troops. The military justice system was the front line in dealing with these issues, and its successes and failures say much about military justice and the U.S. experience in Vietnam. Throughout the 1970s and well into the 1980s, academicians, defense analysts, former and active-duty officers, and others who either followed or were involved in military affairs debated the so-called crisis in discipline or crisis in command in the U.S. armed forces.

By 1971, the mighty U.S. military machine was running roughly and in danger of breaking down altogether. During subsequent years, a multitude of official and unofficial studies scrutinized what had happened to the U.S. military, especially the army, in Vietnam. Dissent by members of the armed forces, combat refusals, fragging, underground newspapers, "search and evade" (making little effort to make contact with the enemy while on patrol), and widespread desertions all pointed to a military on the verge of collapse. The disengagement that came with Vietnamization, the atmosphere of moral decay and corruption in South Vietnam, the antiwar movement in the United States, social instability within the military that reflected racial and social problems in U.S. society, the twelve-month tour of duty that undermined unit cohesion, the access to drugs and the excessive use of drugs among U.S. troops worldwide, poor training and lowered enlistment standards, and the overall decline in the quality of the officer corps all contributed to the state of crisis in which U.S. forces found themselves embroiled in Vietnam. All of these pointed to the idea that the managerial style of command and organization had perhaps failed.[1]

Military crimes were among the more telling indicators of the disintegration of U.S. military forces in South Vietnam. Military offenses outlined in the

Uniform Code of Military Justice, such as being absent without leave (AWOL), desertion, mutiny and combat refusal, sleeping on post, and the like combined with more worldly crimes of rape and murder to threaten the disciplinary core of the army and Marine Corps in Vietnam. Some of these latter crimes committed against civilians could be categorized as war crimes, whereas others might not be. Fragging was one of the better-known crimes of the Vietnam War and tells much about the crisis in discipline and command. Subsequent chapters will look at how military justice combined with other efforts in an attempt to deal with war crimes, drug use, and illicit activities.

These problems are common knowledge to those who study Vietnam and even to those familiar with the conflict through popular culture.[2] What both groups often overlook is that the crisis in discipline and command was not necessarily a Vietnam-centric issue: the crisis engulfed U.S. forces worldwide and continued well into the late 1970s. Still, Vietnam was where the dam nearly burst, and it was the military justice system that played an important role in keeping a finger in the dike to hold back the flood of complete collapse. In this respect, the system could be blamed for being part of the problem. If military justice is indeed supposed to be a deterrent, then it did indeed fail. The very nature of the system lent itself to watered-down sentences. An army court-martial might convict a soldier and give a sentence of five years hard labor and a dishonorable discharge; the convening authority might reduce that sentence to two years and a bad conduct discharge; then the appeals court could reduce the sentence even further; finally, the secretary of the army could reduce the sentence even further to just an administrative discharge. In the 1960s and early 1970s, worse things could happen to a soldier than being kicked out of the military. Moreover, there is little doubt that a range of criminal acts was purposefully overlooked because officers often understandably did not want to bring attention to any blight infesting their command. The deterrent factor perhaps did not function as well as it might have done with harsher sentencing.[3]

Commanders in Vietnam had a variety of means at their disposal to deal with breaches of discipline and more serious offenses against the Uniform Code of Military Justice. Many offenses, rightly or wrongly, found their way to an Article 15 nonjudicial punishment. Article 15s saved time and paperwork and often had an immediate and visible impact as a deterrent. Summary courts-martial had similar advantages. For special and general courts-martial, things became more bureaucratically and logistically complicated. The accused had the right to a military lawyer or a civilian attorney (at his own expense) and could request trial by military judge or by jury. Under Article 31, which predated *Miranda* by several years, an arrested service member had to be informed of his or her rights under the Uniform Code of Military Justice. A general court-martial further required an Article 32 pretrial investigation where a hearing would be held to determine if indeed charges should be brought to trial, which was much like the function of a grand jury.

Military lawyers, their occasional civilian counterparts, and commanders looked to the Uniform Code of Military Justice and the *Manual for Courts-Martial* as their guide. Although most trials were processed relatively quickly, many took a great deal of time, and caseloads on the few military lawyers in Vietnam were heavy. As a consequence, thousands of plea bargains were arranged to save time and effort and to avoid full-blown court-martial trials. Judge advocates sometimes convinced convening authorities to drop trials whenever prosecuting and defense counsels agreed that a trial was unnecessary.[4]

One of the more constant problems plaguing military justice organization in Vietnam was that there barely seemed to be enough judge advocates to handle massive caseloads. An MACV military judges' conference on the Military Justice Act of 1968 in May 1969 requested an additional seventy judge advocates at the rank of captain and seven military judges in response to the changes brought by the 1968 Act and the new *Manual for Courts-Martial*. The new requirement that special courts-martial be presided over by a judge and that accused in special courts-martial had the right to qualified counsel required more legal personnel in Vietnam.

Jurisdictions also had to be reconfigured to spread out the expected increase in trial loads for both judge advocates and judges. A typical special court-martial jurisdiction might have a supervisory judge, three deputy supervisory judges, and four special court-martial judges, with an office run by a warrant officer and two or three clerks. Full-time trial teams were added, and general courts-martial and special courts-martial jurisdictions were ultimately consolidated in a move toward improved efficiency.

Several of these judges' conferences and seminars for judge advocates took place from 1968 to the end of the war, sporadically at first but by 1971 on a regular monthly basis. Predictably, the conferences held in latter years spent time discussing the increasing number of drug and discipline problems. Meetings also took place to work out staffing concerns to better cope with the growing number of trials. The key theme in many of these meetings was flexibility and pragmatism—what worked for one command might not in another. There was indeed a commitment throughout the war to expediently resolve issues to make the system more efficient while maintaining its judicial fairness. For the most part, the structural tinkering worked, and the frequent meetings of judge advocates from across different commands provided a sense of common purpose and camaraderie.[5]

One general court-martial docket for the army in Vietnam in 1969 provides a narrow look at the caseload for judge advocates in Vietnam. The docket lists the disposition of 37 of the 377 general courts-martial tried by the army in Vietnam that year. Charges included 8 counts of larceny, 4 for drug possession, 11 assault charges, 2 rapes, 1 attempted rape, 4 attempted murders, 2 unlawful killings, and 11 counts of murder. Of the cases tried, 13 pleaded not guilty, but only 2 were found so. Eight of those charged were returned to their units for "disposition other than by general court-martial," and 3 had their charges dismissed. At least 5 of the accused chose to stand before a military judge alone instead of a military court (jury). A U.S. civilian working with USARV was charged with murder and two counts of assault with a pistol, but after two days of trial his case was dismissed because the prosecution had failed to obtain the required waiver from the South Vietnamese government.

Detailed in the docket's procedural table is the general court-martial of Private John Pennie of the Fifty-Second Signal Battalion. Pennie's trial shows how a court-martial in Vietnam progressed. He was arrested on February 7, 1969, on a charge of murder (Article 118) and formally charged the next day. The Article 32 pretrial investigation took three days, ending on February 11. On February 20, the unit staff judge advocate examined the Article 32 findings and recommended on February 23 that Pennie be tried by general court-martial. The trial took place on March 25. Pennie pleaded guilty and was sentenced to reduction in rank, total forfeiture of pay, and confinement at hard labor for seven years. The convening authority reviewed the case on April 10, reducing Pennie's hard labor sentence to five years. On May 22, Pennie's sentence was affirmed, and his petition for review was denied on July 14. Pennie's experience with the military justice system lasted almost seven months, a period typical of that for similar trials on the USARV docket for 1969.[6]

For the last six months of 1971, USARV had 221 general court-martial trials, including an impressive 60 in July alone. During this same period, army lawyers dealt with 276 bad-conduct special courts-martial, 1,381 special courts-martial, and 326 summary courts-martial, and they processed 17,963 Article 15 nonjudicial punishments. These were busy people.[7] Table 4.1 gives data for army trials in Vietnam. The number of nonjudicial punishments is staggering.

Table 4.1. Army Disciplinary Actions, Vietnam, 1965–1972

Year	Courts-Martial			Non-Judicial Punishments
	General	Special	Summary	
1965	25	488	301	NA
1966	176	2,723	2,187	NA
1967	283	4,840	2,090	46,392
1968	302	6,798	2,119	59,178
1969	377	7,314	2,231	66,702
1970	300	4,964	597	64,534
1971	350	3,678	434	41,237
1972	113	774	187	8,283

Source: U.S. Army Disciplinary Actions, Republic of Vietnam, Box 3, Vietnam Monograph, Record Group 319, Records of the Army Staff, United States National Archives and Records Administration, College Park, Maryland.

Statistics for the First Cavalry, one of the more famous units that served in Southeast Asia, shed light on the court-martial load for an active combat unit in Vietnam. From February through December 1969, the First Cavalry held 115 general courts-martial, including a high of 19 in August and a low of 2 in December, averaging a little more than 10 per month. Three hundred and four special courts-martial were tried (including one involving an offense against a Vietnamese civilian), with a high load of 41 in April and an atypical low of 4 in August, but still averaging more than 27 cases tried per month. Summary courts-martial made up 107 trials, with a high of 15 in February to a low of 4 in April, averaging just over 9 trials per month. Article 15s provided the most paperwork for First Cavalry judge advocates, processing 3,098 for the eleven-month period, with a high of 363 in October and a low of 203 in April, averaging just fewer than 282 nonjudicial punishments per month. Of these 3,098 Article 15s, 153 were drug-related and one involved an "offense" against a Vietnamese civilian. It is little wonder that the handful of lawyers assigned to the First Cavalry and USARV typically worked twelve to fourteen hours a day.[8]

Charges of desertion and being AWOL also occupied commanders and military lawyers, but the problem was not unique to the Vietnam War. The U.S. military, in particular the army, has a long history of soldiers illegally temporarily or permanently leaving service. During the nineteenth century, peacetime desertion rates reached as high as 50 percent. The Confederate army during the Civil War often had up to two-thirds of its rolls absent. In World War II, the army's desertion rate reached 63 per thousand, and in Korea hit 22.5 per thousand. AWOLs reached a high of 181 per thousand during the Korean War.[9]

During the latter years of the Vietnam War, AWOLs and deserters were a major problem for the U.S. military worldwide (similar to the drug problem). As it did with the drug problem, the military tended to blame excessive AWOLs on "misfits" who had been drafted into the military. Worldwide, the desertion rate for the army had risen from a respectable 14.7 per thousand in 1966 to a disturbing 73.3 per thousand in 1970. In real numbers, the Defense Department reported 40,227 deserters in 1967, 73,121 in 1969, and 90,000 in 1971. AWOLs grew from 57.2 per thousand in 1966 to 176.9 per thousand in 1971. In Vietnam, the army's AWOL rate went from 24.6 in 1967 to 25.2 in 1968, then dropped to 13.9 for the first six months of fiscal year 1969. Desertion rates were much lower: 5.9 per thousand in 1967, 4.5 per thousand in 1968, and 2.3 per thousand for the fist six months of fiscal year 1969.[10]

The Irregular Activities Committee (IAC) took a special interest in AWOLs and deserters. It was these soldiers who contributed heavily to illicit activities in the Saigon area. In a report to the IAC in 1970, the provost marshal of MACV indicated that AWOLs in 1969 had reached a high in February of 1,166 compared to a low in November of 657. The provost marshal suggested that "experience indicates" that about one-third of these soldiers would be arrested, whereas "the major portion of the remainder" would return to their units on their own accord. Fifteen percent usually ended up being listed as deserters after being AWOL for more than thirty days.[11]

The navy and air force had less of a problem with desertion and AWOLs for a variety of reasons. The air force's principal reliance on volunteers and its less rigid hierarchy perhaps reduced the desire for malcontents to desert or go AWOL. In Vietnam, as in the United States, the air force enjoyed far and away the best living quarters, clubs, recreation facilities, and messes. The air force's desertion rate for much of the Vietnam era was less than one per thousand. The air force reported only seven members as AWOL for more than thirty days for 1967 and 1968, and these were all on leave in the United States at the time of their absence. The practical limitations of deserting from a ship may have kept navy desertion rates down. The navy had its share of draftees, but because the highly skilled nature of most jobs in the navy demanded extensive training and technical skills, the navy enjoyed a more motivated sailor than the army's soldier. The navy reported only twenty-two sailors absent for more than thirty days in Vietnam from January 1967 through March 1968. The Marine Corps, however, suffered problems with desertion and AWOLs similar to those of the army. Marine Corps AWOL rates hit 174.3 per thousand worldwide in 1970, then skyrocketed to 234.4 per thousand in 1973. Desertion rates went from

16.1 per thousand in 1966 to 56.2 per thousand in 1971. Of 5,658 Marines listed as AWOL worldwide for more than thirty days in 1968, only 111 were convicted under Article 85. The Marine Corps reported thirty men absent for more than thirty days from January 1967 through March 1968. One Marine Corps officer supposedly remarked, "Let the bastards go. We're all better off without them."[12]

In the Uniform Code of Military Justice, desertion and AWOL are somewhat complicated. Article 85 outlines desertion, and Article 86 covers AWOL. Avoiding hazardous duty was punishable by five years hard labor, dishonorable discharge, and total forfeiture of all pay. For those simply shirking duty, the maximum confinement was only three years at hard labor. If the deserter turned himself or herself in to military authorities, the sentence decreased to two years. A bad conduct discharge could be given in lieu of a dishonorable discharge. First, deserters had to be caught, which was in and of itself not easy. Deserters in Europe could easily melt into the population, and blending into the hustle and bustle of Saigon was almost as easy. Status-of-forces agreements prevented the military from using local authorities to apprehend deserters, and even if they were caught by local authorities, the agreements considered desertion a nonextraditable offense. Those who remained on the rolls as deserters for more than a year were given an undesirable discharge in absentia. If deserters who were thus discharged ended up outside the United States, their names would be listed among those barred from reentering the United States. Instead of being discharged, some deserters and AWOLs in Europe and the United States who were returned to service found themselves transferred to Vietnam.[13]

In Vietnam, local authorities sometimes apprehended deserters, but only because they were caught breaking a Vietnamese law, not because they were AWOL. U.S. military police spent a great deal of time trying to track down deserters in Saigon and other cities. It is difficult to judge success in bringing deserters and AWOLs in for punishment. In 1965, the army had no trials for desertion in Vietnam and had only one in 1966. In 1967, the army tried 14 for desertion, convicting 9 of desertion and the remaining 5 of the lesser offense of AWOL. In 1968, 16 were tried, with 5 convicted of desertion and 11 of the lesser offense. In 1967, the Army tried 35 AWOLs, with 34 convictions, and in 1968 tried 43, with 41 convicted. Of course, in 1967 and 1968 the buildup had added tens of thousands more troops in-country than had been in Vietnam in 1965.

The sentences were inconsistent. In 1968, 8 general courts-martial for the single offense of desertion or AWOL resulted in 4 dishonorable discharges and 3 bad conduct discharges; in addition to being discharged, 1 defendant was sentenced to confinement at hard labor for 3 to 5 months, 2 for 6 to 8 months, 3 for 12 to 17 months, 1 for 36 to 47 months (desertion), and 1 for 48 to 59 months (desertion). The same year, the thirty-four general courts-martial convictions for multiple offenses that included desertion or AWOL resulted in 8 dishonorable discharges and 18 bad conduct discharges. Two soldiers were sentenced to confinement at hard labor for less than 3 months, 2 for 3 to 5 months, 6 for 6 to 8 months, 1 for 9 to 11 months, 11 for 12 to 17 months, 3 for 18 to 23 months, 3 for 24 to 29 months, 1 for 36 to 47 months (desertion), and 1 for 48 to 59 months (desertion). Although the statistics do not clearly delineate total sentencing, many of those discharged likely included confinement at hard labor.[14]

An air force case in Vietnam in 1968 shows how AWOL and desertion were often tied in with other criminal activities. An airman second class was charged with violating Article 86 (AWOL from August 21 to October 4, 1967), Article 92 (violating the MACV regulation against privately owned firearms), and Article 134 (violation of general article, in this case wrongfully discharging a firearm and endangering a human life). The airman pleaded guilty to the Article 86 and 92 specifications and not guilty to the Article 134 charge. A special court-martial found him guilty on all counts, sentencing him with a bad conduct discharge, confinement at hard labor for three months, forfeiture of $86 per month for three months, and reduction in rank to airman basic. The secretary of the air force changed the bad conduct discharge to a general discharge in consideration of prior good service.[15]

Navy trials from the same year show how punishments could vary from unit to unit, pointing to the inconsistency of sentencing and the questionable deterrent role. In one unit, special courts-martial sentenced a sailor (with seven nonjudicial punishments on his record) for being AWOL for 41 days to 6 months confinement at hard labor, forfeiture of $60 per month for 6 months, and discharge from service. In the same unit, a sailor AWOL for 60 days was sentenced to 3 months confinement at hard labor, forfeiture of $68 per month for 3 months, and reduction in rank. By comparison, another unit sentenced a sailor who had been AWOL for 53 days to 2 months confinement at hard labor, forfeiture of $59 per month for 2 months, and reduction in rank, and another unit sentenced a sailor who had been AWOL for 58 days to 3 months confinement at hard labor, forfeiture of $90 per month for 3 months, reduction in rank, and a bad conduct discharge.[16]

Commanders could be caught in a difficult position. They had to maintain discipline and order within their units and make examples of those who broke the rules, but at the same time they often wanted their troops to see them as benevolent leaders. Desertion and AWOL seriously challenged command responsibility. In dealing with desertion and AWOL sentencing, the convening authority often reduced sentences handed down by trials. In 1968, Article 85 convictions in Vietnam averaged a trial sentence of confinement at hard labor for 3.4 years, whereas convening authorities reduced that average to 2.5 years. Article 86 sentences had a similar reduction pattern, going from 5.3 months to 2.8 months. Of seven dishonorable discharges given by courts-martial for desertion in 1968, the convening authority approved five. For Article 86 sentences, convening authorities approved nine bad conduct discharges of the one dishonorable discharge and thirteen bad conduct discharges given at trial. When considering disciplinary effectiveness, however, the Marine Corps may have had the upper hand in dealing with deserters and AWOLs. From 1965 to 1972, the army returned half of its deserters to military control, whereas the Marine Corps returned more than 75 percent. The Marine Corps conviction rate for desertion cases was 80 percent, whereas the army managed 63 percent.[17]

The army's study of Vietnam-era deserters found that most deserted or went AWOL for marital, family, or financial reasons or because they could not make the adjustment to military life. Only 11 to 15 percent admitted that their decision to absent themselves was war related. Absentees were more likely to go AWOL during training but frequently did so later in their service. Like many military studies of the time, the army studies did not focus on the Vietnam deserter/AWOL in specific but treated those as part of the larger, worldwide phenomenon. A similar air force study produced comparable findings. In a survey of convicted deserters and AWOLs in 1971, the air force found that 22 percent went absent for family problems and 16 percent left because they either disliked the military or wanted a discharge to get out of the air force. Only 1.4 percent claimed to have deserted to avoid duty in Southeast Asia, and only 7.6 percent had been involved with drugs. Surely the army AWOL/deserter in Vietnam would have slightly different motivating circumstances than the deserter in the United States or in Europe, but perhaps not. Lower induction standards and inexperienced leadership played a role in absences and were worldwide issues not unique to Vietnam. That many desertions and AWOLs occurred during training may have influenced the army and the Marine Corps to lessen the intensity of basic training before sending new soldiers and marines to Vietnam. Christian Appy, in his study of U.S. combat soldiers in Vietnam, cited one unit that was given a special award for having the fewest AWOLs during basic training. In another unit, commanders lied to recruits to prevent AWOLs, telling them that fewer than 20 percent of them would go to Vietnam. At the end of their training, all but three of 200 men in the basic training cadre were transferred to Southeast Asia.[18]

Other military-oriented crimes challenged the military justice system and pointed toward the disintegration of U.S. forces in Vietnam. Among the more serious were combat refusals. Accurate numbers on combat refusals are difficult to figure, as some incidents went unreported either to protect the record of the officer or noncommissioned officer in command or for fear of reprisals by those involved against the commander. In one of the more memorable television news reports from the war, a rifle company refused to patrol a known dangerous trail right in front of Columbia Broadcasting System (CBS) cameras. Americans at home got to see a combat refusal first-hand.[19] Hearings held by the House Committee on Internal Security found that in 1968, 94 instances occurred in which individuals refused a combat-related order. Of these 94, 82 resulted in convictions. The number increased to 128 with 117 convictions in 1969 and to 152 with 131 convictions in 1970. The First Cavalry by itself had 35 combat refusals in 1970. The Marine Corps claimed only 26 refusals for the entire war, 12 of which occurred in 1968–1969 at the height of Marine Corps fighting in Vietnam.[20]

Combat refusals more often involved individuals rather than groups. Though the latter can be said to be of more danger to a unit, the refusal of an individual is arguably just as dangerous to a unit in the field. When one cog of the machine breaks down, the entire machine is affected. The case of Private First Class Joseph Williams is indicative of the typical individual combat refusal. Williams's squad landed by helicopter in a rice paddy, missing its designated landing zone. As the squad left the helicopters, it came under "moderate to heavy" machine gun and small arms fire from a nearby hamlet. The squad divided into two teams, A and B, to alternatively provide covering fire and maneuver to reach a dike just outside the village, which was the intended landing zone. As the teams moved forward, Williams stayed put, right where he had jumped off of the helicopter. By the time Teams A and B reached the dike, Williams was some 300 feet behind, still in the rice paddy. Sergeant Wolfe, who was in charge of Team B, reported to the squad leader, Sergeant Bowling, that Williams had refused to move with the team. Over the course of the next forty minutes, under fire, Sergeant Bowling yelled at Williams to "move up" and at least once shouted at Williams that he was giving him a "lawful order" to move forward and rejoin the squad.

For the first twenty minutes, Williams responded that he had been wounded, "had a pungi stick in his leg," and could not move. Then, he added that his M-16 had jammed. Sergeant Torres made his way back to where Williams lay, finding neither wound nor jam. Torres finally got Williams to move toward the dike at a "low crawl." Bowling confronted Williams, who told the sergeant that his weapon had jammed. Sergeant Bowling ordered Williams to fire the M-16 into a nearby pond, knowing that "once an M-16 jams," it would not fire again until fixed. Williams pulled the trigger and the weapon fired, then it actually did jam. Sergeant Torres took Williams's weapon and gave him a rifle from a wounded comrade. Over the course of the next fifteen minutes, the squad moved toward the village. Sergeant Bowling did not notice any wounds on Williams, or a limp, and kept Williams in front of him to "prod him along."

After the engagement, Williams was arrested and charged with cowardice before the enemy (Article 99) and disobedience of an order by a superior non-commissioned officer (Article 91). Williams's defense counsel weakly argued that Williams's failure to act did not come from fear. Rather, Williams's failure to move was caused by injury and broken equipment. Moreover, defense counsel argued that Williams had rejoined the squad on his own, evidence he claimed "weighs heavily against any inference of fear." The prosecution easily countered this feeble defense by noting again that Williams claimed to be moving when he actually was not, that he claimed to be wounded when no evidence supported wounds of any kind, that he claimed his rifle had jammed when in fact it had not, and that he only moved forward when Sergeant Torres forced him to do so. Other squad members corroborated the testimony of Sergeants Bowling, Torres, and Wolf. In addition to this damning testimony was the fact that while Williams lay in the rice paddy, several more helicopters unloaded dozens of troops all around Williams, yet he continued to stay put.

Williams was found guilty and sentenced to confinement at hard labor for three years and a dishonorable discharge. He appealed the conviction on the grounds that the evidence against him was insufficient and circumstantial. The Court of Military Appeals, however, found that the evidence was indeed sufficient even though some of it could be considered circumstantial. And even then, circumstantial evidence was admissible, as it could "prove the existence of a fact as direct evidence." The appeal was denied.[21]

In 1971, a unit of the First Cavalry refused to return to an area from which it had recently been evacuated. None of the men was charged with refusal because commanders feared such a massive refusal would expose their thin grip on control of the unit. Such a trial would have ended the careers of more than a few officers. It is interesting to note that black soldiers were ten times more likely than white soldiers to refuse to go to the field, an indication of black feelings toward white authority in the form of officers and belief, whether justified or not, that blacks bore the brunt of the tough fighting.[22]

Whether racially motivated or not, combat refusals only scratched the surface of the disciplinary breakdown of U.S. troops in Vietnam. The most notable and more popularly known crime that best illustrates the U.S. military crisis in Vietnam was fragging, which as noted earlier was the murder or attempted murder of a superior officer. By 1971, fragging had become a frequent fear among officers and noncommissioned officers (NCOs). Fraggings were among the more disturbing of military crimes from the standpoint of military discipline and morale in Vietnam. Killing a superior officer was not unique to Vietnam; it had occurred in all wars fought by the United States, even the American Revolution. The murder or attempted murder of a superior officer or NCO certainly points toward a collapse of discipline in a unit. The Uniform Code of Military Justice, however, dealt with murder in the same manner regardless of the context of the crime—whether it was combat or noncombat related, fragging or otherwise.

The principle method of assault in these cases was the use of a fragmentation grenade, thus the term *fragging*. Fragging was not limited to superior officers or NCOs but was also used against fellow enlisted personnel and Vietnamese. Enlisted men fragged officers and others who were considered incompetent or too "gung ho" or as a way to evade combat patrol duty or to get rid of an officer or other superior who was getting too close to a black-market operation or an illicit drug ring. But fragging was also used by enlisted soldiers to attack other enlisted personnel or Vietnamese for similar reasons—personal feuds, drug deals gone wrong, or in retaliation for a previous fragging attack.[23]

Fragging rarely involved race or political activism. In a study of men convicted by court-martial of fragging a superior officer, Dr. Thomas C. Bond, chief of the Psychiatry Division at the military prison at Fort Leavenworth, found that many perpetrators felt "singled out" by their superiors for punishment. They were tired of being ridden by their sergeant or a superior officer. Most incidents occurred in support units, not combat units. The fragger was frequently intoxicated via alcohol, drugs, or both at the time of the incident, and most did little to avoid being caught. Dr. Bond noted the "macabre ritual" that developed with fragging. Fraggers would often send an anonymous warning in the form of a note or other sign to their intended victim. Although it was common for soldiers in a unit to pool money and offer a bounty to intimidate the officer in question, this rarely motivated the actual perpetrator. Because of company command structures, captains and first sergeants often became the de facto targets. Captains handled unit discipline, promotions, and transfers; first sergeants dealt with duty rosters, work details, and passes, and often it was the NCO who informed the captain of the need for disciplinary action. Bond's study found that 75 percent of the fraggers had had a verbal or physical disagreement with their victim and 90 percent of these had occurred within the three days prior to the fragging act. The offenders, Bond found, came from broken homes, had rarely graduated from high school, and had previously exhibited antisocial behavior. Ironically, many of the convicted troops were volunteers, not draftees.[24]

It should come as no surprise that fragging became a serious problem as the Vietnamization process intensified and the role of U.S. forces declined. Workloads for U.S. troops in support areas decreased, and free, or rather idle, time increased. Troop reductions, lack of immediate objectives, and the overall malaise that slowly infected the U.S. effort in South Vietnam, according to army testimony before the House Committee on Appropriations in 1971, contributed to the alarming increase in fraggings after 1969. There were 126 fragging incidents in the army in Vietnam during 1969 that killed 37 people. In 1970, the army reported 271 incidents, with 34 killed, and in 1971, 333 incidents occurred but with only 12 deaths. For all three years, officers and NCOs made up just more than half of the intended victims. Some of these incidents went unpunished, as the fragging occurred under the cover of darkness, allowing the perpetrator to get away. In 1971, 21 soldiers were convicted under Article 118 of the Uniform Code of Military Justice (murder) for fragging offenses. Four of these had their sentences reduced, and none was executed. In the same year 19 were convicted of manslaughter under Article 119 of the Uniform Code of Military Justice, with 2 having their sentences reduced, 3 suspended, 1 remitted, and 1 commuted. Three more soldiers were convicted of negligent homicide under Article 134 of the Uniform Code of Military Justice. Murder was, after all, a capital offense under the Uniform Code of Military Justice, yet none of the convicted was sentenced to death.[25]

The air force and navy had few incidents. Of the navy's two incidents, both occurred in a "social context" and involved revenge rather than an attack on a superior officer. The Marine Corps, however, had its share of fraggings. Records for fragging in the Marine Corps are incomplete and spotty, but historian and former Marine Corps judge advocate Gary D. Solis has estimated that between 100 and 150 incidents occurred during the war, mainly in the latter stages of Marine Corps involvement. And like those in the army, these incidents tended to occur in rear areas. Through June 1969, the Third Marine Division had had 15 fragging incidents, but a suspect in only 1. In 1970, the First Marine Division recorded 47 fraggings, which killed 1 and wounded 43 others. Thirty-seven marines were arrested in 22 of these incidents. Of these, 21 were court-martialed, and 5 were administratively discharged. No fraggings were recorded in Marine Corps units in 1971, since by then most of those units had left Vietnam.[26]

Marine Corps commanders and military lawyers took extreme steps to root out the evil that was slowly infecting their service in Vietnam. They used informants, and in order to encourage witnesses to testify, they granted transfers to protect witnesses from revenge seekers. Discharge qualifications were liberalized in order to get troublemakers out of the Marine Corps as quickly as possible (the same approach was applied to drug users in the Marine Corps). Officers were told to be on the lookout for potential fraggers and at the slightest sign of trouble to grant administrative discharges. Courts-martial and dishonorable discharges took too much time. In the First Marine Division, Maj. Gen. William K. Jones initiated Operation Freeze, which immediately isolated and investigated any unit in which an internal act of violence occurred. The Third Marine Division instituted curfews and closed clubs at 2130, invigorated an already vigorous intramural sports program to keep marines occupied in rear areas, and worked to make the administrative discharge process quicker. Greater immunity and protection were given to informants and witnesses. Still, the unspoken code of silence tended to prevail.[27]

The only known marine death from a fragging in the First Marine Division occurred in October 1970. On the night of October 23, on Hill 190, near Da Nang, Sgt. Richard L. Tate found Private Gary A. Hendricks asleep at his post. Sergeant Tate gave the marine private a thorough tongue-lashing, then continued his rounds. At about 0100 the next morning, Private Hendricks crawled on top of the sandbagged, concrete bunker in which Sergeant Tate and two other men were asleep. He dropped a fragmentation grenade down the air vent shaft. The grenade landed on Sergeant Tate and exploded, killing Tate and wounding the two other marines. Private Hendricks was quickly arrested after having admitted to the deed to his peers. Charged with aggravated assault and premeditated murder, Private Hendricks signed a confession. His appointed defense counsel, Capt. Philip C. Tower, tried to get Private Hendricks declared mentally incompetent, but evaluations found Hendricks to be mentally stable. Captain Tower knew that no marine had been executed in Vietnam but sensed from the attitude of the commander that Private Hendricks might be the first.

The general court-martial found Hendricks guilty and sentenced him to death. The convening authority reduced the sentence to hard labor for life and a dishonorable discharge. Hendricks attempted to appeal his conviction, claiming his assigned military defense counsel was incompetent, but was denied. Hendricks was paroled after serving only eight years, then went on to college, earning a degree in criminology.[28]

Some murders and assaults upon superiors occurred without the use of a fragmentation grenade but still retained the spirit of a fragging.[29] Such was the case when Army Private First Class Michael McInnis tried to resolve some issues with his sergeant with an M-16 rifle. McInnis, who grew up in Boston, had enlisted for a three-year term in the army in 1967 after failing to graduate from high school. After basic training at Fort Jackson, South Carolina, he was assigned to Fort Gordon, Georgia, then Korea. He completed his general equivalency diploma (GED) and had solid efficiency ratings. His record, however, was not spotless: it included "prior history of a mental disorder," and he had attempted suicide by slitting his wrists in Korea. The suicide attempt resulted in part from an assault on a noncommissioned officer, for which McInnis was convicted by a special court-martial. He was subsequently hospitalized in the Mental Hygiene Clinic at William Beaumont General Hospital in El Paso, Texas, from September to November 1968. His tour in Vietnam began in July 1969 as part of the 595th Signal Company at Phuoc Vinh.

McInnis worked a 24-hour shift from August 18 into the early hours of August 19, 1969. He had been given an Article 15 nonjudicial punishment for some unknown offense the day or so before and was sentenced to kitchen patrol (KP) duty after his 24-hour shift ending the morning of the 19th. Returning to his quarters after his duty shift, McInnis attempted to get some sleep before reporting for KP, but the noise of the housemaids kept him awake. He gave up and went to the Enlisted Men's Club with Private First Class Jay Nelson and had a "few beers." While at the club, McInnis was called to the orderly room to talk with his superior officer, Lt. Robert Thorn, about the Article 15. The talk must not have gone well, as McInnis did not show up for KP but instead went back to the club and had more to drink. He then left the club and supposedly returned to his hooch, where Nelson promised to wake him at 1600 for their next duty shift.

This is where things went awry. At 1945, McInnis burst into the orderly room where Sgt. Martin Pullen, Lieutenant Thorn, Chief Warrant Officer Keither Moore, and Sgt. Augustine Bozant were sitting discussing duty rosters. McInnis was armed with an M-16, clip included. McInnis threw the Article 15 he had received earlier down on the desk and pointed the M-16 at Sergeant Pullen. He yelled, "Sergeant Pullen, do you see this Article 15? Now, do you see this M-16?" Pullen did not respond, but Chief Warrant Officer Moore calmly told McInnis, "Why don't you put the M-16 back and go back to the barracks and act like a human being." At this moment Pullen noticed that the M-16 had a clip in it, and McInnis was alternately pointing the rifle at everyone in the room. McInnis then said, "I have done this before. I done this in Korea to an NCO—I slashed my wrist—I would do it to you." At this moment McInnis had the rifle trained on Moore—he pulled the trigger. The M-16 did not fire. The bolt was back and locked. As McInnis started to fumble with the bolt, Moore rushed him and quickly got the rifle away and into Sergeant Pullen's hands.

McInnis was arrested and charged with attempted murder (of Chief Warrant Officer Moore—an Article 80 violation), lifting a weapon against a superior officer on duty (Lieutenant Thorn—an Article 90 violation), and assault against a superior noncommissioned officer on duty (Sergeants Pullen and Bozant). These were general court-martial offenses and carried a total maximum sentence of a dishonorable discharge, reduction in rank, total forfeiture of pay, and thirty-two years confinement at hard labor. McInnis pleaded not guilty to all charges.

At his trial at Long Binh, McInnis claimed that he recalled going back to his hooch after the beers at the club, but then remembered nothing until he was in the orderly room pointing the M-16 at Moore. Scared to death, he then attempted to put the rifle back into the safe locker when Moore jumped him. McInnis testified that he did not have any issues with or hostility against any of his superiors in the orderly room. The charge sheet clearly stated that McInnis had undergone a psychiatric evaluation after his arrest and was found sane. His defense counsel attempted to sell the court an "insanity by intoxication" defense, but the court was not convinced. The *Manual for Courts Martial* allowed defense to enter evidence that voluntary intoxication could raise reasonable doubt of "knowledge and/or specific intent." Testimony established that McInnis was drunk and had had at least eight beers before the incident. Testimony also noted that McInnis called Pullen and others by name and that he had in fact recognized Pullen as his superior noncommissioned officer. The court ruled that McInnis was not intoxicated to the point of being unable to "form the specific intent to kill."

McInnis took his chances by being tried by a judge instead of a military jury. Military Judge Peter Wondolowski found McInnis guilty on all counts and sentenced him to five years confinement at hard labor, total forfeiture of pay, reduction in rank, and a dishonorable discharge. Testimony from McInnis's direct supervisor, Sgt. John Jaso, may have saved McInnis from a heavier sentence. Jaso called McInnis "one of the best troopers" he had and said that he would gladly take McInnis back to work for him. In his posttrial interview, McInnis claimed that he wanted to complete his military service and obtain an honorable discharge, then go to school back in Boston to study electronics. He claimed again that he "just didn't remember what had happened" but that the judge did not believe him "from the outset." The staff judge advocate recommended that the convening authority approve the sentence as adjudged, which it did on November 30, 1969. The Army Court of Military Review approved the verdict and sentence on September 2, 1970. Records indicate that McInnis served his time at Fort Leavenworth.

Other killings cannot be classified as fraggings per se—they were simply murders. For example, Private Atlas A. Ford shot and killed Private First Class Jerry E. Tow near the Vietnamese Naval Dependent Housing Area at Cam Ranh Bay on October 29, 1972. After being chased down by military police, Ford was arrested with an unauthorized .45 caliber pistol and 1.86 grams of heroin on his person. Ford was tried on four charges, including premeditated murder. He was convicted on all counts, but the court reduced the premeditated murder charge. He was still sentenced to fifty years confinement at hard labor, total forfeiture, and a dishonorable discharge.[30]

Race, of course, accounted for some fraggings and attempted fraggings. One case involved the LMDC, and the charges against ten coconspirators were ultimately dropped. A sergeant, who subsequently refused to offer a written formal statement because he feared reprisals, allegedly overheard the ten soldiers, all black, plotting to kill their company commander, a captain, who was white. The group offered a $500 reward for whoever did the deed. Drugs were also involved, as at least some of the ten had been implicated in a heroin raid the week before, a raid ordered by the company commander. Authorities took the plot seriously enough to temporarily reassign the captain for his own safety and to confine the ten soldiers pending an investigation.

Charges against all ten were dropped in the end because of lack of evidence, which delighted the LMDC lawyer representing them. Three of the ten were given general discharges because of their poor discipline records and reputations as "troublemakers." The other seven apparently spent several weeks in Long Binh jail without being formally charged. The LMDC cried foul and alerted the press, which promptly answered the call. United Press International (UPI) ran a story on the situation, noting that the LMDC had contacted "the new black Assistant Secretary of Defense," Donald L. Miller, demanding an "immediate investigation of racial discrimination." The army investigation found "absolutely no racial overtones" in the case, noting that the sergeant who brought the matter to command attention was himself black. Moreover, the army also noted that the LMDC did not mention to the press that two of the ten soldiers had histories of drug abuse and had been detained for transfer to the army's drug rehabilitation facility at Long Binh. Still, the pressure brought to bear by the LMDC as well as the publicity spurred army action— the remaining five held at Long Binh were released within 24 hours of the completion of the army investigation.[31]

Violent crimes against fellow U.S. soldiers were not the only such offenses that took place in Vietnam. Crimes committed against noncombatants are unfortunately inevitable, and Vietnam was no exception. A group of young men who were well armed and far from home was bound to hurt someone outside the confines of the battlefield. Murder and rape were the most serious of these crimes. From 1965 through 1972, the army held 103 trials of U.S. soldiers accused of murdering Vietnamese civilians. Of these 103, 40 were convicted, 25 convicted on lesser charges, and 38 acquitted. Thirty-eight soldiers were tried for manslaughter, with 17 convicted, 10 convicted on lesser charges, and 11 acquitted. Seventeen were tried for negligent homicide, with 15 convicted and 2 acquitted.[32]

Twenty-seven marines were convicted of murdering a Vietnamese, and 16 were acquitted. The sentences of the 27 are telling. Again, if punishment is supposed to deter, then sentencing appears somewhat inconsistent. Of these 27, 15 received life sentences. The so-called mere gook rule, which implied that courts-martial normally acquitted soldiers accused of serious crimes against Vietnamese because of racial prejudice, was prevalent in U.S. popular culture concerning the war. The review of the disposition of these 15 sentences in Table 4.2 suggests, however, that the rule existed not so much in Vietnam as in the appellate courts and clemency boards. Waldemar Solf's study of courts-martial involving serious crimes committed against Vietnamese found acquittal rates of only 23 percent for murder, 23.5 percent for rape, and 18 percent for manslaughter. These figures compare quite well with Harry Kalven and Hans Zeisel's study of civilian juries in the United States, which found acquittals in 19 percent of murder trials, 40 percent in rape trials, and 45 percent for manslaughter charges.[33] Guenter Lewy was able to put together data on offenses committed by marines against Vietnamese during the war. Table 4.3 presents this data.

Table 4.2. Confinement Adjudged in Cases of Marines Convicted of Murdering a Vietnamese, 1965–1971

Individual	Sentence Adjudged at Trial (in years)	Sentence Approved by Convening Authority (in years)	Sentence Approved by Naval Court of Military Review (in years)	Action by U.S. Court of Military Appeals	Sentence from Parole (P) or Clemency (C) (in years)
1	Life	Life	25	Appeal denied	C: 6 ½
2	Life	Life	3	Appeal denied	NA
3	Life	25	5	Appeal denied	C: 2 ¾
4	Life	Life	Life	Appeal denied	C: 12
5	Life	35	5	Appeal denied	C: 2 ⁵/₁₂
6	Life	30	30	Appeal denied	C: 3
7	Life	Life	Life	Appeal denied	C: 9
8	Life	20	20	Appeal denied	C: 7 ½
9	Life	20	20	Appeal denied	C: 7
10	Life	Life	3	Appeal denied	NA
11	Life	30	3	Appeal denied	NA
12	Life	30	15	10 years	P: 3
13	Life	40	15	Appeal denied	P: 3 ¾
14	Life	1	1	Did not petition	C: Denied
15	Life	25	25	Appeal dismissed	C: 19

Sources: Guenter Lewy, *American in Vietnam* (New York: Oxford University Press, 1978), 458; Gary D. Solis, *Trial by Fire: Marines and Military Law in Vietnam* (Washington, D.C.: Marine Corps History and Museums Division, 1989), 280–281.

It appears that white soldiers rather than black troops were more likely to commit a crime against a Vietnamese. Race has been a consistent and important focus in scholarship on the war, and relations between white U.S. troops and black U.S. troops and between both white and black U.S. troops and Vietnamese were important during the Vietnam War. Dr. Jerome Kroll of the Rockland Psychiatric Center in Orangeburg, New York, examined 293 soldiers serving sentences of six months or more in Fort Leavenworth for crimes committed in Vietnam. His study, published in *Psychiatry* in February 1976, found that black soldiers were twice as likely as white soldiers to be imprisoned for crimes against fellow soldiers. White soldiers, on the other hand, were six times more likely to be imprisoned for crimes committed against

Table 4.3. Serious Offenses Committed by Marines against Vietnamese, 1965–1971

Offense	Convicted	Acquitted
Murder	27	16
Attempted murder	1	2
Rape	16	10
Attempted rape	2	0
Assault with intent to commit murder, rape, or indecent assault	10	8
Indecent acts with a female	8	0
Manslaughter	15	7
Negligent homicide	6	1
Mutilation of a corpse	1	0
Arson	1	0
Kidnapping	1	2
Officer filing false report to cover up murders or failing to report murders	2	0
Total number of offenses	90	46

Source: Guenter Lewy, *America in Vietnam* (New York: Oxford University Press, 1978), 456.

Vietnamese. More than 50 percent of murders committed in Vietnam by U.S. troops, regardless of race, were committed against victims known to the accused. Kroll's thesis suggested that white soldiers simply transferred traditionally held racial prejudices to Vietnamese, whereas black soldiers tended to "sympathize" with the plight of the Vietnamese as an oppressed and exploited people. Combat apparently forced both whites and blacks to put aside their racial issues and focus on the task at hand, but when off of the line, white and black troops went their separate ways, attempting to create distinct segregated worlds outside the combat zone. Combat relationships forged in the field buckled under the tedium of the rear area. Kroll concluded that with all the stresses in Vietnam, it was rather amazing that more assaults and murders had not occurred. Of all the thousands of troops who served in Vietnam, "these [comparatively few] men put into action some of the fears, hostilities, and temptations that all men felt."[34]

These murder cases show the strain of race relations in Vietnam. For example, a nineteen-year-old white soldier from Mississippi was convicted of aggravated assault in 1967 after cracking the skull of a Vietnamese civilian as the trooper rode by in a truck. It seems the soldier wanted a Vietnamese hat and had tried knocking hats off of Vietnamese bicyclists with his rifle as his truck sped by. He "finally connected," hitting an unsuspecting Vietnamese man with the butt of his rifle, causing a fatal skull fracture. The soldier was sentenced to five years confinement at hard labor and a dishonorable discharge. The confinement was reduced to eleven months by the convening authority.

Another case involved the murder of a white soldier by a black soldier. Both soldiers had become close "buddies" in their short time in Vietnam, but the strain of a short turnaround for field duty proved too much for the relationship to bear. The white soldier returned to quarters drunk one evening, forcing the black soldier to deal with the white man's drunken rage and to get him into bed for the next morning's early patrol. That morning, the white soldier, who outranked the black soldier, ordered the black soldier to carry extra mortar shells in addition to his already overloaded gear. The black soldier refused, left the room, and then returned a short time later after cooling off. The white soldier had not cooled off, however, and "bawled out" the black trooper further. The white soldier got carried away, pulling his knife and threatening the black soldier. Now aware that he was the only black man in the room with four other whites and his white "buddy," the black soldier stepped over to his bunk to pull out a wooden slat to protect himself. The slat would not budge, so he grabbed the nearest thing to him—his M-16. He pointed the weapon at the white soldier. The black soldier claimed to have been trying to fix the safety when the rifle discharged, killing his white "buddy" instantly. The other witnesses, all white, testified that he had not been trying to fix the safety. A court-martial convicted the black soldier of murder, sentencing him to confinement at hard labor for life. The Army Court of Military Review, however, overturned this sentence and ordered a retrial, resulting in the lesser conviction of manslaughter and a ten-year sentence.[35]

One case involving the death of a Cambodian suspected of being a double agent highlights the peculiar conditions in which murders sometimes took place in Vietnam.[36] Capt. John J. McCarthy Jr., a Green Beret, was part of an intelligence program known as Operation Cherry. A top-secret mission, Operation Cherry was intended to learn more about the Khmer Serai and its plans to overthrow the government of Cambodia. Finding that the Khmer Serai was not organized enough to pull off such a coup, the army terminated Operation Cherry in November 1967. McCarthy's role in this mission was to "remove" the Cambodian contacts from U.S. military bases in order to wipe the slate clean and end contact between the Green Berets and the Khmer Serai.

On the night of November 24, 1967, McCarthy and a sergeant took one of these Cambodians, Inchin Hia Lam—known as "Jimmie" to the Americans—

for a ride in an unmarked Datsun sedan. On a deserted road some miles out-side of Saigon, McCarthy ordered the sergeant to turn the car around. Jimmie was sitting in the middle of the front seat, with McCarthy at his side holding a loaded .38 pistol. Suddenly a shot was fired, striking Jimmie in the head and shattering the windshield. After stopping the car, the sergeant and McCarthy removed Jimmie's body from the car, stripped it, burned Jimmie's clothes, and then "disposed of the body." The next day McCarthy was arrested for the mur-der of Inchin Hia Lam.

With Capt. Stewart Davis and Capt. James Mathews as defense counsel, McCarthy's trial began on January 29, 1968. Mathews had just arrived in Viet-nam and had tried one murder case while stationed at Fort Sill. Davis had never tried a murder case. McCarthy's defense was not hopeful. He had been heard on more than one occasion to claim that Jimmie was in fact a double agent and should be "killed." McCarthy also admitted that his .38 had indeed discharged but claimed it was not the weapon that killed Jimmie. The only ex-planation Davis and Mathews could come up with was that a sniper had killed Jimmie.

Davis and McCarthy did not have much faith in their client's claim of in-nocence, but they were duty-bound to defend him. In his opening state-ment, Davis briefly noted that McCarthy had no motive and that no ballistic evidence could link McCarthy's weapon to the wound that killed Jimmie. The prosecution characterized McCarthy as a highly trained "super assas-sin." McCarthy took the stand in his own defense, but it was to no avail. The members of the court found McCarthy guilty after a trial of only one and a half days. In the sentencing phase Mathews pleaded for McCarthy's life, claiming that McCarthy's excellent service record warranted life imprison-ment rather than the death penalty. After forty-three minutes of delibera-tion, the members agreed, sentencing McCarthy to life imprisonment at Fort Leavenworth.

Later in the summer of 1968, Davis, now back in Washington, D.C., was by chance assigned to handle McCarthy's appeal. Original defense counsel rarely would also handle the appeal. In 1971, the Court of Military Appeals finally ruled on McCarthy's case. New ballistics evidence obtained by Davis shed rea-sonable doubt on McCarthy's conviction. The court ordered a retrial, but the army decided to let it go, and as a consequence, set McCarthy free.

Military justice had a rough time of it in attempting to maintain discipline and prosecute violent crimes in Vietnam. The conditions made it difficult, as did the military situation and the political circumstances. The lawyers them-selves had a variety of abnormal obstacles to overcome. Could military justice as outlined by the Uniform Code of Military Justice really be effective and fair in combat conditions? And in a politically charged war? The record was mixed, but the lessons taken from the experience helped improve the process and thereby the system.

CHAPTER FIVE
VIOLATIONS OF THE LAWS OF WAR

As disturbing as fragging and assaults became in Vietnam, it is often war crimes and other atrocities that people first think of when asked about the Vietnam War. The brutal killing of noncombatants, torture and mutilation of enemy prisoners, and other acts of violence have become so ingrained in U.S. popular culture that many people believe these crimes against humanity were the norm rather than the exception. They were not commonplace, but they did happen, and some crimes doubtless went unreported. War crimes are violations of the laws of war, which are outlined in various Hague and Geneva Conventions; the Nuremberg Principles, which include the provision that obeying orders is not a valid defense; and the U.S. military's *The Law of Land Warfare*. These laws are meant to protect noncombatants, combatants on the battle-field, and prisoners of war, and they provide a framework in which warfare can be conducted in a manner that eliminates needless suffering.[1]

There were no "war crimes" trials in Vietnam because of jurisdiction and se-mantics. Although the term *atrocities* is commonly used in connection with the war, a U.S. combatant cannot be charged with an atrocity or war crime per se, only with underlying violations of the Uniform Code of Military Justice. International law normally associates war crimes with brutal acts, such as murder, rape, and mutilation, committed during times of war against *enemy* combatants and *enemy* noncombatants. In Vietnam, U.S. soldiers perpetrated such acts against South Vietnamese (who were technically *allies* of the United States and thus not enemy noncombatants in the traditional sense of the term), Viet Cong insurgents, and North Vietnamese military personnel. Fortu-nately, the Uniform Code of Military Justice is broad enough to effectively cover such crimes committed by U.S. soldiers against combatants and non-combatants, friend or foe. Moreover, *The Law of Land Warfare* clearly states that "war crimes are within the jurisdiction of general courts-martial" and other authorized courts of the United States. Furthermore, "violations of the law of war committed by persons subject to the military law of the United States will usually constitute violations of the Uniform Code of Military Jus-tice and, if so, will be prosecuted under that Code."[2]

The Law of Land Warfare, Manual for Courts-Martial, and the Uniform Code of Military Justice also determine valid defenses against war crimes charges. For example, Article 90 of the Uniform Code of Military Justice covers willfully disobeying a superior commissioned officer, asserting that "an order requiring the performance of a military duty or act may be inferred to be lawful and it is disobeyed at the peril of the subordinate. This inference does not apply to a patently illegal order, such as one that directs the commission of a crime."[3] Article 92 covers failure to obey an order, focusing on lawful orders.[4] The Uniform Code of Military Justice also provides for a soldier's legal and moral responsibility to disobey an order that is unlawful. Of course, the burden on the soldier to prove the order was indeed unlawful is enormous. Article 92 states: "A general order or regulation is lawful unless it is contrary to the Constitution, the laws of the United States, or lawful superior orders or for some other reason is beyond the authority of the official issuing it."[5]

In discussion of acceptable defenses, the *Manual for Courts-Martial* suggests that although actions resulting from a lawful order are justified, a crime committed resulting from an unlawful order is excused unless the perpetrator knew the order was unlawful. Such a defense would rarely succeed: "It is a defense to any offense that the accused was acting pursuant to orders unless the accused knew the orders to be unlawful or a person of ordinary sense and understanding would have known the orders to be unlawful."[6] *The Law of Land Warfare* clarifies using "obeying orders" as a defense:

> The fact that the law of war has been violated pursuant to an order of a superior authority, whether military or civil, does not deprive the act in question of its character of a war crime, nor does it constitute a defense in the trial of an accused individual, unless he did not know and could not reasonably have been expected to know that the act ordered was unlawful. In all cases where the order is held not to constitute a defense to an allegation of war crime, the fact that the individual was acting pursuant to orders may be considered in mitigation of punishment.[7]

In his work on the dilemma of atrocities and "following orders," law professor Mark J. Osiel contended that such a defense is dependent upon the "verbal artistry" of the courts. If instructions to court members ask them to find whether or not the accused intentionally killed noncombatants, then the crime is murder. But if asked to find out whether or not the accused followed a lawful order, then the crime is negligent manslaughter. As Osiel suggested, the second scenario "mitigates or exculpates, while the first does not." The case could, and sometimes did, boil down to semantics or description to determine what a soldier might be charged with if accused of such a crime.

Moreover, how an alleged war crime is described is greatly influenced by what motivates the prosecution. Is military justice motivated by a need to "preserve military discipline through order-following" or a moral obligation to prevent atrocities?[8]

From training to active duty, there were several avenues to educating military personnel on proper treatment of prisoners of war and noncombatants and on the procedure for reporting war crimes. The level of intensity for such instruction, however, was inconsistent. The several weeks of recruit training included only a few hours covering *The Law of Land Warfare* and the Hague and Geneva conventions. Even when more time was spent on these concepts, putting them into practice was never certain. An August 1971 article in *Soldiers*, the army's official magazine, pointed out the great void between the classroom and the battlefield: "In the classroom, the law of land warfare is elementary—then the GI is in combat—the situation is critical—and suddenly he is judge and jury with only a split second to return the correct verdict."[9] In Vietnam, as in all wars before or since, soldiers sometimes got it wrong.

Once in Vietnam, orientation included several cards that were to be kept on one's person at all times. These cards covered treatment of prisoners of war and noncombatants as well as how to report war crimes. Periodic training included unit sessions on atrocities and the respectful treatment of prisoners of war and noncombatants. MACV also issued numerous directives on the same subject, including a November 1967 directive titled "War Crimes and Other Prohibited Acts," all of which could be prosecuted under the Uniform Code of Military Justice.[10] A May 1968 directive outlined procedures for reporting war crimes and initiating war crimes investigations.[11]

The extreme nature of warfare, with its inherent fear and chaos, will contribute to acts of inhuman violence against combatants and noncombatants alike. Intensive training, and perhaps more so leadership, can minimize though not wholly prevent such acts from occurring amid the savagery of combat. Although an effort was made to educate officers and soldiers in Vietnam about war crimes and the laws of war, in unusual incidents those efforts, along with leadership, fell far short. The two most notorious acts of brutality committed in Vietnam, which were by far the most influential in shaping U.S. popular memory of the Vietnam experience, were the incidents at My Lai and Son Thang. The events themselves are vital to understanding the U.S. experience in Vietnam, but so too are the investigations and trials of those involved important to understanding military justice. The record of prosecution; the abilities of the military judges, lawyers, and court members; and the defense strategies used in each of the trials related to these two events shed a great deal of light on this grave challenge to U.S. military justice.

My Lai, of course, is the obvious and best-known such incident of the war, perhaps of any war. U.S. military justice came under incredibly intense scrutiny after the incident became publicly known and the trials commenced in late 1969 and into 1970. The killings at My Lai technically do not qualify as a war crime because the victims were South Vietnamese civilians who could be described as allied noncombatants. But because My Lai was located in an area considered under the control of the Viet Cong, the victims could also just as logically be considered enemy noncombatants, which would then fall under the rubric for war crimes. Be it war crime, atrocity, or murder, the My Lai incident was a horrific though isolated episode that is perhaps most accurately described as a mass murder investigated and brought to trial under appropriate articles of the Uniform Code of Military Justice.

On March 16, 1968, Task Force Barker of the American Division conducted a "tactical operation" in the village of Son My, which included the hamlet designated My Lai 4. Commanded by Lt. Col. Frank A. Barker, the battalion-sized unit was to locate and destroy a Viet Cong battalion that operated in the area and used Son My as a logistical base. Two previous operations had failed to achieve this objective and had resulted in several U.S. casualties from mines and booby traps. With Col. Oran K. Henderson, new commander of the Eleventh Brigade of which Task Force Barker was a part, Lieutenant Colonel Barker ordered another assault on the area, claiming that the people of Son My were mostly Viet Cong or at least Viet Cong sympathizers. The plan was typical of air mobility operations during Vietnam. Companies A, B, and C would assault the area by helicopter from different positions after a brief artillery barrage and then sweep into the area.

Company C, under the command of Capt. Ernest Medina, moved toward My Lai just before 0800 on March 16. Things began to go tragically wrong. After killing several Vietnamese who were fleeing down a road, Medina ordered First Platoon, commanded by Lt. William Calley, into My Lai. As the unit moved into the hamlet, the men rounded up the inhabitants, destroying their huts. Officers on ground, however, soon lost control, as several of Calley's troops allegedly began raping and sodomizing, then killing, women and young girls. A large group of terrified villagers was gathered along a ditch to the east, where U.S. soldiers gunned them down. To the south, U.S. soldiers allegedly slaughtered perhaps as many as fifty villagers alongside a trail. Second Platoon also allegedly committed several rapes and killings as it passed through the northern part of My Lai and into the hamlet of Bin Tay just a few hundred feet to the north. They killed perhaps as many as seventy Vietnamese. Third Platoon came into My Lai behind First and Second Platoons, burning whatever structures remained and killing livestock. The unit allegedly took the time to kill a group of seven to twelve women and children along the way.

At 0920, Second Platoon was ordered to cease fire, which it did. First Platoon either ignored or did not receive the order and continued killing until 1030, when an order to stop was finally obeyed. By the time Company C moved out of My Lai that afternoon, the soldiers had allegedly killed at least 200, perhaps as many as 500, Vietnamese. Subsequent investigations found that only a small handful of the dead were suspected Viet Cong.

Company B made its way into nearby My Khe, just across the river from My Lai. Company B's First Platoon, commanded by Lt. Thomas K. Willingham, allegedly fired into the hamlet, killing several inhabitants, then moved in to destroy huts and other structures, killing seven more people. Perhaps as many as ninety civilians were killed by Company B's First Platoon that morning, but the unit reported killing thirty-eight Viet Cong.[12]

The publicity that followed the cover-up of this incident means that many Americans are familiar with the actions to be described here. Later that day, March 16, initial reports of civilian deaths made by Lieutenant Colonel Barker to his commander, Colonel Henderson, claimed that fewer than thirty Vietnamese civilians had been killed. Henderson would later, on April 24, report that only twenty had been killed. Maj. Gen. Samuel W. Koster, commander of the Americal Division, prevented further on-site inspections of the My Lai area by division officers and press early the next day after learning there had been some civilian casualties. Later on the 17th, Lt. Col. John L. Holladay and Maj. Frederic Watke reported to Brig. Gen. George H. Young, the deputy commander of the Americal Division, that a large number of women and children had been killed during the operation on March 16. Stemming from reports by several helicopter pilots, notably Warrant Officer Hugh Thompson, Holladay and Watke felt they had done the right thing in reporting the alleged deaths to General Young. Young, however, reported only a confrontation that Thompson had had with ground units and urged Koster to have Colonel Henderson investigate that aspect of the day's operation.

Some days later, local Vietnamese officials reported the deaths to division headquarters, but these reports were covered up as well. No reports from Company B or C suggested any criminal acts, nor did after-action reports from Task Force Barker. From company to division, every level of command had been apprised of possible mass killings of noncombatants, but all either failed to act or acted deliberately to conceal the crime.[13]

The army had not only a massive war crime on its hands but also an equally massive cover-up to prevent action against those responsible for committing the crime. It was the conscientious efforts of Ronald L. Ridenhour, a soldier whose tour in Vietnam began shortly after the incident occurred, that brought the My Lai massacre to the attention of the U.S. Congress and the Department of Defense. Ridenhour learned of the massacre through fellow soldiers who served in the American Division. Disbelieving at first, the more he heard and the more he asked around, the more he knew that something heinous had occurred at My Lai. In March 1969, Ridenhour described what he had heard in letters to Congress, the army, and the Department of Defense.[14] A year after the March 16, 1968, operation in My Lai, the silence had been broken. Responding to congressional inquiries, Maj. Gen. William Enmark, the army inspector general, ordered an investigation. Col. William Wilson, a highly decorated Special Forces officer, volunteered to be in charge of the investigation after seeing Ridenhour's letter in the inspector general's office. Wilson interviewed thirty individuals directly or indirectly tied to the events at My Lai. In less than four months, he had discovered the awful truth about the massacre itself as well as the fact that there had been startling irregularities in reports from units involved in the incident. There had been an attempt to hide what had happened at My Lai.[15]

Enough had been discovered by Wilson to warrant a criminal investigation. In August 1969, Gen. William Westmoreland, by then the army chief of staff, ordered the army Criminal Investigation Division (CID) to investigate possible criminal charges in the My Lai incident. A month later, just before Calley was to rotate out of the army, he was charged with premeditated murder of 109 noncombatants. Had he already been discharged, bringing charges against him would have been extremely difficult, as case precedent held that once a soldier had been honorably discharged, he could not be subsequently charged with crimes committed while on active duty.[16]

As the army began preferring charges against individuals directly involved with the killing, Westmoreland appointed army lieutenant general William Peers to conduct a massive investigation into the broader issue of a possible cover-up. Beginning in November 1969, Peers spent the next four months producing a shockingly detailed report that ultimately recommended that thirty officers and men, from Major General Koster down to Specialist Jay Roberts, be charged for their direct or indirect involvement in the My Lai killings and/or the subsequent cover-up. The Peers Report on the My Lai allegations found that from MACV down to the Eleventh Brigade, all MACV directives and policies concerning the treatment of prisoners and noncombatants, rules of engagement (including those for villages and hamlets), and reporting war crimes had been disseminated properly. In other words, from Major General Koster down to the privates who had killed and raped at My Lai, all had been informed of what was expected in relation to war crimes activity. But, as the Peers Report noted, directives, information cards, and other publications are "not a substitute for leadership."[17]

The Peers Report, unfortunately, did not help army prosecutors build the cases they needed to aggressively pursue those implicated in the My Lai killings. Ultimately, fourteen of the thirty officers and enlisted men that Peers recommended for charges had charges preferred against them. These included Maj. Gen. Samuel Koster, Brig. Gen. George H. Young, and Col. Oran K. Henderson. Charges that General Young, Col. Nels Parson (American Division chief of staff), Col. Robert B. Luper (artillery battalion commander), and Maj. Robert W. McKnight (Task Force Barker's executive officer) had been involved in the cover-up were dismissed for lack of evidence. Major General Koster was subjected to an Article 32 investigation for his failure to report the deaths and subsequent perjury before the Peers commission. The Article 32 hearing, chaired by Brig. Gen. B. L. Evans, clearly showed that Koster had known that some level of killing had taken place, that he had been informed that at least twenty civilians had been killed, and that he had failed to order a proper investigation of the allegations. Koster was nearing the end of his long and mostly distinguished military career—he was superintendent of West Point at the time. In an astonishing move, Lt. Gen. Jonathan Seaman, commander of the First U.S Army, approved Brigadier General Evans's recommendation that all charges against Koster be dismissed.

Public outcry over the killings, now made very public by journalist Seymour Hersh and *Life* magazine's publication of disturbing photographs of the massacre taken by army photojournalist Ronald Haeberle, demanded justice. General Seaman demoted Koster to brigadier general and withdrew Koster's Distinguished Service Medal. Brig. Gen. George Young, Koster's deputy in the American Division, was subjected to administrative punishment and given a letter of censure by the secretary of the army; his Distinguished Service Medal was also revoked. The investigations of both men were conducted behind closed doors, an action that only fed the public's perception of a conspiratorial cover-up.[18]

The resulting trials brought by the army CID investigation did not fare well. Sgt. David Mitchell was tried at Fort Hood in October 1970. He had been identified as being at the ditch where Calley had ordered more than 100 women and children shot. The most crucial evidence came from four helicopter crewmen, including Hugh Thompson, who had seen Mitchell in the act of killing. All four men had testified before a secret session of a congressional committee investigating My Lai a few months earlier. Having been given during a classified hearing, their testimony was not available to prosecution or defense. Congressman F. Edward Herbert, the committee chairman, refused to release the testimony transcript, which led the military judge, George R. Robinson, to deny testimony from any witness who had also appeared before Herbert's committee because Mitchell's defense team would not be able to cross-examine these witnesses to discover inconsistencies between their testimony before the committee against that before the court-martial. Prosecuting Capt. Michael Swann was left with an empty witness list, as he could now call only three of the dozens of witnesses he had originally planned to call to testify against Mitchell. These three were not strong enough to convict Mitchell. Ossie Brown, a civilian attorney who had volunteered his time and services to defend Mitchell, called several witnesses to either counter the prosecution's witnesses or cause doubt as to their reliability. Mitchell testified on the stand that he had done nothing and seen nothing. Left with no presented evidence to convict, the court-martial members acquitted Mitchell.[19]

In January 1971, the court-martial of Sgt. Charles Hutto got underway at Fort McPherson. Hutto had told CID investigators that the company's orders were to kill everyone they found and that he had fired an M-60 machine gun at unarmed civilians, killing them. Prosecution witnesses, however, could not say with certainty that they had seen Hutto fire a single shot. His statement to CID investigators was read to the court-martial panel, and Hutto's defense team did not contest it. Instead, Hutto's civilian defense team, led by Miami attorney Edward Magill, focused on Hutto's ability to determine a legal order. A clinical psychologist, Dr. Norman Reichenberg, offered testimony that indicated Hutto had a simplistic, black-and-white view of the world. In the case of My Lai, Hutto sincerely believed that those who had ordered him to shoot innocent civilians were doing the right thing. He believed in authority, willingly took orders, and trusted blindly. Hutto, according to the defense, had been following orders, orders that he did not have the mental capability to determine were either right or wrong. The court members, after only two hours of deliberation, agreed and acquitted Hutto. The success of the defense was truly significant.

The Nuremberg precedent that "obeying orders" was not a valid defense to committing war crimes had been rather patently pushed aside by allowances in the *Manual for Courts-Martial*. Moreover, if Hutto was indeed incapable of determining a legal order from an illegal one, then his assignment to a combat unit must also be questioned.[20]

The commanding officer of the U.S. Third Army, Lt. Gen. Albert O. Connor, had convening authority in the My Lai cases tried at Fort McPherson. After the Hutto verdict, Connor determined that seven others who had been charged in the My Lai killings were being held under evidence that was less damning than that against Hutto. This included the notorious Sgt. Kenneth Hodges, who had been accused of multiple rapes and sodomy. Since Hutto had been acquitted, Connor therefore determined that charges against these seven should be dropped. All were administratively discharged from the army but not punished for what they had done at My Lai. Michal Belknap, in his book on My Lai, pointed to the central problem in the courts-martial of My Lai offenders—officers who sat on these panels tended to believe that obeying orders was a *valid* defense, not an *invalid* defense as had been established at Nuremberg.[21]

The court-martial of Lt. William Calley at the courthouse at Fort Benning proceeded in November 1970 amid these other developments. Calley's trial is certainly among the most sensational courts-martial in U.S. history. A panel of six members—all officers, all combat veterans, five of whom had served in Vietnam—were to judge Calley. Col. Reid W. Kennedy presided over the trial and quickly realized that he had a media frenzy on his hands. His problem, however, was that he felt his hands were also tied as to how far he could legally go to curb media interference from prejudicing the case.[22]

The prosecution and defense teams were not going to make Kennedy's job any easier. Captains Aubrey Daniel and John Partin, both in their twenties, led the prosecution team, and Calley brought to his defense the noted civilian attorney and former U.S. Court of Military Appeals judge George Latimer, civilian attorney Richard B. Kay, and military lawyers Maj. Kenneth Albert Raby and Capt. Brooks S. Doyle Jr. Latimer was highly regarded and was working on Calley's case for free. Kay turned out to be a liability to the team, as he knew little about military justice. Raby was considered a keen legal scholar but not that effective in the courtroom, and Doyle had the job of researcher in the case. Captain Daniel, for the prosecution, got the Calley case on a coin toss with three other captains and relished the opportunity to prove himself. He had apparently become disillusioned by the Vietnam ordeal but regardless of his own feelings about the war believed that Calley should be held responsible. Partin served as an able assistant and, like Doyle for the prosecution, did hundreds of interviews and hours of research in preparation for the trial. This was the My Lai trial that the public had come to focus upon—it was the center ring of the circus.[23]

Calley was on trial for the premeditated murder of more than 100 Vietnamese civilians, four specifications in all. Dozens of witnesses, some willing, others not so, described what happened at My Lai and Calley's role in the killings. Several who had themselves killed and raped either exercised their Fifth Amendment right to avoid self-incrimination or testified under immunity. In the other Article 32 investigations and trials, Calley had been heavily implicated, but none of this could be entered as evidence—all testimony had to be for this trial and this trial alone. It took weeks, throughout which Calley maintained his composure.

Calley's defense was straightforward—he had followed orders. On the stand he did not deny killing civilians but fervently maintained that he had been ordered to do so by Captain Medina. Calley clearly meant to portray his actions as acts against the enemy, not noncombatants. Both prosecution and defense dug deep into their respective legal bags for whatever tools, including psychiatry, they could use to promote their sides of the case. Calley's mental and emotional state dominated one phase of the trial. Kennedy recessed the trial for one week and ordered Calley to undergo psychiatric examination at Walter Reed Army Hospital. The results were "normal." Calley's defense team placed "experts" on the stand to testify to the unique psychiatric nature of a combat veteran such as Calley. In each instance, Daniel was able to riddle the testimony of these "experts" through vigorous and relentless cross-examination. Latimer attempted every stalling technique in a defense lawyer's handbook—he moved for mistrial based upon intrusive publicity, command influence, and lack of access to classified evidence (testimony from the Herbert congressional hearings). Kay removed all doubt about his lack of expertise in military courts by wasting Judge Kennedy's time with frivolous motions and by violating procedure time and time again. Throughout it all, Kennedy proved patient, good natured, and consistent in denying defense petitions.[24]

Captain Medina took the stand and denied having given the order to kill the villagers of My Lai. Although he admitted to covering up what had occurred, a crime for which the statute of limitations had run out for Medina, he went so far as to suggest that the few dead he had seen might have been killed by artillery or fire from helicopter gunships. Still, after all the damning testimony, Medina's denial of giving the order to shoot everyone in My Lai seemed to remove the last hope for Calley. On March 15, 1971, Daniel gave a methodical but eloquent summation to the court members, noting that the prosecution had clearly proven that Calley had given orders to kill civilians and had himself killed civilians at My Lai. He reminded the members that their task was to convict or acquit Calley, not anyone else who committed crimes at My Lai on March 16, 1968. Moreover, Calley had not been following orders—he had committed these acts on his own, and even if he had been ordered, Calley was intelligent enough to have known such orders were not legal. Latimer's summation was not so persuasive. In fact, he basically alienated whatever sympathy he had built in the members by suggesting that infantrymen had a tendency to exaggerate "war stories." The court members were combat veterans who knew that combat need not be exaggerated.[25]

Judge Kennedy gave the court members instructions to guide their findings. Like Daniels, he reminded the panel that obeying orders actually had little to do with how they might find in the case. The issue on trial was whether Calley had killed and whether illegal killings had taken place under his command. If the members acquitted Calley of premeditated murder, then they were obligated to consider lesser charges. As Kennedy put it:

> A determination that an order is illegal does not, of itself, assign criminal responsibility to the person following the order for acts done in compliance with it. Soldiers are taught to follow orders, and special attention is given to obedience of orders on the battlefield. Military effectiveness depends upon obedience to orders. On the other hand, the obedience of a soldier is not the obedience of an automaton. A soldier is a reasoning agent, obliged to respond, not as a machine, but as a person. The law takes the factors into account in assessing criminal responsibility for acts done in compliance with illegal orders. The acts of a subordinate done in compliance with an unlawful order given him by his superior are excused and impose no criminal liability upon him unless the superior's order is one which a man of ordinary sense and understanding would, under the circumstances, know to be unlawful, or if the order in question is actually known to the accused to be unlawful.[26]

The members then retired and for ten days considered the testimony and evidence. After intensive deliberation, they convicted Calley on each of the four specifications. In all Calley was convicted of killing not fewer than twenty-two individuals. The exact number could not be determined based upon the evidence available, though it was less than the 109 originally charged. Still, murder is murder is murder—all it took was one. Once the verdict had been reached, it was left to the members to sentence Calley. The choices were limited—life or death. Latimer argued for his client's life, citing all sorts of mitigating circumstances. Calley spoke briefly, stating that he had lost his honor, but now he begged the court to preserve the honor of future soldiers. Daniel said only that Calley's actions had already denied him his honor—the court could not restore it. Daniel did not argue for the death penalty. The members returned after several hours of deliberation the following day and sentenced Calley to spend the remainder of his natural life in prison.[27]

Calley's lawyers immediately appealed, and President Richard M. Nixon, responding to public sympathy that portrayed Calley as a scapegoat, immediately ordered Calley confined to his apartment pending appeal. The convening authority, Lieutenant General Connor, reviewed the court-martial's findings and concurred, but, as was his prerogative, he reduced Calley's sentence to twenty years. In January 1972, Calley's lawyers wrote Nixon, requesting executive clemency be granted to Calley, which Nixon denied. The appeal to the Army Court of Military Review, citing thirty-two possible errors in the trial, was rejected in a lengthy opinion. In April 1973, Calley's defense team appealed the Army Court of Military Review's decision to the Court of Military Appeals, the court of last resort, and was again rejected. Calley then turned to the federal court system, where his lawyers argued that Calley's right to a fair trial and proper due process had been denied. They filed a petition for a writ of habeas corpus with Judge J. Robert Elliott of the United States District Court for the Middle District of Georgia, which included the Columbus–Fort Benning region. Elliott ruled that Calley be released on bond until the review had been completed. The army appealed this decision to the United States Court of Appeals for the Fifth Circuit and won. The court remanded Calley to army custody and ordered his sentence carried out until Judge Elliott had ruled on the habeas corpus petition. Calley had been incarcerated at Fort Leavenworth for only a few weeks, however, when Judge Elliott completed his review of the habeas corpus petition. He ruled for the petitioner.

Judge Elliott ordered Calley freed. In a sixty-three-page opinion, Elliott cited numerous violations of Calley's right to due process and a fair trial. First and foremost, intense media coverage of the My Lai incident and Calley's prosecution had virtually assured that there could be no fair and impartial jury. The case had become a trial of the entire Vietnam War, not just Calley, Elliott noted, and that had infringed upon Calley's Fifth Amendment right to a fair trial. Moreover, the court-martial judge, Judge Kennedy, had denied several subpoenas for witness requested by Calley's defense team, many of which might have countered prosecution witnesses. Calley, according to Judge Elliott, had been convicted for following orders. The army, of course, appealed to the Fifth Circuit, which stayed Calley's release for fifteen days, then decided to hear the appeal. In the meantime, Calley had become eligible for parole. The secretary of the army, Howard Calloway, reduced Calley's sentence again to just ten years, which meant that with time already served he would shortly fall within the three-year minimum time served to qualify for parole. Then the Fifth Circuit court overturned Elliott's ruling and confirmed Calley's conviction. Just before the court announced its verdict, Secretary Calloway approved Calley's petition for parole. On November 9, 1974, more than six years after Calley had ordered, participated in, and witnessed the slaughter at My Lai, he was a free man.[28]

Beginning in August 1971, Medina's trial was uneventful compared to Calley's. The focus of army prosecutors, led by William G. Eckhardt, on the Medina court-martial was command responsibility—Medina should be held responsible for the actions of his men at My Lai. Medina denied everything, including any knowledge that illegal killings had occurred and participating in any subsequent cover-up. His defense counsel, F. Lee Bailey, himself a former Marine Corps lawyer, made a mockery of prosecution witnesses, especially Michael Bernhardt, a member of Company C who had suggested to Medina's military counsel that he might lie under oath. Bailey struck him with this damning allegation in court the following day, destroying Bernhardt's credibility as a prosecution witness. Bailey also convinced the judge, Col. Kenneth Howard, not to allow the Haeberle photographs to be admitted as evidence. The court members took less than an hour to acquit Medina of all charges. Shortly afterward, Medina left the army and admitted to filing false reports to cover up the My Lai killings. He was out of the army and could not be charged with perjury.[29]

Of the Peers Report's "Omissions and Commissions," Henderson's case was the only one that made it to trial and was the last of the My Lai–related trials to take place. Accused of lying to the Peers inquiry and covering up evidence of the massacre, Henderson was defended by Henry Rothblatt. Rothblatt portrayed Henderson as a valiant soldier who had sacrificed for his country in three wars. Rothblatt failed to keep Henderson's statements to the inspector general's inquest and to the Peers inquiry from being entered as evidence by the prosecution. The prosecution attacked Henderson's motivation for covering up the massacre—he feared losing his command and knew that if men under his command were investigated for war crimes, he would never be promoted to general. On the stand, Henderson claimed that if he had known the true extent of the killings at My Lai, he would certainly have ordered a proper investigation. He claimed ignorance, and it worked. The court-martial panel acquitted him of all charges. Henderson went public with his frustration with the army, including that charges of cover-ups extended well beyond his command. According to Henderson, almost every brigade in Vietnam had a "My Lai."[30]

The killings at My Lai had contributed to a change in Americans' perception of the war, the military, and undoubtedly military justice. Calley had been hailed as a hero, of sorts, across the United States. Political pressure from Congress and the White House on the army not to pursue those who had not been charged left the U.S. public with questions about the effectiveness of military justice. Still, in the public's view, Calley's indictment had been an indictment of the war rather than an indictment against a soldier accused of wanton slaughter of innocent civilian noncombatants.

The Marine Corps had a "My Lai" as well and learned from the army's mistakes. There would be no cover-up, and military justice, at least procedurally, would be carried out to the letter of the law. The atrocities committed at Son Thang on February 19, 1970, rank as the most serious crime committed by marines on a combat patrol for the entire war. Moreover, the way the Marine Corps dealt with the matter was directly influenced by the public outcry over the My Lai incident. Company B, First Battalion, Seventh Marines had had a tough few months since the fall of 1969. Since November, fourteen members of the unit had been killed, and eighty-five had been wounded in action. The unit operated in the southern part of the I Corps area, which differed greatly from the mainly depopulated demilitarized zone (DMZ) to the north. Although some civilians had been relocated away from the southern area, many had remained, heightening suspicions that many of these were Viet Cong sympathizers, at the very least, and perhaps actually Viet Cong themselves.

Unit commanders made an extensive effort to educate new arrivals about restraint in dealing with local civilians. Part of the problem, however, was that experience had led marines to consider women, even children, as the enemy. Two weeks before the incident occurred, two Vietnamese women had led a patrol into an ambush, and a week later a patrol fell into a firefight with what turned out to be Vietnamese boys with automatic weapons. One of the boys, thought to be nine to twelve years old, was killed. The very day of the incident, a marine had been shot and killed in yet another ambush. Tensions were certainly high.[31]

Company B was commanded by 1st Lt. Louis R. Ambort, considered by his superiors as an experienced and effective combat leader. On the evening of February 19, Ambort organized a so-called killer team to seek revenge on the enemy who had done the unit so much damage over the previous weeks. A killer team, which was not authorized by the Marine Corps, was a short patrol designed to be light and quick, to hit with surprise, and to kill as many of the enemy as possible, then extricate itself without taking extensive casualties. Ambort chose Lance Corporal Randell D. Herrod, who had combat experience in the northern part of I Corps in the Third Marine Division and had previously led several such teams for B Company, to lead the team. Considered "bush wise" and "more mature" than his fellow marines, Herrod was thus chosen for his supposed "natural" leadership capabilities and experience. But he had been in trouble before, including a special court-martial conviction for being AWOL for two months. The other four members of the killer team volunteered for the patrol and were approved by Herrod: Lance Corporal Michael S. Krichten, Private First Class Thomas R. Boyd, Private First Class Samuel G. Green Jr., and Private Michael A. Schwarz. Green and Schwarz were new to the unit, having only recently arrived in Vietnam. Green was truly just that—green. This was his first combat patrol.[32]

Lieutenant Ambort addressed the team before it set out, giving a Patton-like speech that recalled their fallen comrades and urged revenge: "Don't let them get us anymore. I want you to pay these little bastards back!" Each man recalled hearing roughly the same thing from Ambort—go out and kill whoever was out there. At 1930 the team departed. The first hamlet they came across was Son Thang 4.[33]

The first hooch in Son Thang yielded six Vietnamese: one woman, three young boys, and two thirteen-year-old girls. Forcing the occupants outside, Herrod allegedly ordered the team to kill them. There was brief discussion, to which Herrod replied that he was under orders from the company commander and again gave the order to shoot, which the team obeyed. At the next hooch, Herrod again allegedly gave the order to shoot, which was again obeyed, this time leaving two women and two young girls dead. A third hooch fell under Herrod's alleged order to shoot, leaving two more women, two girls, and two young boys dead. Because the team was such a short distance from Company B's perimeter, the firing was easily heard. Ambort had the team called back in, not wanting to risk more casualties than had already been suffered over the previous days.

Herrod reported to Ambort that as many as sixteen enemy had been killed, but he must have let on that something had gone wrong as he gave his report. He and Ambort then conspired to submit a false report to battalion headquarters. The report stated that fifteen to twenty Viet Cong had been spotted moving along a trail. The team had set up an ambush, which netted seven killed, including one female. Ambort added an SKS rifle (common among North Vietnamese Army and Viet Cong units) that had been found earlier in the week to add legitimacy to the report, make sure the unit got credit for the supposed enemy kills, and perhaps to protect his men.[34]

Maj. Richard E. Theer, the battalion operation officer, received reports the next day from an intelligence officer who had toured the Son Thang area that morning and had seen the bodies. Suspicious, Theer contacted the battalion commander, Lt. Col. Charles G. Cooper. Theer and Cooper agreed that Company B should be moved back to battalion headquarters and that the reports should be investigated. At first, Theer understandably assumed that these people might have been killed in the cross fire between the marines and the enemy. Enemy contact had been made near Son Thang before, and the fact had previously been established that enemy combatants might be women and children in the area.

Theer interviewed Lieutenant Ambort, who admitted that he had falsified the spot report, particularly the part concerning the captured enemy rifle. All five members of the killer team provided written statements that Theer slowly realized were much too similar for comfort. The men had declined legal counsel when providing these statements. Theer then returned to see Son Thang and quickly came to the conclusion, judging from the positions of the team, the bodies, and shell casings, that there could have been no enemy fire as each marine had claimed. Upon returning to battalion headquarters, Major Theer recommended that a First Marine Division legal team be brought in to conduct an investigation.[35]

At the suggestion of the division legal personnel, Theer gave each member of the patrol an opportunity to withdraw his previous statement, which would not be used against him if withdrawn, and to make a new one. Herrod refused. Green refused to offer a new statement but opened himself to oral questioning, to which he reacted hostilely. Schwarz at first refused but then wrote out a new statement, admitting that there had been no sniper fire, that he had been ordered to fire on the civilians, and that he had feared court-martial if he did not obey the order. Boyd also changed his statement, admitting that no sniper fire had been received. Krichten did the same thing and, like Schwarz and Boyd, implicated Herrod as the one who gave the order to fire and kill the civilians. Each man was advised of his Article 31 rights and had now signed a written statement to a formal investigation. Theer now had a clear idea of what had occurred at Son Thang. All five patrol members were placed in custody, and Lieutenant Ambort was relieved.[36]

The Article 32 investigation began on February 24 and was completed eleven days later. Maj. Robert Blum, an experienced judge advocate, conducted the investigation. Marine Corps lawyers assigned to the case now represented each man, and Herrod had a civilian lawyer coming from his native Oklahoma. First Division had astutely alerted the press to the incident and allowed reporters to visit Company B's area, including Son Thang, as well as battalion headquarters. My Lai was shocking the nation, and the Marine Corps wanted no armylike cover-up on their hands. They wanted to come clean with the public, and nothing was hidden.

Blum recommended that Herrod and Schwarz be tried for premeditated murder, that Boyd and Green be charged with unpremeditated murder, and that all be tried by general court-martial. The South Vietnamese government waived its jurisdiction despite the seriousness of the allegations. Lt. Col. Cooper agreed with the recommendations except for the case of Krichten, who had apparently fired over the heads of all of the civilians shot at Son Thang. None of the other killer team members contradicted this. Krichten was given immunity to testify in each trial. Using his prerogative as convening authority, Cooper decreed that all four cases be tried as noncapital offenses. The death penalty was out, but life imprisonment was still a possibility.[37]

Schwarz's court-martial convened first. Defended by Capt. Daniel H. LeGear Jr., Schwarz chose to be tried before a seven-member panel versus before a judge alone. LeGear first tried to persuade the panel members that Son Thang was indeed in a hostile area and that there had been several instances where women and children turned out to be enemy combatants. The Vietnamese district chief testified that among the dead women were three Viet Cong. Then LeGear tried to prevent Schwarz's written statement from being admitted as evidence but failed. Only then was LeGear left to offer "obeying orders" as Schwarz's defense. Herrod had ordered Schwarz to shoot the villagers—he was simply following orders. The prosecution team, Captains Franz P. Jevne and Charles E. Brown, presented a tight case against Schwarz. Krichten, in particular, offered damning testimony, which LeGear was unable to offset in cross examination. Lieutenant Ambort and Lieutenant Colonel Cooper also testified. In all, the testimony pointed to Herrod as the judge and jury and Schwarz as chief executioner of the civilians at Son Thang.

The court members convicted Schwarz on twelve of the sixteen counts of premeditated murder that had been filed against him. The four killings at the first hooch were excused, as reasonable doubt existed that the team might have been fired upon at that location. Such was not the case at the other hooches. Schwarz already had a long and colorful record in the Marine Corps, including five Article 15s, one summary court-martial, and two special courts-martial convictions. Schwarz was dishonorably discharged, forced to forfeit all pay, and sentenced to serve the rest of his life at hard labor. The court members had sent a clear message about following orders: Schwarz knew that Herrod's order to kill these noncombatants was illegal, yet he had chosen to follow that order.[38]

Boyd's court-martial came next. Having heard the ruling on Schwarz outside the courtroom, Boyd decided to take his chances by being tried before a judge alone. The same judge as in the Schwarz court-martial, Lt. Col. Paul St. Amour, presided over the Boyd trial. Boyd was charged with unpremeditated murder. His defense team included Howard P. Trockman, a civilian attorney from Boyd's hometown of Evansville, Indiana. Capt. Michael P. Merrill sat as Boyd's military cocounsel. Trockman, like LeGear, tried to have Boyd's statement given to Major Theer made inadmissible and even alleged command influence had been brought to bear on Boyd when he made his statement. Trockman also brought to the court's attention the fact that no autopsies had been performed on the dead and that no ballistics evidence had been gathered. St. Amour denied these and other motions made by the defense. Krichten testified again for the prosecution, but surprised all by stating that Boyd had fired over the heads of the villagers at each hooch and that Boyd had been the last to fire his weapon in each instance. This dramatically helped Boyd's case. When Boyd took the stand, he repeated what Krichten had said occurred and what he had vaguely said in his written statement. He had fired over their heads and not killed anyone. Further, it was substantiated that he had not even qualified with the rifle at boot camp, had been AWOL for four weeks before coming to Vietnam, and was considering applying for a conscientious objector exemption. The prosecution's case had fallen flat. St. Amour took only a few hours to acquit Boyd.[39]

Lieutenant Colonel St. Amour also presided over the next trial, that of Private First Class Green. Prosecuted by Captains Jevne and Brown, Green was defended by Capt. John J. Hargrove. Green opted for trial before court members, in this instance three officers and two enlisted men. Green was charged with sixteen counts of unpremeditated murder. Once again, Krichten appeared as the star witness for the prosecution, and as in the Boyd trial, he disappointed. Although he was certain that Green had fired his weapon, he could not say for certain that Green had actually hit anyone. Hargrove tried the "obeying orders" defense, noting that Green had been in-country for only a short time before the incident and had been in the Marine Corps for less than six months. As in the Schwarz case, the court members (a different panel, of course), found that Green could not have believed that Herrod's order to shoot noncombatants was legal. They convicted Green on fifteen of the sixteen counts (testimony clearly showed that Herrod had killed one of the victims himself). The sentence was lenient—dishonorable discharge, reduction in grade, total forfeiture, and confinement of five years at hard labor.[40]

Herrod's trial was last. It seemed an open-and-shut case, but remember that what had been said in the previous trials did not prejudice Herrod's trial. The prosecution team of Captains Brown, Gary E. Bushell, and J. Len Skiles would have to show that Herrod had committed sixteen counts of premeditated murder. Defending Herrod was a rather large team of civilian lawyers and Captain Williams, who took a backseat in the trial proceedings. Oklahoma state senators Denzil D. Garrison and Gene Stipe came to Vietnam at their own expense to defend native son Herrod. Assisting them were civilian attorneys Richard Miller and Harry Palmer. Armour had been transferred to Japan, so navy commander Keith B. Lawrence presided over the seven-member panel, made up of all officers. The defense team used five days of trial time presenting numerous motions, including change of venue, a new Article 32 investigation, and a request for a panel of members made up entirely of enlisted personnel; each of these motions was denied. Major Theer and Lieutenant Colonel Cooper, both of whom had by now rotated back to the United States, returned to Vietnam, Theer to testify against Herrod and Cooper to be a witness on his behalf.

Clever civilian attorneys from Oklahoma outmatched the prosecution. They somehow produced testimony that marines in Company B had heard an M-60 machine gun in the vicinity of Son Thang while the killer team was out on patrol there. Then they actually produced an M-60 that had been captured near Son Thang a few days after the killings. In a coup d'grâce, the defense established that Herrod's team could have been responding to enemy machine gun fire. The prosecution could not corroborate the other four team members' often conflicting testimony as to who actually fired at what, and when. Lt. Oliver North testified in the trial as Herrod's previous company commander (North had recommended Herrod for the Silver Star) and as a witness to support the suggestion that Herrod could not get a fair trial in Vietnam since his case was being discussed by just about every marine eligible to sit on his panel of members. Herrod took the stand in his own defense and repeated what he had said in his original statement to Theer—his team had been fired upon, and the victims had been killed by cross fire. The defense team continued to bombard the court with motions, even one to declare a mistrial. All were denied.

The court members took three hours to acquit Herrod on all counts. It took a two-thirds majority to find a defendant guilty and apparently the members were stuck at a four-to-three vote for conviction, which was not enough. The members could have found Herrod guilty of a lesser charge, and even though they apparently considered lesser charges, the panel inexplicably did not convict. The prosecution had failed, and Herrod walked a free Marine.[41] Herrod wrote a book of his experience, titled *Blue's Bastards: A True Story of Valor under Fire*.[42]

Lieutenant Ambort received what amounted to a slap on the wrist. Having admitted to filing a false report, an Article 32 investigation concurred and recommended Ambort receive nonjudicial punishment. Maj. Gen. Charles Widdecke, new commander of the First Marine Division, gave Ambort a formal letter of reprimand and ordered that he forfeit $250 pay for two months. Ambort did not appeal the punishment. His thirteen-month tour was almost over, and as a reserve officer, his career as a marine was probably finished because of the career-ending letter of reprimand.[43]

Green and Schwarz, the only two of the five marines convicted in these killings, both served only a year of the original sentences, each sentence being reduced by Widdecke as convening authority. Both appealed based upon Herrod's acquittal, but the appellate court denied both petitions, citing the premise that aiding and abetting a crime is the equivalent of committing an independent crime. As a young lawyer in the mid-1970s, James H. Webb Jr., a heavily decorated Marine Corps combat veteran who had commanded a rifle company in Vietnam in 1969 and who later served as secretary of the navy in the Ronald Reagan administration from 1987 to 1988, took an intense interest in the Son Thang trials. He eventually convinced the Navy Department in 1978 to throw out Green's dishonorable discharge. Green, however, did not live to see this slight vindication: he committed suicide in 1975.[44]

My Lai and Son Thang may be the more familiar atrocities committed by U.S. forces in Vietnam, but other allegations, whether confirmed or unproven, occurred as well. The Winter Soldier investigation and its controversial testimony at hearings organized by Vietnam Veterans Against the War in Detroit in

1971 and the hearings sponsored by the National Committee for Citizens' Commission of Inquiry on U.S. War Crimes in Vietnam brought even deeper interest in alleged violations of the laws of war committed in Vietnam. Dozens of veterans came forward with claims that they had participated in, witnessed, or (mostly) heard of war crimes committed in Vietnam. There is much debate on the validity of this testimony alleging all manner of war crimes. The hearings cited numerous incidents of rape, murder, mutilation, torture, and other inhumane acts, so much so that such crimes appeared commonplace in Vietnam. Both commissions placed blame on corrupt command, racism, failure to understand cultural differences, and numerous other supposed failings of the U.S. effort in Vietnam. Many witnesses charged that the military justice system was incapable of dealing with the problem.[45]

Yet U.S. troops were held responsible. Violations of the Uniform Code of Military Justice that constituted war crimes were prosecuted. Specialist Fourth Class George Pawlaczyk and Specialist Fifth Class Franklin Passantino, both of the army's First Battalion, Eighteenth Regiment of the First Division, were convicted by special court-martial for "bringing discredit upon the armed forces" by mutilating enemy corpses, in this case cutting the ears off of dead Viet Cong for souvenirs. Pawlaczyk was demoted and forced to forfeit two-thirds of his pay for two months; Passantino was demoted and forced to give up two-thirds of his pay for four months.[46]

In another case, Marine Corps sergeant Charles Wilkerson claimed that his lieutenant had ordered him to shoot a Viet Cong prisoner. Wilkerson had indeed taken the prisoner off the trail and killed him. Wilkerson's court-martial sentenced him to life imprisonment, which was reduced to thirty years by the reviewing authority. The lieutenant, David Yorck, also had charges brought against him but was acquitted of giving the order to kill the prisoner. A *Time* article describing Wilkerson's case also noted the conviction of four soldiers who had raped a Vietnamese girl—all four were dishonorably discharged and given sentences ranging from eight years to life. The article seemed to applaud the vigorous defense by military lawyers of soldiers accused of these crimes and gave a sympathetic ear to the "following orders" defense. Aside from the fact that a military lawyer would assuredly uphold his obligation to do his best for his client, the "following orders" defense sometimes was the only alternative left as a defense strategy. Lt. Col. Bill Wander, a Marine Corps lawyer, suggested in the article that the "following orders" defense often fell on deaf ears, as courts-martial members "rarely sympathized" with soldiers who had committed such crimes, especially those who claimed they were "following orders."[47]

Occasionally, the "following orders" defense had traction. Army lieutenant James B. Duffy was accused of premeditated murder of a Vietnamese noncombatant, a farmer named Do Van Man. Man was found hiding in an air-raid bunker near the village of Phouctanhung and, as was the case with many Vietnamese found in hiding, was suspected of being Viet Cong. Found unarmed and offering no resistance when brought out of his hiding place, Do Van Man claimed to be a South Vietnamese soldier on leave. Although he had on his person a South Vietnamese army pay voucher, a sick slip, and photographs of himself and fellow soldiers in uniform, his identification card was not found. Duffy radioed the command post that a suspected Viet Cong had been taken prisoner. The reply, according to testimony, asked whether the "prisoner had escaped yet"—apparently unspoken code for "had the prisoner been shot yet." At trial, assistant defense counsel Capt. Tom Thomsen claimed that Duffy understood this to mean that he should shoot the prisoner under the guise that the prisoner tried to escape. Duffy ordered Do Van Man tied to a stake overnight and in the morning ordered Sgt. John L. Nasa to execute him. Afterward, according to Specialist 4 David Walsted, Lieutenant Duffy "got on the horn and informed command that the prisoner had tried to escape and we shot him."

In the court-martial, Duffy admitted all of this and added further that he was told to get a body count rather than "bring in prisoners." He was following orders. Duffy's lead defense counsel was a civilian, Henry B. Rothblatt, the same attorney who had defended Henderson in the My Lai trials. Rothblatt contended that it was not Duffy who should be on trial, but rather the army itself. By placing so much emphasis on "body counts," the army had in essence ordered Duffy not to take prisoners. Do Van Man had been taken in a free fire zone, where it was understood that whoever was found in such zones was assumed to be Viet Cong and therefore eliminated. Duffy's fellow lieutenants corroborated this practice. Lt. John Kruger testified that prisoners were not taken and that "everything in the kill zone was killed." The unit's command would get "very angry" if prisoners were indeed taken alive. Lt. Ralph C. Krueger put it more bluntly: "If a VC comes out of a fight to give himself up, that man is dead." Other testimony suggested that the unit's supplies might even be held up if it did not turn in an acceptable body count.

The military judge in the case, the same Col. Peter Wondolowski of the previously mentioned McInnis trial, did not allow this defense to be considered by the court members. The Uniform Code of Military Justice and *The Law of Land Warfare* were clear: it does not matter who gives the order or carries out the order; both parties are equally guilty. By all accounts, including that of an army psychiatrist, the twenty-two-year-old Duffy was "just as apple pie and all-American as you can find, a damn good kid." His commander, Capt. Howard Turner, called Duffy "one of my best officers." Nonetheless, the court members convicted Duffy of premeditated murder, which carried a mandatory life sentence. Despite being told not to consider the defense position, court members felt such a punishment was too harsh under the circumstances. Wondolowski allowed the members to reconsider their finding. They instead convicted Duffy of the lesser charge of involuntary manslaughter and sentenced him to six months confinement at hard labor and a $1,500 fine.[48]

The Duffy trial received a great deal of media attention, and some commentators suggested that the "mere gook rule" had played a significant role in the outcome. The mere gook rule informally held that offenses committed against Vietnamese would be punished with lighter sentences, if indeed punished at all, than sentences for similar offenses against non-Vietnamese. The *Nation*, not surprisingly, strongly defended Duffy, claiming that although he was certainly a "minor criminal," he was more a victim of the system, which made soldiers "criminally subordinate to the government of the United States, which sent them across the sea to invade a small country and to wipe out inoffensive people in a fanatical crusade to crush communism and, not incidentally, to provide profits for American business and employment for American labor." Perhaps the mere gook rule was at play in this case, but the unlikely claims of Rothblatt and The *Nation* certainly did not excuse the order that Duffy clearly and admittedly gave. It is unclear what became of the sergeant Duffy ordered to execute Do Van Man.[49]

A Marine Corps case highlights the difficulty in getting a conviction for murdering a North Vietnamese prisoner. Marine Corps captain Robert W. Poolaw, a Native American from Oklahoma, was charged with murdering a prisoner of war on August 11, 1969.[50] Poolaw, commander of Company H of the Second Battalion, Fifth Marine Regiment, led his company on a "sweep and destroy" mission south of An Hoa. Typical of such operations, Poolaw had his three platoons lined up abreast with the squads of each platoon in column. Poolaw and his command post were with the center platoon as the formation moved forward. At about 1000, a North Vietnamese Army (NVA) soldier, Nguyen Van Hoc, was captured along the trail the center platoon was following. As Hoc was severely wounded from an earlier engagement, Poolaw ordered a litter made to carry the NVA prisoner. A few minutes later, Private First Class Frank Williams, on point, spotted another wounded NVA soldier in a hammock off the trail. Delirious with fever, the NVA soldier could not respond to Williams's attempts to force him out of the hammock, whereupon Williams severely beat the man.

Poolaw arrived on the scene, angry at Williams for having moved too far ahead of the platoon. Poolaw told Williams to leave the NVA soldier in the hammock alone and ordered Williams to the rear of the column to help carry the litter bearing the other prisoner. Williams refused and "put up a bitch" that he had captured the NVA soldier and was therefore entitled to a three-day in-country rest-and-relaxation (R and R) pass, as had apparently been the unit's custom to reward those who captured enemy soldiers or Viet Cong. Poolaw again ordered Williams to the rear, an order Williams again refused. The company gunnery sergeant, Anthony H. Marengo, stepped in and ordered Williams to obey Poolaw's order. Williams verbally assaulted Sergeant Marengo, giving the sergeant good cause for delivering two solid slaps to Williams's face. Williams finally relented and was heard saying in reference to the NVA soldier, "I would rather kill him than carry him because of the way he smells. . . . I hate gooks anyway."

Sergeant Marengo cleared away the marines who had gathered around the commotion, but Williams lingered on the edge of the clearing where they had found the NVA soldier. Talking with Lance Corporal Edward W. Hendrix, Williams claimed he heard Captain Poolaw load a round into the chamber of his .45 pistol. Looking toward Poolaw, whose back was to the men, both Hendrix and Williams claimed that Poolaw's arm was extended toward the NVA soldier. Neither man could state for certain that Poolaw had unholstered his .45 because the thick underbrush obstructed a full view. A shot rang out, then the NVA soldier's body slumped backward. Sergeant Marengo was already headed back down the trail and did not see the incident and testified that he did not hear a shot. Williams and Corporal Hendrix made their way to the corpse, which was lying on its front side, thus exposing the large fracture on the back of the skull. Williams turned the body on its back to get a look at the NVA soldier's face, noting the bullet hole in the man's forehead. Poolaw noticed the two marines examining the corpse and ordered them to move out. As they did so, Poolaw turned the body back on its front and pushed it off the trail.

Only Williams seemed willing to pursue charges against Poolaw. Hendrix and the others did not agree with what Poolaw had supposedly done but also did not want to cause trouble. Williams, on the other hand, had a reputation for making trouble and for being a "loudmouth" and had revenge as motivation. Gunnery Sergeant Marengo saw no need to initiate an investigation based upon Williams's charges and his reputation. Williams, however, made enough of an issue of it that the Naval Investigation Service initiated an investigation in October 1969, finding enough evidence to authorize an Article 32 investigation in the next month. By this time, as was often the case in investigations and trials in Vietnam, Hendrix had completed his tour and had been discharged from service. Poolaw, Marengo, Williams, and other principal witnesses were still in Vietnam. Poolaw refused to offer any statement. Marengo was interviewed four times, proving uncooperative during the first two interviews; he was then ordered by the commanding general of the First Marine Division to give a "full, complete, and truthful" account of the events of August 11. Marengo, however, continued to contradict Williams's story, stating that Williams was nowhere near Poolaw and that he had personally escorted Williams to the rear. Hendrix and two other witnesses contradicted Marengo. Naval Investigation Service agents interviewed Williams several times, and Williams apparently changed his story more than once. It was apparent that Williams wanted revenge on Poolaw for not granting the three-day R and R and that Marengo was protecting his captain.

Poolaw's trial occurred amid the storm of the My Lai investigation, and the First Marines understandably wanted to avoid any unnecessary press attention: "All of us here are keeping our fingers crossed that the press doesn't become aware of the incident. Toward this end maximum local effort is being devoted."[51] Poolaw was charged with a violation of Article 118 for premeditated murder rather than a "war crime." Conflicting testimony and intense assaults on trustworthiness of witnesses hurt the prosecution's case. Defense counsel Capt. Theodore J. Padden was able to place enough doubt, particularly on the testimony of Hendrix, to persuade the general court-martial members not to convict Poolaw. Padden had done his homework on Hendrix, exposing a fraudulent Purple Heart application and a combat refusal, both of which seriously undermined his credibility as a key prosecution witness. Moreover, no one was able to state with complete certainty that Poolaw indeed had a pistol in the hand of his extended arm. Poolaw was acquitted.

War crimes cannot be completely prevented or even eradicated. As proactive as directives, manuals, training, and leadership can be, none of these means can provide 100 percent assurance to prevent crimes of war. Proactive and reactive measures can, however, at least help military forces put in place better procedures to deal with war crimes. My Lai had brought violations of the law of war to the U.S. public's attention in late 1969, but U.S. military forces in Vietnam already had measures in place to deal with such acts, and the Uniform Code of

Military Justice provided for their prosecution. It is one thing to order anyone with knowledge of a possible war crime to report it, but it is quite another to actually convince them to do it, and it is a credit to the army's military lawyers that they prosecuted cases, especially the My Lai cases, with such vigor despite risking harm to their military careers. Military lawyers and investigators investigated 241 cases of alleged violations of the laws of war. Only 36 of these cases could be substantiated enough to prefer charges under corresponding articles in the Uniform Code of Military Justice. Of these 36, 20 cases resulted in the conviction of 31 U.S. soldiers.[52]

Many factors contributed to the conditions in which U.S. soldiers committed war crimes. The emotional and physical stress of combat, seeking revenge for a fallen comrade, peer pressure, poor leadership, vague orders, unclear chains of command, morale confusion, poor decision making, and countless other causes influenced a small number of U.S. soldiers in Vietnam to commit horrid acts, including murder, rape, and mutilation.

The more soldiers know about the laws of war, the better they will appreciate the reasoning behind such laws. The more a nation and its military institutions value and comply with conventions regulating war behavior, the more these principles will shape the behavior and decision-making capability of soldiers in the field—at least that is the hope. The United States unquestionably values these ideals of battlefield behavior and promotes proactive education and legal deterrents to persuade and train its military personnel to act accordingly in the chaos of combat. Perhaps this is what makes My Lai, Son Thang, and other barbaric acts allegedly committed by U.S. troops in Vietnam so shocking and appalling. The fact remains that Americans committed these acts and will do so again. Combat is a universal human activity, not limited to Americans; like other soldiers, Americans made terrible errors in judgment in Vietnam and will make similar mistakes in other conflicts.[53]

Military lawyers and the Uniform Code of Military Justice, especially after its 1968 revision, were adequately equipped to deal with war crimes. Sometimes inexperienced judge advocates, for whatever reason, prosecuted and defended in these critical cases when more able and experienced lawyers might have performed better. As in the case of Son Thang, the conditions of a combat zone, manpower shortages, transport limitations, time, and the ripple effect of command and judicial decisions influenced the manner in which a case was investigated, tried, and decided. Aside from the jurisdictional shortcoming that a person who has been honorably discharged cannot be charged with crimes committed while in service, the system supporting military justice faltered rather than the Uniform Code of Military Justice itself. In Vietnam, wartime conditions may well have demanded a different "combat" judicial code. The fact remains, however, that the Uniform Code of Military Justice was *the* code during the Vietnam War and as such commanders and judge advocates had to use *that* system. Deficient or not, in dealing with war crimes by using corresponding articles of the Uniform Code of Military Justice to prosecute war crimes, military justice in Vietnam did not fail, nor was it perfect.[54]

CHAPTER SIX
THE DRUG PROBLEM

As is the case with war crimes, illegal drugs and Vietnam remain firmly linked in the popular culture and historiography of the U.S. war in Southeast Asia, a connection that began during the war itself. In many ways, the U.S. experience with drugs in Vietnam merely continued Vietnam's colonial experience dating back to the nineteenth century. Demands placed upon Vietnam by the United States and earlier by France brought dramatic changes in Vietnamese attitudes toward illicit drug use, profiting from drug production and sales, and general corruption. How the United States and Vietnam arrived at this caustic crossroads is intriguing, to say the least, and tells us much about how the United States lived a dual life by waging war on the new drug culture at home while allowing drugs to play a significant role in morally and militarily undermining a real war in Southeast Asia. Cultural differences, political necessities, and economic realities relating to drugs, corruption, and respect for the rule of law widened the gap between the United States and South Vietnam as both countries tried to stop the North Vietnamese insurgency and preserve South Vietnam's independence. U.S. military justice played a vital role in fighting the drug problem in Vietnam.

There has always been a conspiratorial aspect of the drug puzzle in Southeast Asia. Before the arrival of Europeans, local peoples used opium principally for medicinal purposes. This rather innocent use changed when Spanish and Portuguese traders inadvertently triggered the Western opium trade by introducing tobacco to Asia. Chinese in Southeast Asia took the Spanish tobacco pipe, mixed a bit of opium with the tobacco, and enjoyed a soothing smoke. European traders began exporting opium around Asian coastal regions. British India brought the first large, organized monopoly of opium cultivation and production by the late 1700s, exporting tons of the stuff to China to meet the needs of the Western-induced "fad" that had by this time taken hold of Chinese bureaucrats. So concerned was the Chinese imperial house that it banned opium imports in 1800, but the East India Company ignored the edict, beginning decades of tense conflict that erupted in two infamous opium wars (1839–1842 and 1856–1858).

The trade spread as Western military superiority allowed European merchants to control China's ports and thus import opium at will. As European imperialism colored the map of Southeast Asia and Chinese immigrants flooded the region to fill the needs of manual labor, they brought with them their addiction. Colonial administrations sensed profit and set up state-run opium dens. Before long, opium monopolies supplied the needs of over 15 million addicts in China alone and enticed more in Southeast Asia into addiction each year. Profits from the opium trade, official opium dens, and related corruption made up more than 40 percent of colonial revenues in Southeast Asia, which is rather ironic considering that opium was illegal in western European countries.[1]

By 1900, demand for opium had expanded beyond Asia and even become well established in western Europe. Even the United States had its share of opium addicts, who required a vast illegal trade to keep supplied. Opium demand also created a thriving black market in Asia, as colonial governments raised prices, inadvertently forcing addicts to find cheaper opium through illegal sources.[2] This black market and associated corruption became the norm in Southeast Asia, lasting well after the U.S. war in Vietnam.

Many farmers in Indochina's central highlands, an area long known for growing opium poppies and processing opium, made a good living from harvesting the crop for heroin suppliers in Thailand, Cambodia, and Vietnam. The French, who conquered Indochina piece by piece between 1859 and 1893, encouraged the opium trade by granting monopolies to companies that grew poppies and processed opium. A share of the profits made such generosity possible. French colonial officials bought raw opium from producers in China, India, and Indochina and had it processed in dozens of small household factories in and around Saigon. The final product was sold at commissaries run by the French administration at a markup of 400 to 500 percent. The French administration became so addicted to its opium monopoly that it had to spend a great deal of its time and resources enforcing black-market and smuggling laws to prevent loss of trade and revenue. High taxation, forced labor, and an opium monopoly—Western imperialism at its finest, indeed.

Opium use among Vietnamese had never been high because of the cultural stigma attached to habitual use of the drug, but under French rule, up to 20 percent of Vietnamese officials who worked for the French colonial administration became addicts, compared to only 2 percent of the population at large. This does not include the tens of thousands of Chinese and other immigrant laborers who fell prey to the drug, which significantly increased the number of addicts overall. Opium use was illegal in France, but in French Indochina the law was indeed ignored, and the sale and use of the drug was officially encouraged.[3]

By the 1930s, however, the subsidized drug trade began to backfire on the French colonial administration. Vietnamese nationalists in Vietnam as well as in Europe began condemning the horrific effects of opium use on the Vietnamese people. It was killing the Vietnamese workforce, legitimizing graft and corruption among the Vietnamese elite who worked for the French colonial administration, and undermining hopes for Vietnamese independence. World War II exacerbated the situation. The demand of the addicts remained, but the war certainly threatened the delicate opium supply. Poppies from China and other parts of Southeast Asia could not reach Indochina—there was no transportation, and in many cases the farmers themselves could not plant or harvest their crop because of the war. French colonial officials, allowed to administer Indochina during the Japanese occupation, struggled to find a new source of poppies. The French tried to solve the problem by convincing the Meo in Laos to dramatically expand their crop. This program worked with stunning success, despite a few rather bloody Meo uprisings over what the tribe saw as pure exploitation: more land to grow poppies meant less to support the Meo's subsistence farming. The French did not seem interested in making up the difference. Short-term profit, however, apparently appeased the Meo. Crop yields increased to the point that the opium trade provided the chief source of revenue in Laos, and opium-related revenues in Indochina actually increased during the war.[4]

Into the postwar power vacuum of Indochina stepped Ho Chi Minh. A man keenly aware of the opium trade and its impact on the Vietnamese people, Ho included his concern about that impact among his list of grievances against the French government in his declaration of independence (much like the American declaration listed grievances against King George III) on September 2, 1945: "To weaken our race, they have forced us to use their manufactured opium and alcohol."[5] Ho attempted to outlaw opium production and drug use, which was a tall order indeed considering the war he had to fight against the French until 1954, the continuation of the French monopoly to that time, and the expanding underground of illegal opium smugglers. The French-Indochina War drastically cut domestic opium production. The Chinese source of raw opium dried up in 1949 when Mao's communist forces ended regularized opium trade in southern China. Vietnam turned to Iran as its principal source, but this too ended in 1955 with an Iranian government edict outlawing opium production and trade. From that point, the black market took over. Smuggling and illegal crop production fed the addiction in Southeast Asia.

The 1950s brought the cold war to Southeast Asia and with it came clandestine support for the illegal drug trade. The Golden Triangle (the highlands of Burma, Thailand, Laos, and Vietnam) was filled with small tribal communities that grew opium poppies and were not thrilled with the prospect of communism. Working with these tribes as well as with Chinese mafia during World War II to sabotage Japanese occupation forces, the U.S. Office of Strategic Services (OSS) tried to look the other way when faced with the reality of opium. U.S. agents allowed drug trafficking as a trade-off for securing support of local peoples. The Central Intelligence Agency (CIA), the successor to the OSS, maintained and often enhanced these contacts to organize and support resistance against the new threat of communist insurgency. U.S. money and arms allowed the illegal opium trade to flourish in part to win the support of these peoples against communism as well as to finance military operations.[6]

The role of the CIA in the drug trade in Vietnam is indeed controversial. Air America planes allegedly transported opium and heroin around Southeast Asia. U.S. aid sometimes indirectly supported drug trafficking, which enabled the drug trade to flourish during the Vietnam War. The Diem regime and successive South Vietnamese governments each profited from the illegal drug trade, which by 1968 was supplying U.S. soldiers with marijuana, opium, and heroin. The irony surpasses absurdity—South Vietnamese government officials supplied drugs to the very U.S. soldiers who kept those officials in power. Moreover, some of these drugs ultimately reached lucrative markets in the United States, expanding the problem well beyond the narrow borders of Vietnam.[7]

Vietnamese opium and marijuana farmers became financially dependent upon their illicit crops, as did corrupt government officials who profited by accepting bribes to facilitate the trade. Payoffs, bribes, and corruption had become common in Vietnam. Vietnamese looked upon the Western concept of corruption as simple "commission sharing." By Western standards, the puppet governments supported by France and later the United States each reached new heights in egregious corruption. Culturally, corruption served a purpose in Vietnamese society, helping the Vietnamese people cope with the destructive forces of nearly thirty years of constant war. Corruption acted as a "social lubricant" that was "probably [as] deeply rooted as tipping in other cultures."[8] In Vietnam, as in many places, money equaled power. To have power, one must have money to pay off potential adversaries at all levels and maintain the pyramid of factions necessary to support power. The problem of course was how to get cash. Drug trafficking and the black market provided a steady and ready source.[9]

Drug trafficking, the black market, and other corruption had at the height of the U.S. war created a new class of nouveau riche that undermined the old social system in which bureaucrats and monks enjoyed wealth and respect in society. The traditional peasant ways gave way to rapid urbanization as people left the fields to move to cities and towns near U.S. military installations, in order to experience capitalism at its most barefaced level. The service industry boomed at the expense of agricultural reform and industrial production. South Vietnam became dependent upon the U.S. presence, and drugs played a role. The slow and gradual shift to adapt to the ever-increasing presence of U.S. goods and dollars altered Vietnamese society to become even more accepting of corruption and drugs and to allow profiteering in the moment to overtake building for the future.[10]

Decades of corruption culminated in the dilemma that faced U.S. policymakers by 1969. The problem had become so threatening that it was having a politically and militarily destructive impact on the U.S. war effort. To completely clean out corruption, close the black market, and end the drug trade in South Vietnam would undermine what the United States had struggled for years to build in South Vietnam—stable government. For the United States to attack the drug trade at its roots would risk the possible economic, if not political, collapse of local and perhaps even national government in Vietnam, opening the doors of insurgency even wider. It was a mess, and one that became even messier as its full impact on the U.S. soldier became known to the U.S. public.[11]

Drug use among U.S. soldiers in Vietnam is one of the more enduring tragedies of the conflict. Although drugs had certainly been available and used in previous wars, Vietnam was the first time drug use became so prevalent that it threatened to break the U.S. military. Controlling drug use did not offer obvious solutions. A soldier using narcotics or other dangerous drugs would not be able to perform required duties; furthermore, the soldier could become addicted to the drug and be incapacitated for the long term. In fact, he or she might never recover from his or her addiction. A single soldier on drugs could destroy the combat effectiveness of an entire unit. During the first years of the conflict, drug use was not a problem. Some attribute this to the career officers and volunteer service members who made up the bulk of U.S. forces in Vietnam at that time. Conventional wisdom held that as dedicated, professional soldiers, they had no need for drugs and knew what drugs could do to their mission. The increasing reliance upon draftees to supply troops in Vietnam, however, altered the drug landscape. By 1968 drug use became a serious issue. By 1970 it had erupted into a crisis of potentially catastrophic consequences.

With Vietnamization and the feeling of lost purpose came a malaise that rapidly spread through U.S. forces, especially among draftees and noncareer officers. Drug use was indicative of this crisis. As the combat role of U.S. troops lessened and more soldiers spent time in rear areas, drugs became one of the more popular means of dealing with the everyday boredom of rear echelon duty. Add to this the fact that the emergent drug culture among youths in the United States had found its way to Vietnam by the late 1960s; as many as 30 percent of U.S. troops may have used drugs *before* coming to Vietnam. That marijuana and heroin were abundant in Vietnam compounded the problem. Marijuana grew naturally in the lush, humid countryside and rivaled the most potent "weed" in the world. Marijuana use among U.S. soldiers in Vietnam began as early as 1963 and increased dramatically in 1967 and 1968. Often seen as a social drug used among groups of buddies in Vietnam, it was also used to calm down after combat actions. Studies rarely found marijuana use by troops in the field during combat operations, however.

Prepackaged marijuana cigarettes could be purchased from taxi drivers and street vendors and at bars for less than $1 per pack. Heroin, also incredibly potent, could be purchased just about anywhere for as little as $2 for a 250 milligram vial; the same vial could sell for as much as $200 in the United States. As inconceivable as it may sound, some U.S. soldiers may have volunteered to go to Vietnam because drugs were cheaper and more readily available than in the United States. Add the lucrative black-market situation to the scenario, and what one had in Vietnam was, in essence, a drug user's paradise.[12]

Acknowledging the problem, MACV went on the attack, producing anti-drug films (one narrated by Sonny Bono) and radio spots and inundating units with circulars and posters detailing the ill effects of marijuana use, some creatively titled "Keep off the Grass" and "Don't Blow It." New arrivals to Vietnam now had to take a special orientation course on what Frank Bartimo called the "moral, medical, social, and legal consequences" of drug use. Command chaplains were enlisted to work the dangers of marijuana use into their character guidance programs. On the law enforcement end, military police and base security troops cracked down on marijuana suppliers as well as users, using drug-sniffing dogs and surprise inspections of billets. Special investigation teams established several field offices to root out suppliers and growers. The CID under MACV added a special lab specifically to analyze and identify suspected illegal substances as part of its crime lab at Long Binh. Lab technicians could testify to their findings at courts-martial.[13]

MACV hoped that better cooperation with Vietnamese police would broaden the search for suppliers, many of whom were Vietnamese, but corruption in Vietnamese courts and loopholes in Vietnamese drug-trafficking laws allowed suppliers, both large and small, to slip through bureaucratic cracks. The South Vietnamese government, whose officials made thousands of dollars from the drug trade, at least made a show of dealing with the problem by issuing a directive in October 1968 instructing mayors, provincial chiefs, and local police to increase their efforts to track down and catch drug traffickers. In addition, U.S. military police and CID units, along with judge advocates, formed joint committees, much as they had to combat the black market, to fight the drug problem. These Combined Anti-Narcotics Enforcement Committees did not begin operating until December 1970. With the unrelenting corruption of the South Vietnamese government, these joint efforts in the end had little impact.[14]

The focus on marijuana brought some positive results; although the rate of individuals investigated per thousand for marijuana use doubled from 1968 to 1969, by 1970, as shown in Table 6.1, it had actually slowed somewhat. It is important to understand that marijuana use was not isolated to Vietnam; it was a problem among U.S. forces in the United States and worldwide. Of course, it was impossible to investigate all suspected users and suppliers; thus the numbers for courts-martial underrepresent the extent of the problem. More telling for conditions specifically in Vietnam is a breakdown of marijuana use by service (see Table 6.2). Numbers are understandably higher for cases investigated in the army, which had the bulk of U.S. troops in Vietnam. What is more important is that the rate per thousand figures really show that marijuana use had become a substantial problem in each service. Judge advocates certainly had their hands full with the increase in drug-related investigations and courts-martial.

The campaign against marijuana may have worked too well, even though it did not completely eradicate the drug's use. Marijuana is a visible drug. Its smell, the distinctive look of the cigarette, and the bulkiness of its raw form make marijuana easy to detect. A soldier using marijuana would not get away with it for long in such a tight-knit, military environment as Vietnam. For those wanting to continue using a drug and not be so obvious about it, heroin provided an excessively effective but undoubtedly deadly alternative. No smoke, small amounts that were easily hidden, and a longer-lasting, more-intense "high" than what marijuana could deliver made heroin increasingly popular among troops in Vietnam from 1970 through 1972.

Table 6.1. Marijuana Use: Number of Cases Investigated and Rates of Individuals Investigated per Thousand, 1966–1970

	Cases/Rate		
Year	Worldwide	United States	Vietnam
1966	3,096/.98	1,892/.89	503/1.80
1967	5,536/1.63	3,493/1.62	1,267/2.69
1968	11,507/4.84	6,335/4.65	4,188/7.99
1969	19,129/7.60	8,809/6.21	7,737/14.77
1970	26,902/10.56	13,999/9.20	8,412/20.27

Source: United States Congress, Senate, Committee on Labor and Public Welfare, Sub-committee on Alcoholism and Narcotics, *Military Drug Abuse, 1971: Hearings*, 92nd Cong., 1st sess., June 9 and 22, 1971 (Washington, D.C.: Government Printing Office, 1971), 120–127.

Cheap and available, heroin challenged marijuana as the military's more dangerous drug problem even though thousands continued to smoke grass.

Heroin in Vietnam, like marijuana, was extraordinarily potent. The 250-milligram vials for sale just outside some U.S. military installations often contained 95 percent pure heroin, a drug which is highly addictive and often lethal. Rumors in Vietnam accused the North Vietnamese of artificially deflating the price of heroin to promote its use by U.S. forces. "Good American boys" would not have dirtied themselves with the awful drug otherwise, so the thinking went. Wherever it came from and regardless of its price, the fact remained that heroin had become a serious and deadly problem. The saying went that one "saluted with one hand and took a hit with the other."[15] Like the numbers for marijuana, the investigation numbers for heroin and dangerous drugs in Tables 6.3 and 6.4 give an idea of the scope of the problem, showing that the issue again was not unique to Vietnam.

Looking at a breakdown of cases in each service involving hard narcotics (Table 6.5) and dangerous drugs (Table 6.6) shows that the army and the Marine Corps had a more difficult time with narcotics and dangerous drugs, respectively. The numbers and rates show that the drug problem did not really improve and in fact got worse for each service in Vietnam through 1970. The Marine Corps, in particular, had a serious problem with dangerous drug use worldwide, especially in Europe, where the rate per thousand reached 34.94.

Short of catching a soldier in the act of using, purchasing, or selling drugs, prosecuting service members for drug-related offenses could be difficult because of rigid search-and-seizure procedures and strict rules of evidence. This perhaps challenged military lawyers most in their struggle against drugs. If the offense involved Vietnamese, which it often did, Vietnamese police could be unreliable, and getting Vietnamese witnesses to testify in courts-martial was difficult. Only rarely was a U.S. soldier convicted of drug-related charges in a Vietnamese court, mainly because of the evolving practice of leaving U.S. offenses to the U.S. courts. Convicted drug offenders generally received a bad conduct discharge, occasionally combined with suspended hard labor sentences. Once discharged, the drug-addicted soldier faced a very uncertain future.[16]

The military did attempt rehabilitating some of these drug abusers to return them to service as clean soldiers. It was an ambitious, if not controversial, idea, and the results were indeed mixed. The Pentagon tried this rehabilitation concept through experimental amnesty programs in the United States and in Vietnam. Judge advocates played a key role in creating and running these programs, which were by no means perfect, but nonetheless were a creative means of combating the drug problem. The amnesty program in Vietnam had varied results; with no clear chain of command over the amnesty program, the range of interest and effort U.S. units in Vietnam put into the program varied tremendously. The program, initiated in late 1969, allowed a soldier to voluntarily turn himself or herself in to a chaplain, judge advocate, doctor, or commander for rehabilitation without fear of disciplinary action. Once the abuser had made contact with an authority figure within the unit, doctors evaluated the soldier to determine the extent of addiction and decide upon a psychological or physiological program for recovery. In addition, the soldier in question had to ask a respected fellow soldier in the unit to act as a lay counselor, who would keep an eye on the abuser and help the soldier stay sober.

The amnesty program had restrictions and limitations. Anyone under investigation for drug abuse or in possession of drugs when applying for the program would not be immune from disciplinary action. Likewise, anyone already in the program discovered under the influence of drugs or in possession

Table 6.2. Marijuana Use: Number of Cases Investigated and Rates of Cases Investigated, per Thousand, by Service in Vietnam, 1968–1970

	Cases/Rate		
Service	1968	1969	1970
Army	2,956/8.92	5,251/15.63	6,790/23.68
Navy	336/9.65	295/8.45	329/16.21
Air Force	168/3.11	263/4.90	254/5.67
Marine Corps	738/9.06	1,828/25.25	1,039/29.81

Source: See Table 6.1.

Table 6.3. Hard Narcotics (Heroin) Use: Number of Cases Investigated and Rates of Individuals Investigated per Thousand, 1966–1970

Year	Cases/Rate		
	Worldwide	United States	Vietnam
1966	521/.16	275/.13	39/.14
1967	573/.17	274/.13	89/.19
1968	940/.32	608/.41	174/.33
1969	1,871/.67	1,479/.89	309/.59
1970	3,401/1.29	2,368/1.57	854/2.06

Source: United States Congress, Senate, Committee on Labor and Public Welfare, Sub-committee on Alcoholism and Narcotics, *Military Drug Abuse, 1971: Hearings*, 92nd Cong., 1st sess., June 9 and 22, 1971 (Washington, D.C.: Government Printing Office, 1971), 120–127.

of drugs lost "amnesty" and could thus be prosecuted. In addition, those who chose not to volunteer did not get the benefit of rehabilitation. If one received a bad conduct discharge, one lost veteran's benefits, a factor that provided motivation for joining the program. If drug-abusing soldiers could make it through the program, at least an administrative discharge—even for those not deemed fit for duty—would ensure the possibility of continuing treatment once out of the military. As might be expected, it was predominantly hard drug users who considered taking part in the amnesty program. Marijuana users often simply assumed that they were not addicted and could stop smoking at any time; thus they felt that they did not need rehabilitation and ignored the program. Others, quite understandably, did not trust the "amnesty" part and feared disciplinary action.

One of the most visible symbols of the program was the amnesty box. Each day at a certain time, usually for an hour in the morning and an hour in the afternoon, soldiers could voluntarily drop any drugs in their possession into a designated box without fear of disciplinary action or of being apprehended going to or from the box site. Ideally, men using the box would not be questioned or searched at a later time or even placed under surveillance. Nor would anything be added to their record reflecting use of the amnesty box. Of course, what was ideal and real often differed, as commanders could easily abuse the box arrangement. Surprisingly, some troops actually used the boxes.[17]

The amnesty program exposed itself to other abuses. One commander placed his entire unit under investigation for possible drug use, thus prohibiting anyone from taking part in the program. Despite assurances that voluntary

participation in the program would not appear on their records, some participants found just such a notation in their permanent files. Once an amnesty
program soldier returned to his unit, he often did not find the support he
needed to stay clean. Instead, he found animosity and isolation from his fellow
soldiers because he was a known drug user.[18]

In 1971 alone, 703 of 3,458 participants did not successfully complete the
amnesty program. At Long Binh's Pioneer House rehabilitation center inside
the stockade, only 149 could be declared "clean" out of 532 who entered, and
there is no indication that they stayed clean. Taking into account the fact that
two counselors at Pioneer House were arrested for doing drugs while working
at the center, getting help to just 20 percent who entered the program was perhaps better than no help at all.[19] A January 1971 briefing by the army's II Field
Force Headquarters, which included the First Cavalry and the Twenty-fifth Division, for visiting members of Congress who were investigating the drug
problem pointed to positive interest in the amnesty program while showing
that drug users who did not participate in the amnesty program found themselves on the receiving end of military justice. The amnesty program of II Field
Force differed from others in that it also had a sort of halfway house, run by re-
habilitated users, where troops could take three days to "dry out." From October to December 1970, the II Field Force amnesty program treated 784 drug
users. Of those, 291 were given "probable" chance of success in the program,
and 145 were declared likely to fail. It is interesting to note that 292 participants had returned to the United States while in the program because either
their tour had ended or they had been transferred to another unit and could

**Table 6.4. Dangerous Drugs (Amphetamines and Barbiturates)
Use: Number of Cases Investigated and Rates of Individuals
Investigated per Thousand, 1966–1970**

| | Cases/Rate | | |
Year	Worldwide	United States	Vietnam
1966	917/.29	648/.31	20/.07
1967	1532/.45	1144/.54	34/.07
1968	1594/.50	1078/.69	109/.21
1969	3,357/1.21	1,849/1.21	892/1.68
1970	7,541/2.55	2,695/2.62	1,549/3.73

Source: United States Congress, Senate, Committee on Labor and Public Welfare, Subcommittee on Alcoholism and Narcotics, *Military Drug Abuse, 1971: Hearings*, 92nd
Cong., 1st sess., June 9 and 22, 1971 (Washington, D.C.: Government Printing Office,
1971), 120–127.

Table 6.5. Hard Narcotics (Heroin) Use: Number of Cases
Investigated and Rates of Cases Investigated per Thousand, by
Service in Vietnam, 1968–1970

Service	Cases/Rate		
	1968	1969	1970
Army	119/.36	257/.74	726/2.51
Navy	3/.08	3/.08	24/1.09
Air Force	6/.11	9/.17	50/1.13
Marines	46/.58	40/.60	54/1.55

Source: United States Congress, Senate, Committee on Labor and Public Welfare, Sub-committee on Alcoholism and Narcotics, *Military Drug Abuse, 1971: Hearings,* 92nd Cong., 1st sess., June 9 and 22, 1971 (Washington, D.C.: Government Printing Office, 1971), 120–127.

not be tracked because of the amnesty part of the program. Three hundred and sixteen of the participants had to be hospitalized, and six died.

Many did not qualify or participate in the amnesty program for a variety of reasons, and as a consequence were either court-martialed or received nonjudicial punishment. During 1970, II Field Force tried 8 general courts-martial involving dangerous drugs. Fifty-eight special courts-martial were held for dangerous drug offenses, along with 136 others involving marijuana. II Field Force issued 80 Article 15s for dangerous drugs and 560 for marijuana the same year. Sixteen servicemen received administrative discharges because of drug use, and dozens of others received bad conduct discharges as part of their court-martial sentences.[20]

The First Cavalry, one of the better-known units of the Vietnam War, constituted a large part of II Field Force. At the division level, the First Cavalry administered its own drug program with the assistance of army judge advocates. A drug council, which included the staff judge advocate, focused its efforts on education, amnesty, and discipline. For education, First Cavalry used newsletters, directives, posters, and other means to get the word out that drugs endangered both soldier and unit. Over half of the 22,000 soldiers in the First Cavalry attended classes or seminars on drug abuse in 1970.

The First Cavalry's amnesty program had not been in place long, but because it had eight former users assisting with the program, drug users apparently were more willing to give it a try. In December 1970 alone, 121 troops, many of whom were heroin addicts, entered the amnesty program. Despite the large numbers involved in the amnesty program, however, discipline remained the stronger and longer arm of the law for the First

Cavalry's response to the drug problem. Twenty-seven special courts-martial resulted in thirteen convictions for using or selling drugs during 1970. One hundred and twenty-eight received Article 15s. Thirty-five servicemen resigned in lieu of court-martial. Cooperating with Vietnamese police, CID investigations managed to apprehend three U.S. soldiers dealing drugs along with forty-eight Vietnamese drug dealers. In December 1970, the CID confiscated 4,280 grams of marijuana, almost 200 vials of heroin, and 21 packets of amphetamines, among other drugs and drug paraphernalia. During the First Cavalry briefing, the members of Congress wanted to see statistics from years previous, but like many units in Vietnam, the First Cavalry had kept no specific statistics on drug-related issues until these issues became serious problems. First Cavalry did not begin consistently keeping good statistics on drugs until 1970.[21]

The American Division (Twenty-third Infantry) had a longer history of drug trouble, recognizing as early as 1969 that drugs were a significant problem. Like the First Cavalry, the American Division used education, amnesty, and discipline to attack the problem and established a Marijuana and Drug Suppression Council, again including the staff judge advocate, to oversee the program. All enlisted personnel were required to attend a one-hour program on drug abuse each month. Officers and NCOs also had to participate in monthly orientation presentations to learn how to detect and deal with drug users. From September 1 to December 31, 1970, 165 participated in the American Division's amnesty program. Of the 165, 97 percent used heroin or some combination of heroin and other narcotics. One hundred and four had used drugs before coming to Vietnam. Hospital admissions included 153 drug users who were

Table 6.6. Dangerous Drugs (Amphetamines and Barbiturates) Use: Number of Cases Investigated and Rates of Cases Investigated per Thousand, by Service in Vietnam, 1968–1970

Service	Cases/Rate		
	1968	1969	1970
Army	37/.11	604/1.75	1,066/3.83
Navy	5/.03	14/.42	57/2.02
Air Force	6/.11	15/.28	32/.71
Marines	61/.74	259/3.84	394/10.49

Source: United States Congress, Senate, Committee on Labor and Public Welfare, Subcommittee on Alcoholism and Narcotics, *Military Drug Abuse, 1971: Hearings*, 92nd Cong., 1st sess., June 9 and 22, 1971 (Washington, D.C.: Government Printing Office, 1971), 120–127.

not part of the amnesty program. Nine American Division soldiers died from drug abuse during these four months.

The American Division's disciplinary actions against drug use indicate that army judge advocates spent a lot of time on drug-related offenses with the Americal. In 1969 and 1970, the division CID investigated over 900 alleged drug offenses. In 1970, judge advocates tried 7 general courts-martial and 136 special courts-martial and issued 113 Article 15s for drug offenses. Overall for 1970, for a force of 25,000 soldiers, American Division lawyers handled over 5,500 disciplinary actions, including 638 courts-martial. For the year, military police and CID investigators confiscated almost 70,000 grams of marijuana, more than 4,300 barbiturate tablets, and hundreds of grams of heroin, opium, cocaine, lysergic acid diethylamide (LSD), and morphine.[22]

The navy in Vietnam also had to cope with drugs.[23] By the end of 1970, NAVFORV numbered only around 16,000 sailors, most of whom served in noncombat or advisory capacities. With discharges and rotations back to the United States accelerated because of Vietnamization and deescalation, trying to discourage drug abuse and maintain tight discipline was difficult. The "correlation" between this situation and the drug problem, according to the briefing given to Congress in early 1971, was a "possibility." Compared to the other services in Vietnam, NAVFORV had a small antidrug program. The drug information program consisted of only a few two-man teams that traveled from unit to unit giving presentations that focused solely on facts and figures while avoiding discussion of the descriptive dangers of drug abuse. Education was not the mainstay of the navy program.

Tough enforcement, however, was. Unlike the other units described above, the navy had no amnesty program in Vietnam. Identifying drug users for punishment was the main thrust of the navy antidrug effort. In 1966, only 8 percent of Naval Investigative Service investigations involved drug use. By 1970, 38 percent involved alleged drug violations, and by that time navy lawyers had also realized that some of those investigated were using drugs as a means to get discharged from service. When possible, navy judge advocates used courts-martial rather than pleas for administrative discharge as a means to discipline drug users and dealers. Often, those deemed "experimental users" received nonjudicial punishment or summary courts-martial. If their records were otherwise acceptable, these sailors were reinstated into service. More habitual users received more severe disciplinary action and were often discharged. Those with severe addiction to heroin or LSD, for example, were given medical treatment, and with no hope of retention, they were then discharged. The navy could crack down on "strikers" who used drugs to get out of the navy, but in the process there was little to no effort to really help those in need of medical or psychological attention without fear of disciplinary repercussions.

The Seventh Air Force in Vietnam also had no amnesty program but did attempt rehabilitation on an individual basis.[24] Air force commanders, judge advocates, and doctors had reached no consensus on the effectiveness of an amnesty program. Those users seeking help could be sent to Lowry Air Force Base in Colorado for "retraining" and hopefully reinstatement. Many, however, did not seek help and faced disciplinary action when caught using or selling drugs. In 1970, 61 of 226 courts-martial in the Seventh Air Force involved drug abuse, mostly marijuana. Only 11 of the 61 resulted in acquittals. Convictions resulted in confinement, reduction in grade, and/or forfeiture. Seventeen air force personnel received administrative discharges in lieu of disciplinary action by court-martial or Article 15.

Education, as with other services, played a major role in the Seventh Air Force antidrug program. Air Force regulations stipulated that all air force personnel, regardless of location, had to complete a drug abuse orientation program, then take refresher courses each year thereafter. In addition to the education program, the Seventh Air Force had a special narcotics investigation unit and put in place a Combined Anti-Narcotics Enforcement Committee at the end of 1971.

Drug use in Marine Corps units in Vietnam seemed an unmanageable problem that increased rather dramatically from 1969 to 1971, during which time both the Third Marine Division and the First Marine Division withdrew from Vietnam. For the Third Marine, the problem continued at Okinawa through the mid-1970s. The Marine Corps approach to the issue was straightforward: experimental users would be punished, and addicts would be kicked out of the Marine Corps. In stereotypical no-nonsense Marine Corps fashion, the antidrug program consisted of a "three-pronged attack" to rid the corps of drugs. First, make drugs "hot, . . . expensive, . . . dangerous," so much so that drugs would become unavailable and the risk of use too great. Second, apprehend drug users and "pushers," then "move them out." Third, through education and "moral guidance," convince marines, especially recruits, to "reject drugs and the whole drug culture."[25]

The Marine Corps resisted amnesty programs, standing by a perfectly logical desire to keep all drug users out of the corps. In a single year, 1970, the First Marine Division prosecuted 142 drug-related courts-martial and administratively discharged 211 individuals for drug abuse. Once out of the corps, they became either the Veterans Administration's problem or were on their own. It was a hard-core approach, but one that reflected a hard-core situation. Fortunately for the Marine Corps, the I Corps area of northern South Vietnam was not a center for drug trafficking like the southern areas around Saigon and the Mekong River delta. Hard narcotics, such as heroin, were not as available, but marijuana flourished just as it did all over South Vietnam.[26]

Cases and judge advocate experiences give a feel for the drug problem in Vietnam. The following examples are representative, yet each has some unique aspect that helps put an individual face on the statistics presented above. Many possession cases were straightforward. Take, for example, the special court-martial of Airman First Class James Daniels. Daniels, of the 336th Security Police Squadron at Da Nang Air Base, was caught with 3.32 grams of marijuana in his possession on March 1, 1968. Daniels pleaded not guilty but was found in violation of Article 134. He was reduced to airman basic, confined to hard labor for six months, and required to forfeit ninety dollars pay per month for six months. The convening authority approved the guilty verdict and the reduction to airman basic but reduced confinement and forfeiture of pay to four months. For marijuana possession, this sentence appears typical.[27]

Other cases were more complex, demonstrating how difficult it could be to prosecute for drug offenses. One such case involved a very conscientious army corporal named Mark Russello.[28] In January 1968, Russello moved into a room in the Da Nang Hotel occupied by army corporals Ernie Mitchell and John Watson. It was not long before Russello discovered that the two men were regular marijuana smokers. Three other corporals, Jeffrey Hynyr, Jack Mobley, and Lawrence Salerno, usually joined Mitchell and Watson in the room to smoke. Each night at 1900, the men gathered and smoked for a couple of hours.

Russello was in an awkward position. He did not do drugs and realized that his roommates not only were going to get into trouble but also were probably going to drag him down with them. Never mind the insect spray they used to cover the smell; Russello knew it was only a matter of time before they were caught. He reported the matter to the Da Nang field office of the 252nd Military Police CID detachment in late February. CID investigators quickly obtained authority to search the hotel room. That night, the same day that Russello reported to CID, Marine Corps lieutenant Carlos Espinoza of the 3rd Military Police battalion arrived at 1920 to conduct a search of the room and hopefully catch the soldiers in the act. Entering the room Lieutenant Espinoza explained who he was and his purpose and began searching.

THE DRUG PROBLEM   133

Unfortunately, the corporals had not started smoking yet, but Lieutenant Espinoza did find their marijuana. He quickly discovered an envelope containing forty rolled marijuana cigarettes in Salerno's field jacket. He failed to notice ten more cigarettes in Mitchell's right boot located under his bed. A half-smoked marijuana cigarette was found behind a *Playboy* centerfold hanging near the door. Several more cigarettes were discovered in Mitchell's nightstand. Mobley's wall locker in the adjacent room yielded another half-smoked cigarette. Lieutenant Espinoza confiscated all of these items as evidence.

Salerno claimed he knew nothing. Mitchell admitted experimenting with marijuana on occasion, but he did not know of any of his buddies using the drug. Mobley asserted the same. Watson, like Salerno, denied everything. Hynyr also denied using marijuana. In the end, none of the men could be charged with using marijuana, but Salerno, Mitchell, and Mobley were charged with wrongful possession and convicted by a special court-martial. There was not enough evidence to do anything about Hynyr and Watson.

Many cases involving drugs had multiple charges, usually unauthorized weapons possession or AWOL. The case of Private First Class Charles Heggie is one such case that also provides a good example of how the court-martial review process worked.[29] Heggie, of the army 459th Signal Support Battalion at Nha Trang, was charged with wrongful possession of heroin and barbiturates as well as unlawfully carrying a concealed weapon. He was also charged with being AWOL. Lt. John Smeriglio detained Heggie at Nha Trang on April 23, 1971. Heggie had been reassigned to Cam Ranh Bay some time before, and when Smeriglio spotted him at Nha Trang he ordered Heggie to report to the post orderly room. Heggie reported the next morning, where Lieutenant Smeriglio quickly ascertained that Heggie had no authorization to be in Nha Trang. Smeriglio became suspicious of drug use when he noticed Heggie's slurred speech. Smeriglio called in Sgt. Lawrence Smith of the 218th Military Police Company to arrest Heggie. Lieutenant Smeriglio informed Sergeant Smith that Heggie was in Nha Trang without authorization, possibly under the influence of drugs, and further that Heggie might be carrying a concealed weapon. Sergeant Smith then placed Heggie under arrest and informed him of his Article 31 rights. Sergeant Smith proceeded to search Heggie, finding two vials of heroin in his sleeve pocket. Heggie began to resist but was restrained by Sergeant Smith and Lieutenant Smeriglio. The search further yielded two more vials of heroin, eleven Binoctal tablets, and a black knife sheath.

Testimony at the special court-martial concurred with the above recounting of the facts save for one important disparity. Lieutenant Smeriglio testified that in the struggle of the search, Heggie pulled a knife from under his shirt and threw it to the ground. Smeriglio further testified that he was certain Sergeant Smith must have seen the knife. Under cross-examination, Sergeant Smith stated he did not see a knife nor did he recall Lieutenant Smeriglio telling him specifically about a knife. The knife was not produced in evidence.

Heggie pleaded not guilty to all four charges but was convicted on the wrongful possession of heroin and barbiturates counts and of carrying a concealed weapon. He was acquitted of the AWOL charge. Heggie's military service record was excellent, and nothing in his personnel file indicated a tendency to wrongdoing. Character witnesses testified that Heggie was a good soldier and an effective and quiet worker. The maximum sentence for the charges was a bad conduct discharge, forfeiture of two-thirds pay for six months, confinement at hard labor for six months, and reduction to lowest enlisted grade. The trial judge, in light of Heggie's record and character testimony, sentenced Heggie to ninety days hard labor, forfeiture of ninety dollars pay per month for three months, reduction to private, and a bad conduct discharge. The judge recommended to the convening authority that the bad conduct discharge be suspended. The convening authority, however, upheld the entire sentence.

Bad conduct discharges are automatically appealed. During the trial, defense counsel had objected to admitting evidence found during the search of Heggie's person on the grounds that the items were the result of an unreasonable search and seizure. Appellate defense counsel argued that probable cause did not exist and that the arrest was a pretext for a search. In overruling defense counsel's objection during the trial to this effect, the judge, according to the appeal, had erred. Moreover, the absence of the knife as evidence and the inconsistent testimony as to the knife's existence should have been cause of reasonable doubt as to the charge of carrying an unauthorized concealed weapon. And even if the knife did exist, reasonable doubt existed in determining whether the knife was a dangerous weapon and used with dangerous intent. Because of these alleged shortcomings in the trial, the appeal asked that the bad conduct discharge be withdrawn, as the trial judge had originally recommended. The Army Court of Military Review, however, disagreed, finding that there indeed was probable cause, that the military policeman had acted appropriately, and that the trial judge had also acted appropriately. Owing to the seriousness of the collective offenses, the review court upheld the conviction on all counts and affirmed the sentence with the bad conduct discharge.

U.S. civilians also contributed to the military drug problem, but because of jurisdictional issues they were more likely to escape punishment. In 1969, when the ruling against trying civilians by courts-martial came down, a mechanic for the Dynalectron Corporation was charged and convicted on two of three counts involving drugs. In a general court-martial, Anthony Simonaro pleaded not guilty to possession of marijuana, possession of opium, and selling marijuana. A helicopter mechanic at Ban Me Thuot, Simonaro was arrested in July 1969 with several grams of marijuana, some marijuana cigarettes, and five grams of opium in his possession. Testimony from two privates indicated that Simonaro often smoked marijuana and sold some cigarettes to them. Simonaro was charged under Article 134, alleging that Simonaro's conduct was prejudicial to the good order and discipline of the armed forces and/or would bring discredit to the armed forces. As a civilian serving with or accompanying armed forces in the field during time of war, Simonaro could be tried. Defense and prosecution counsel argued this point for the bulk of the short trial. Defense then moved to dismiss charges because the prosecution failed to show that a civilian's drug use or possession violated Article 134.

The court found Simonaro guilty of possession of marijuana and opium but not guilty of selling marijuana because of lack of evidence. Simonaro was sentenced to pay a fine of $1,000 and serve time at hard labor at Long Binh until the fine was paid. The sentence was approved in November 1969, and there is no indication that Simonaro appealed it. Since the *Averette* decision was handed down in the midst of Simonaro's trial, his conviction could have been thrown out.[30] As with crimes committed by U.S. civilians in Vietnam, the question remained as to what to do with U.S. civilians involved with drugs in Vietnam.

Occasionally, taking legal and disciplinary action against a drug ring created other, potentially serious problems. One such situation arose with the base security detachment at Cam Ranh Bay in early 1971.[31] In late 1970, the air base at Pleiku had closed down, transferring part of its base security force to replace those rotating out of Cam Ranh Bay. Drug use and dealing, in particular heroin and amphetamines, had been widespread among the Pleiku base security force. The supply of drugs easily fed the demand at Pleiku, but at Cam Ranh Bay, these troops found satisfying their addiction a bit more difficult. Cam Ranh Bay had had little trouble with drugs before the Pleiku replacements arrived in December 1970. Access to the base was limited, and the only ground route to the peninsula base was via Tiger Bridge, helping keep drugs out of the base. That changed in December. The Pleiku heroin addicts now made up a large proportion of the

Cam Ranh Bay base security force, which inspected and controlled transportation in and out of the base via Tiger Bridge. In no time, it seemed, drugs became a problem at Cam Ranh Bay. Suppliers paid off guards to get dope into the base. Hooch maids entering the base each day were the carriers.

From 1970 through 1971, only one American was killed at Cam Ranh Bay from enemy rocket attacks, but in early 1971 alone, fifteen American servicemen overdosed on heroin and died. Step one for the staff judge advocate and clean security police at Cam Ranh Bay was to cut off the source of drugs. One morning they set up a roadblock in front of the base gate to search for drugs being brought in by hooch maids and others on the incoming trucks. In the first fifteen minutes, more than 300 vials of heroin were confiscated, most of which were picked up from the ground after being discarded by hooch maids on board the trucks. After the first fifteen minutes, searchers found nothing. They did the same thing the next day, and the next, finding drugs at first then none as word spread down the line of trucks that military police were searching for drugs. To avoid falling into a predictable routine, random searches became standard procedure. It was only partially effective, as pushers found other ways to get drugs into the base.

A preliminary investigation netted three of the Pleiku security police, who each independently agreed to act undercover in exchange for immunity from prosecution. Undercover work in these circumstances was indeed difficult. As base security troops, the three men had to continue their normal duties, continue to use drugs, and socialize with their fellow guards, all so that they would not be discovered, which would have resulted in injury or death. These were not professional undercover agents by any means. They did well, however, and by February 1971 the investigation had identified eighty-seven airmen involved with the use or sale of heroin at Cam Ranh Bay.

Investigators wanted to quickly wrap up the investigation, fearing that the three undercover guards would be discovered and that a leak would alert the heroin users that they were about to be arrested. The problem was that by arresting such a large number of the base security team, who would be left to defend the base? Replacements had to be arranged for and brought on base but without arousing suspicions. Commanders had to be briefed, and witnesses evacuated for protection. A new staff judge advocate, Maj. Harold Teeter, arrived only days before the bust. Teeter and the staff judge advocate of Seventh Air Force made the decision not to hold the subsequent trials at Cam Ranh Bay. No one wanted the fragging of a military judge added to the list of crimes. As it turned out, by the day of the big bust, forty of the suspects (some of whom had been discharged from the air force) had already been rotated back to the United States. Forty-seven, however, remained and were arrested.

Cam Ranh Bay's stockade had room for only 12 prisoners, so an unused wing of the base hospital was used to detain the 47. Keeping all 47 in pretrial confinement was impossible because of the time it would take to process all 47. With the base commander, Teeter decided that the 47 had to be whittled down to a more practical number. Releasing those charged only with possession would cut the number by 25. Teeter released 25 and now had 22 left. Just as the 25 walked out the door, the alarm sounded that Viet Cong had breached an outer perimeter. The authorities had forgotten to pull the prisoners' gun cards when they were arrested, unwittingly authorizing the 25 to quickly draw their weapons from the gun locker and join other security personnel in manning positions to defend the base. Fortunately, all did their duty, but Teeter feared they could have turned on him and the commander.

The twenty-two still presented a large number. Releasing those charged with distributing but not selling heroin cut the number down to eight charged with selling heroin. One of the eight was a very heavy user and had gone into withdrawal. Fearing that the man would overdose if let free, they tried to talk him into voluntarily checking into the hospital. He refused at first, wrapped in several blankets, shivering uncontrollably in the ninety-degree heat. He finally relented, as Teeter convinced the man that there was already ample evidence to convict him of drug use. The fact that the man was going through the severe pain of withdrawal right in front of Teeter was superfluous. The man thought Teeter just wanted to use his withdrawal as evidence! After ten days in detoxification, the man discharged himself and immediately began shooting up again. He was reconfined and given a voluntary administrative discharge in lieu of court-martial. He was discharged and in the United States within twenty-four hours. His addiction required up to eight vials of pure heroin a day, which would have been impossible to acquire, much less afford, in the United States. It is not known if he survived.

One of the detained pushers turned out to be the victim of mistaken identity and was subsequently released. The rest were either tried at Tan Son Nhut or discharged in lieu of court-martial. In the meantime, more heroin incidents surfaced at Cam Ranh Bay. The scope and scale of the problem at Cam Ranh Bay was extraordinary and shows just how serious the threat of drug use was to the function of a military unit. Teeter recalled Operation Lotus Blossom, as the heroin bust was known, as one of the most out-of-the-ordinary incidents of his time as a judge advocate in Vietnam.

Countless serious, intriguing, and some simply comical incidents occurred involving drugs. One case centered on the smuggling by air of 700 pounds of opium that the air force navigator thought were boxes of pornographic magazines and stolen antiques. The pilot had loaded the boxes; after landing, the navigator found one of the boxes had accidentally opened, exposing large gray bricks. He had no idea what it was and took one of the bricks to base security police, who immediately identified it as opium. The pilot was presently arrested.[32]

Another incident involved the informal side of punishment for dealing with the drug problem. Just before departure on helicopters for an extended patrol operation near the geographic formation near the DMZ known as the Rockpile, a Marine Corps sergeant caught a private putting a pack of odd-looking cigarettes into his knapsack as he was preparing for a three-day leave. Discovering opium-soaked marijuana cigarettes, the sergeant notified the company executive officer, who was in the midst of getting the company away on the helicopters. The executive officer quickly and curtly told the sergeant to "deal with it," which he did. Moments later, the young marine was seated behind a tent eating the cigarettes one by one, as the sergeant supervised. Apparently the young man was never again found with drugs or under the influence of drugs for the rest of his time with the company.[33]

Officers were not immune to the drug problem. An air force colonel with twenty-eight years of service was arrested while hosting a party with his men in 1971 and was subsequently convicted of possession of, soliciting for, and transfer of marijuana. He was convicted by a general court-martial of two brigadier generals and seven colonels, who heard testimony from several witnesses, some of whom had to be flown back to Vietnam from the United States and given immunity. The sentence—three years at hard labor and a $15,000 fine—obviously ended this colonel's career.[34]

It is certain that drug abuse had a negative effect on the later years of the U.S. war in Vietnam. Military justice, education programs, and amnesty initiatives were among the several strategies used to combat the problem. None solved it, nor did any one strategy overwhelmingly prove more effective than any other. For judge advocates, the effort to control the drug problem took badly needed resources away from more productive duties, as it did medical personnel, CID investigators, and military police. Perhaps the only strategy to defeat the drug problem was to get U.S. forces out of Vietnam; such a withdrawal had already been in place for other reasons since 1969. The sad irony, of course, is that the drug problem in the U.S. military was not restricted to troops in Vietnam, as it was indeed a worldwide problem among U.S. forces that would take most of the 1970s to sort out and resolve.[35]

And what of the tens of thousands of Vietnamese involved in the drug problem as users or dealers? They found very little help from their own government and still less when the North Vietnamese conquered South Vietnam in 1975. Despite efforts to stamp out the drug trade, it continued throughout the 1970s under a slippery but lucrative black market run mainly by Chinese in and around Saigon. The 1980s saw a dramatic decrease in the Vietnamese drug problem as immigration and trade in general were much more strictly regulated. Beginning in the mid-1990s, however, the problem returned. A policy of openness allowed drugs and looser Western attitudes to return to Saigon. The government of Vietnam today is seriously concerned about a growing antiauthority attitude among the increasing number of drug-using youth in Saigon as well as the role of drug users in the spread of acquired immunodeficiency syndrome (AIDS).[36]

Imperialism of both the French and the U.S. variety provided the fertile environment for the drug trade to flourish. As a consequence, the outsiders found themselves wittingly and unwittingly both promoters and victims of the drug trade. The Vietnamese suffered a similar fate. Differences in attitudes toward drug use, toward corruption, and toward solutions to the problem influenced the way the Americans and South Vietnamese dealt with the problem, which in the end was not solvable and has come to characterize the U.S. experience in Vietnam. From the standpoint of military justice, consider the thousands of staff-hours that military lawyers and criminal investigators could have put toward more serious crime and nation-building duties had drugs not been such a serious problem in Vietnam.

CHAPTER SEVEN
THE BLACK MARKET,
CURRENCY MANIPULATION,
AND CORRUPTION

In a broad sense, black markets, currency manipulation, and corruption violate the principles of legal free enterprise and respect for the rule of law in a capitalist society. As political objectives in Vietnam, fighting the black market and curbing corruption were meant not only to help the United States save money but also to be part of the nation-building program designed to instill democratic and capitalist values in Vietnamese society and thus to dissuade the Vietnamese from the communist insurgency. To do this, the United States turned to the military justice system, government programs, and intragovernmental cooperative efforts, none of which could solve what in the end was, like drugs, an unsolvable problem. In fighting corruption, military justice and military lawyers were once again in the vanguard of nation-building in Vietnam.[1]

Black markets seem to be a common phenomenon of war; such a black market for misappropriated goods and currency manipulation developed in Vietnam over the course of World War II, the French-Indochina War, and the U.S. war. U.S. military and civilian agencies neither anticipated nor were prepared for this development despite recent experience in World War II and Korea. Building materials, dry goods, weapons, Jeep and truck parts, machinery, clothing, and even laundry detergent could be purchased on the black market in Vietnam. In 1968, one could buy a heavy mortar for $400 and M-16s for $80 apiece. Uniforms of almost every style and class from each of the U.S. armed services could be bought and sold. As ludicrous as it may seem, diamond rings, furs, stereo equipment, lingerie, and other luxury items that were astonishingly but plentifully available at U.S. PX stores located in South Vietnam, a combat zone, easily found their way onto the black market. One had to have a much-valued PX card to purchase goods at PX stores. Of course, most Vietnamese did not have such privileges and therefore willingly paid more for these goods on the black market, which even then offered cheaper prices than most legitimate Vietnamese merchants. One of the more flourishing illicit purchasing grounds, the so-called Little Black Market, was open for business almost every day just down the street from the American Embassy in Saigon. Much of this material was intended for U.S. aid programs and U.S. and South Vietnamese forces, and still more was meant to stimulate economic growth in

South Vietnam. Considerable money could be made selling these goods on the streets of Saigon, Hue, and Da Nang.[2]

In addition to the illegal trade of goods, the black market also provided a profitable place for currency manipulation, which cost the Vietnamese economy and the U.S. government hundreds of millions of dollars over the course of the conflict. The South Vietnamese government, U.S. aid programs, and the U.S. military PX, club, and mess systems located on military installations across the country liberally fertilized an already well-tilled black market with cash, from which the weedy seeds of corruption took even deeper root. Enterprising individuals, including U.S. soldiers and sailors, could make anywhere from a little extra cash to sizable fortunes off of the war by capitalizing on the intrinsic relationship among the black market, currency manipulation, and corruption.[3]

U.S. counterinsurgency policy unintentionally exacerbated the already dire economic and political conditions in South Vietnam. War-torn underdeveloped countries are ripe for black markets and currency manipulation. War tends to cause people to lose faith in their own currency and then to display an exaggerated confidence in and demand for foreign currency and imported goods. In theory, a black market for commercial goods under these conditions should act as a positive price control mechanism, using competition as the chief tool, and should help the economy stabilize over the long run. Such a theory, however, wrongly discounts price gouging and misinterprets corruptive relationships between black-market operators and government officials. On the other hand, a black market for currency is universally considered as a negative, if not destructive, influence on wartime economies. This was certainly the case in Vietnam. Part of the U.S. strategy to combat both of these phenomena was to fight inflation by maximizing imports and minimizing the influx of U.S. dollars into Vietnam. Both ultimately failed: the U.S. Agency for International Development (USAID) admitted in its final report that at best U.S. aid could only struggle to stabilize the Vietnamese economy as opposed to developing it for significant long-term growth.[4]

Corrupt Vietnamese government officials became the real beneficiaries of these illegal activities and thus, for the most part, showed little enthusiasm for doing something about the problem. As long as U.S. dollars and material goods poured into the country, they could continue to make money and acquire luxury items. From this rather sordid standpoint, they arguably had little incentive to make any effort to diminish the U.S. presence in Vietnam or even to work toward an end to the war. Considering the millions of dollars of goods and currency that exchanged hands on the black market, the potential wealth for an impoverished population was indeed staggering. Flagrant corruption among Vietnamese and Americans flourished, and because of it U.S. efforts to combat the black market made little headway against the tide of illegal trade. Without a real cooperative effort by the Vietnamese government, the problem continued and in fact worsened as the war dragged on.[5]

The U.S. role in Vietnam's economic woes began well before U.S. combat troops arrived in Vietnam. A country with a centuries-old barter economy corrupted by French imperialism, Vietnam had a thriving black market and intense illegal currency trade during World War II and the French-Indochina War. Officials in the government of Vietnamese emperor Bao Dai bought and sold political and administrative offices with cash profits from illegal exchanges of French francs and Vietnamese piasters. French businesspeople took both their legal and illegal profits back to France, and Vietnamese who could afford it also deposited their gains abroad rather than reinvesting in Vietnam. Vietnamese black marketeers became financially dependent upon their illicit trade, as did corrupt government officials who facilitated the trade themselves and profited by accepting bribes to look the other way.[6]

Looking for a new benefactor as the French military effort collapsed, corrupt officials and businesspeople in Vietnam rather suddenly discovered U.S. goods and dollars brought to Vietnam through the Commercial Import Program (CIP). In Uncle Sam they found a new "Uncle Sugar." Beginning in 1955, the CIP provided funding and commodities to stimulate Vietnamese commercial growth, with the goal of strengthening the Vietnamese economy to the point that it could stand on its own. Profits from sales of goods from the CIP were given to the South Vietnamese government to cover its operating expenses. This economic stability would supposedly place the government on a solid footing while simultaneously strengthening the counterinsurgency effort. It was a delicate proposition. The CIP was supposed to counteract South Vietnam's foreign exchange deficit without the massive inflation that such a large infusion of U.S. dollars might potentially bring (see Table 7.1).[7]

It looked good on paper. Vietnamese businesspeople imported U.S. goods paid for by the U.S. government. In exchange for the goods, they deposited piasters in "counterpart funds" administered by the South Vietnamese government in Saigon. The government, in turn, used these funds to subsidize financial development projects and cover its own operating expenses. This strategy initially moderated high inflation despite the millions of piasters generated by the South Vietnamese treasury, but in the long term the economy failed to

Table 7.1. U.S. Aid and Import Support, 1955–1973 (in millions of U.S. dollars)

Fiscal Year	$ Commercial Import Program (1)	$ Food for Peace I (2)	$ Food for Peace II (3)	$ Projects & Other Aid (4)	$ Piaster Purchases (5)	$ Total Aid (1+2+3+4) (6)	$ Total Import Support (1+2+5) (7)
1955	253.7	—	2.2	66.5	3	322.4	257
1956	174.7	—	14.3	21.0	3	210.0	178
1957	210.9	—	22.8	48.5	3	282.2	214
1958	151.9	4.4	5.2	27.5	3	289.0	159
1959	146.4	—	6.5	54.5	4	207.4	150
1960	135.6	5.0	6.3	34.9	5	181.8	145
1961	111.2	7.0	4.5	29.3	6	152.0	124
1962	94.1	26.8	5.1	30.0	7	156.0	128
1963	95.0	23.7	28.9	48.3	11	195.9	130
1964	113.0	34.3	24.8	52.7	15	224.8	162
1965	150.0	41.4	8.5	75.0	126	274.9	317
1966	399.3	98.2	44.8	194.2	333	736.5	830
1967	160.0	73.3	.4	334.4	327	568.1	560
1968	160.1	96.6	41.9	238.1	301	536.7	558
1969	130.0	60.8	38.65	184.1	347	413.5	538
1970	238.5	164.9	35.2	127.4	318	476.7	632
1971	281.0	62.5	23.1	106.7	403	575.7	849
1972	313.0	179.0	5.3	73.8	213	454.6	591
1973	226.2	268.9	9.3	87.2	96	501.7	532

Source: United States Agency for International Development, Office of Vietnam Affairs, *United States Economic Assistance to South Vietnam, 1954–1975: Terminal Report* (Washington, D.C.: U.S. Agency for International Development, 1975), 238, Table 1.

strengthen. Many Vietnamese tended to buy consumer goods and luxury items, because of their availability, rather than investing in machinery and other items critical to establishing light industry and promoting modern agricultural production. With the flood of U.S. consumer goods overwhelming the market for Vietnamese manufactured goods and Viet Cong insurgents stagnating agricultural efforts in the countryside, the Vietnamese people had little motivation to do otherwise. Early on, corruption among South Vietnamese government officials who desired U.S. luxury items resulted in lax credit policies and exaggerated import demand figures, placing the program in near constant jeopardy. Unrealistic exchange rates and the absence of effective monetary controls fueled this corruption and increased inflationary spikes.

Inundating the Vietnamese economy with U.S. goods without effective fiscal control mechanisms had essentially robbed the United States and the Vietnamese government of the ultimate intended success of the program.[8]

U.S. policymakers might have seen this situation coming, based upon similar experiences during World War II and in Korea. The Korean experience in particular had revealed that inflation could quickly run out of control without appropriate economic mechanisms in place to minimize its impact and that inflation made things tough for the local people, which in turn made them more sympathetic toward insurgents. Few U.S. military leaders and government officials made the connection between what had happened in Korea and what was happening in Vietnam.[9]

One of the more recurrent forms of corruption in the CIP involved the commissions earned by agents arranging sales between U.S. manufacturers and Vietnamese buyers. Vietnamese and foreign sales agents often also acted as suppliers; thus they were able to buy CIP goods at a lower U.S. government price and then sell the goods at higher prices and pocket the difference. In addition to the net profit gained from this arrangement, these dual agents also received the mandatory sales commission from USAID. The commission was initially paid in U.S. dollars, but in order to limit the dispersal of dollars in Vietnam, CIP changed its regulations to make commission payments in piasters, which it could recoup in dollars from an escrow account housed at the National Bank of Vietnam. USAID officials in Vietnam ran the program in conjunction with the South Vietnamese government but frequently encountered bureaucratic delays, lack of interagency cooperation, and the usual problem of government corruption.[10]

The rapid growth of the CIP created additional complications. Many shipments originated from third-party countries where U.S. consuls had scarce resources and limited capacity to properly inspect shipments to Vietnam. Substandard equipment, shoddy products, and falsified shipping manifests created huge headaches for buyers, suppliers, and CIP officials alike. Forty percent of all CIP imports to Vietnam came from countries other than the United States. Sixty percent of these goods had to be inspected before shipment, according to CIP regulations. In 1966 alone, there were over 30,000 separate shipments to Vietnam from ports in the United States and third-party countries. Budgetary constraints and the human expense made inspecting even a small percentage of these shipments impractical.

USAID had a daunting task enforcing these regulations and trying to punish those who violated them. Military and civilian lawyers working with the program ran into roadblocks set up by bureaucrats in Washington. Worried about upsetting this country or that by suspending an exporter who violated CIP regulations, the State Department occasionally insisted on maintaining "diplomatic niceties" rather than enforcing the rules. Suspension procedures against violators moved at a snail's pace, usually taking months to investigate and process. Moreover, suppliers and buyers who tried to take legal action against USAID for restitution for inferior goods or delayed reimbursements ran into similar barriers, as USAID often pushed their complaints along to the Vietnamese government and courts, both of which were understandably hesitant to take on the U.S. agency that supplied such large amounts of material goods for the Vietnamese economy and wealth for themselves. Add the corruption factor to the mix on both the U.S. and Vietnamese sides, and it is understandable why the problems existed and seemed unfixable.[11]

Black marketeers often stole U.S. goods brought into Vietnam through the CIP to illegally sell again for profit. Because these goods were legally and illegally shipped primarily to cities, enterprising people in the cities took advantage and enjoyed financial and material gain. Under the Diem regime, a small number of CIP importers began to monopolize the program. By 1969, fewer than 100 importers, based mostly in Saigon, controlled two-thirds of CIP trade, making substantial fortunes from kickbacks and overbilling. The multitudes in the countryside found themselves mostly excluded from both the availability of CIP goods as well as the profit that could be had from the illegal trade of these goods. Black markets thrived in Saigon, Hue, and other larger population centers, whereas in rural areas only small operators were able to make any gain from illegal trade. This was a major problem for the U.S. nation-building process in Vietnam: corruption abounded in the cities while people in the countryside failed to realize benefits of the CIP. Corruption wasted money and resources, and without the rural population's support, the counterinsurgency effort could not succeed and the South Vietnamese government would certainly fail.[12]

In addition to commodities brought into the country by the CIP, goods for supporting U.S. forces as well as for supplying the various civilian and military pacification and counterinsurgency programs arrived through various ports of entry and were then distributed to PX stores and warehouses across Vietnam. The illegal sale and acquisition of PX goods and other materials on the black market involved both U.S. and Vietnamese military and civilian personnel. Vietnamese authorities willingly allowed the U.S. military to investigate black market violations involving Americans because the Uniform Code of

Military Justice covered these offenses, and, again, Vietnamese authorities seemed more than willing to let the Americans take care of their own legal problems.[13] Moreover, Vietnamese law enforcement agencies often found obtaining enough evidence to successfully prosecute offenders quite difficult because of loopholes in Vietnamese law and simple lack of effort.[14]

Trafficking stolen goods was not the only black-market activity that caused headaches for the U.S. military. A more sophisticated and equally costly problem was currency fraud. This involved the illegal exchange of MPCs and illegal purchase of money orders as well as selling U.S. dollars and Vietnamese piasters through unofficial means. With the injection of so many U.S. dollars into the Vietnamese economy, the temptation to speculate and profit on currency was too great for some Americans and Vietnamese to resist. According to a 1970 congressional report, the U.S. dollar was the "most sought-after commodity in Vietnam."[15] Currency manipulation was easy, relatively low risk, and extremely profitable. If selling stolen goods from the CIP and PX stores could cause inflation and potentially wreck the fragile Vietnamese economy, currency fraud could devastate it. In fact, early in the U.S. involvement in Vietnam, the U.S. military worried that this problem could "have a serious effect . . . on the conduct of the war."[16]

According to Gabriel Kerekes, an economist testifying before the Senate Committee on Government Operations in 1969, "local capital seeking foreign haven simply outbids legitimate demand" and thus encouraged a black market for currency exchange at rates "substantially in excess" of official rates. Hoping to set aside nest eggs to use after the war, some Vietnamese, Chinese, Indian, and French businesspeople who could afford it sent Vietnamese capital out of the country in the form of illegally purchased U.S. dollars at a furious but debilitating pace. The colossal presence of goods from the United States, copious amounts of U.S. currency, and the escalating number of U.S. troops had first created and now sustained the problem. Moreover, Vietnamese law, which required flagrante delicto evidence to prosecute black-market-related violations, and U.S. legal obstacles, which mainly involved jurisdiction, meant that it was extremely difficult to make a firm statement against such activities through rapid convictions with harsh sentences. Kerekes maintained that the United States should have foreseen this problem well before the present crisis because of similar experiences in World War II and Korea.[17]

Estimates vary on the exact dollar amounts of illegal currency traded in Vietnam, but even the lowest estimate is rather staggering. Additional testimony before the Senate Committee on Government Operations in 1969 attempted to grasp the scope of the problem. Francis Pick, who copublished *Pick's Currency Yearbook*, which noted black-market currency exchange rates around the world, believed the Vietnamese illegal currency market involved $35 to $45 million annually from 1965 through 1968. The subcommittee's own investigation placed the estimate much higher, at $75 million annually. Other witnesses put the figure closer to $150 to $250 million per year. Despite the range of tens of millions of dollars, the estimates confirm that the problem was so large that currency fraud by itself significantly undermined the U.S.-supported Vietnamese economy (see Table 7.2).[18]

U.S. military personnel, U.S. civilians attached to the military, and Vietnamese who worked on U.S. military installations were all paid in MPCs in order to minimize the number of U.S. dollars in circulation. MPCs could not be converted into green U.S. dollars but could be transferred through postal money orders. This policy was designed to deter black-market use of dollars, keep U.S. and Vietnamese currency separate, and prohibit inflation.

Of course, those with a bit of ingenuity found ways to circumvent the intricate MPC system. Vietnamese, especially women, often played the role of go-between in these schemes. For example, a soldier might get wind of an upcoming MPC conversion date (when old MPCs were collected and new ones issued) and before the exchange date purchase old MPCs at a good rate, giving piasters or dollars in exchange. The soldier would then take the old MPCs to the conversion, get new MPCs, and have a Vietnamese or U.S. coconspirator exchange those for dollars or piasters on the black market, usually making a considerable profit. The illegal exchange of dollars for piasters could also easily turn a worthwhile return. A soldier would take X piasters to the American exchange at a particular installation and purchase U.S. dollars. He (or perhaps his Vietnamese house servant or girlfriend) would then take the dollars to the black market and purchase X + Y piasters, Y being the difference between the rate at the U.S. exchange and the black-market rate of exchange. For example, the official rate of 118 piasters to the dollar might rise to 200 piasters to the dollar on the black market.[19]

Cases involving currency manipulation and the black market abound and offer both a broad look at the problem and a glimpse of the distinctiveness of individual cases. The case involving Marine Corps private James Dunbar is both typical and illustrative.[20] Dunbar and two Marine Corps comrades deserted from Khe Sanh during the siege in February 1968. Deserting the besieged outpost was not as difficult as one might think. With daily flights in and out of Khe Sanh, stowing away aboard a cargo plane or some such aircraft

Table 7.2. Black Market and Legal Exchange Rates (in piasters), 1965–1974, by Quarter

Year	Black Market Rate (1st quarter)	Legal Rate (1st quarter)	Black Market Rate (2nd quarter)	Legal Rate (2nd quarter)	Black Market Rate (3rd quarter)	Legal Rate (3rd quarter)	Black Market Rate (4th quarter)	Legal Rate (4th quarter)
1965	143	73.5	140	73.5	152	118	169	118
1966	166	118	188	118	168	118	172	118
1967	173	118	158	118	151	118	167	118
1968	166	118	178	118	203	118	200	118
1969	194	118	202	118	225	118	360	118
1970	418	118	382	118	426	118	388	275
1971	403	275	374	275	366	275	414	410
1972	445	410	417	425	424	435	495	465
1973	540	475	491	500	518	510	554	550
1974	600	605	621	620	665	670	795	685

Source: United States Agency for International Development, Office of Vietnam Affairs, *United States Economic Assistance to South Vietnam, 1954–1975: Terminal Report* (Washington, D.C: United States Agency for International Development, 1975), 252.

between chaotic landings and rapid departures was actually not that risky and was fairly common. In Da Nang, the deserters managed to steal a few items from Marine Corps and air force administrative offices, the most valuable and useful of which were two air force typewriters. With a typewriter, the men could easily forge travel orders and other forms to make getting around the country as deserters rather easy. They sold most of the stolen goods, including one of the typewriters, on the black market, providing the men with much-needed cash.

With forged travel orders, the three made their way to Saigon, where they sought out and found the several colonies of U.S. deserters that managed to melt into the Cholon area of the teeming wartime city. As was common, these groups lived off of the black market. Dunbar and his comrades allegedly became involved in one of the largest black market/currency manipulation rings in Saigon. Made up mostly of army deserters, the ring of about fifty men operated with amazing efficiency and made a substantial monthly profit, sometimes well over $250,000. Stolen money orders were the ring's specialty. The ring operated out of a Saigon apartment building, renting an entire floor of apartments for a dual headquarters and living area. Strict rules for behavior,

appearance, and "off duty" activity governed the operation. The most important aspect of the scam was deception, which was surprisingly simple to
achieve by personal appearance. Looking like a deserter guaranteed attention
from military police. If one did not, however, one could get away with it. Each
deserter kept a clean, "squared away" appearance and thus did not draw unnecessary attention to himself.

Each day, the men would cash a check for $50 (the maximum amount al-
lowable) at as many PXs as they could get to, using checks from an account at
the Chase Manhattan Bank of Saigon. They then took the cash to base post offices and purchased $100 money orders, again the maximum amount allow-
able. On the black market, a postal money order with the payee line filled in
was not near as valuable as one with the payee line left blank. Postal clerks
were, of course, required to fill in the payee line, but $20 slid under the counter
usually left the line blank. The $20 "service charge" was well worth the extra
profit from a blank money order. Black marketeers bought the money orders
for $150, sometimes as much as $250, and would then sell the money orders
for piasters, which they could then exchange for dollars on the black market. It
was quite an intricate but profitable circle.

With forty-five or so men collecting the money orders, they often accumu-
lated over 500 money orders per day, which were sold the same day on the
black market. The profit was then deposited in the Chase Bank that afternoon
to easily cover the morning's fifty-dollar checks that had started the process.
With creative organization and large amounts of cash, the ring easily moved
about Saigon via forged orders and bribes. They even had some military police
on the take to warn them in case of a raid. Army military police did occasionally manage to apprehend some of the ring, but the loss to the ring was easily
replaced. Dunbar himself was actually caught a few times but managed to
bribe his holders, or "chasers" as they were called, on their way to Tan Son
Nhut airport for transfer to Da Nang. He presented them with an interesting
option: either accept the $100 bribe to let him go, or his friends would kill
them at the terminal. The chasers took the $100.

Enter here three military lawyers sent from Da Nang to bring Dunbar in once
and for all. Marine Corps captains Hays Parks and Pat Matthews (acting as defense attorney), along with navy lieutenant Bill Cosgriff (to conduct the Article
32 investigation), arrived in Saigon and had Dunbar arrested. At the time of his
arrest, Dunbar had almost $1,000 in MPCs and twenty-eight $100 money orders in his possession. He also had a contract for a brand-new Buick in the
United States that he had just purchased with cash. The three lawyers had to get

Dunbar and one other Marine Corps deserter in the ring back to the Da Nang brig, which no one had managed to do to this point. On the way to the airport, Dunbar offered the usual bribe, but Parks and the others would not play along. Parks had once been a traveling guard for the U.S. Marshal's Service and employed some tricks of that trade to keep the two deserters in line. Taking their shoe laces and belts, Parks had the two men restricted to the point that if they tried to run, their loose pants and boots would bring them to the ground in short order. Parks's loaded 12-gauge shotgun also persuaded the two deserters that running was not in the cards, and the weapon further served as a visible deterrent to any friends who might try to intimidate the lawyers. By the end of the day, Dunbar and his friend were safely locked in the Da Nang brig.

Prosecuting Dunbar for money order fraud proved difficult because of lack of hard evidence. Instead, Parks was able to convict Dunbar on the more provable and less complex charge of desertion from Khe Sanh. The court sentenced Dunbar to ten years imprisonment and a dishonorable discharge. Because Dunbar had not been convicted on the fraud charges, he was able to claim the cash and money orders upon his release from prison (after two years). Army investigators and lawyers ultimately managed to break up the ring, but one ring was only a drop in the bucket contrasted to the dozens that continued to operate in Saigon's black market.

A similar racket operated out of Phu Bai from December 1968 through February 1969, placing thousands of dollars in money orders each day. Three U.S. civilians working for army contractors Dynalectron and Consolidated Engineers ran the ring and used U.S. soldiers to do the legwork. CID investigators broke the ring up in March 1969, arresting several soldiers and the three civilians. Courts-martial sentenced two soldiers to two-year prison terms, and a third received a six-month sentence. The three civilians managed to escape court-martial because of jurisdictional issues, but they were debarred from working for U.S. contractors in Vietnam and most likely deported.[21]

Indeed, U.S. soldiers were not the only ones arrested for such crimes. Records reveal that it was not uncommon to catch U.S. civilians and their Vietnamese coconspirators with several thousand dollars in illegally gained currency or MPCs. Of seventeen currency violations tried from December 1965 through May 1966 (when this was a relatively minor problem), twelve of the defendants were U.S. civilians. All twelve were convicted under the Uniform Code of Military Justice and sent back to the United States, forfeiting their employment.[22]

Jurisdictional issues caused serious problems for the U.S. military justice effort in fighting black-market activities and currency fraud in Vietnam, as after

1969 U.S. civilians no longer needed to fear court-martial, much less the Vietnamese courts. After 1970, Vietnamese courts had jurisdiction over U.S. civilians in Vietnam but proved reluctant to vigorously prosecute Americans despite the efforts of some defiant and dedicated Vietnamese prosecutors and investigators.[23] This aspect of nation-building had hit an obstacle that would continue to impede the anti-black-market effort. As La Verne J. Duffy, an assistant counsel to the Senate Committee on Government Operations, pointed out, the judicial "inequities" between civilian and military personnel in Vietnam made the problem worse and sent the wrong signal to the Vietnamese concerning the rule of law.[24]

The black market for currency continued uninterrupted up to the end of the war, and even then the money apparently could still tempt even the most honest of U.S. soldiers. The case of army staff sergeant James Walters, 344th Supply Company, is a good example. A general court-martial convicted Walters of illegally obtaining more than $34,000 in MPCs during the first half of 1972. Walters, a ten-year veteran of the army and of two previous tours of Vietnam (noncombat tours, as Walters was a baker), had a spotless record—no previous courts-martial, no Article 15s. Walters pleaded guilty to the charge of obtaining MPCs from an unauthorized source, so only the sentencing phase of the trial took place. Several officers and men testified on behalf of Walters, noting his service record, absence of previous convictions, and his amiable character. Walters apparently made little profit on the transactions, since the MPC exchange rate inside the base at Da Nang had recently been adjusted to meet the black-market price at 410 piasters to the dollar MPC, whereas outside the rate fluctuated around 390 piasters to the dollar MPC. Two Vietnamese women, one of whom was Walters's girlfriend, purchased the MPCs outside the base; Walters then took the MPCs inside the base to exchange back into piasters. Because this was his first conviction, the court's sentence was light; only two months at hard labor plus reduction in rank. This case suggests that it was not just repeat offenders and troublemakers who were involved in these activities, even at the end of U.S. involvement in the war.[25]

Major black-market operations, however, went far beyond the amiable sergeant being tempted by quick profit. One of the largest black-market currency syndicates uncovered by investigators was the so-called Prysumeen Account.[26] The actual physical bank account under the name Prysumeen resided at the Manufacturers Hanover Trust Company in New York. The brains behind the account belonged to a part-time legitimate trader and alleged full-time smuggler and black marketeer based in Hong Kong named Rahman, who ran a large organization of Indian and Asian traders and gem dealers. Prysumeen was a code name made up from the names of Rahman's principal front men. In fact, it was the Manufacturers Hanover Trust Company that came up with the name after informing Rahman that under U.S. law it could not create confidential numbered accounts like those popular among Swiss banks. In 1968, more than $1.5 million went into the account each month. As early as 1967, the Prysumeen account held more than $51 million. Illicit money exchange became one of Rahman's more profitable operations, and his Vietnam syndicate accounted for over 40 percent of his currency exchange scams.

Rahman's biggest clients were U.S. companies under contract with the Vietnamese government. Many of these same companies also held contracts with the Defense Department, USAID, and other U.S. government agencies for services in Vietnam. According to testimony in 1970 before the U.S. Senate Permanent Subcommittee on Investigations of the Committee on Government Operations, the DeGill Corporation, Elleget Enterprises, Sarl Electronics, Star Distributing Company, Tectonics Asia Incorporated, and World Wide Consultants allegedly used contractual piaster payments from the Vietnamese government to cash in on black-market currency manipulation. Otherwise, there was no other way to exchange piasters for dollars. They used Rahman's syndicate to trade the piasters paid to them by the Vietnamese government for dollars minus a commission. The dollars were then deposited into the Prysumeen account in New York, then at a later date transferred to other banks, mainly in the Middle East, for payment. Companies paid in U.S. dollars in Vietnam (usually via U.S. government contracts) would exchange dollars for piasters on the black market, getting an extremely good rate, to pay their subcontractors in Vietnam in piasters. Investigators found that more than 200 individuals, companies, and banks had used Rahman's services in this way and had deposits in the Prysumeen account.

Investigative inquiries at several banks, including Manufacturers Hanover in New York, alerted Rahman's gang that their assets might be frozen by a federal court order, so they quickly withdrew most of their funds from Manufacturers Hanover in early 1968, leaving only a few thousand dollars in the account. The operation shifted to banks in Dubai, where the local government shied away from interfering in private banking affairs. In the end, Rahman's scams continued with little interference from U.S. investigators. U.S. and Vietnamese authorities apprehended only small-time operators at the fringe of the operation, including some U.S. soldiers who had unwittingly used Rahman's sources.

Such creative schemes required creative measures to combat them. Using the Uniform Code of Military Justice to prosecute these illegal activities was a resourceful means of attacking the black market. Courts-martial for black-market activities and currency violations began appearing in MACV monthly military justice activity reports in 1966. Among the four services, twenty-eight black-market and fifty-five currency cases were brought to trial in the 1965–1966 period, with the majority of violations occurring in the army, representing the largest group of U.S. forces in Vietnam. The value of goods stolen or sold on the black market in these cases ranged from $30 to $10,000. As more U.S. military and civilian personnel streamed into Vietnam in the 1967–1968 period, black-market activities and currency violations increased accordingly. In 1967, judge advocates took sixty-four cases to trial. After 1967, monthly and quarterly summaries no longer mentioned exact figures, simply the problem. Judge advocates spent an increasing amount of time dealing with these issues as the U.S. presence in Vietnam escalated.

Punishment was not prorated to the estimated value of the offense. An army private caught dealing $10,000 worth of black-market goods received six months confinement to hard labor and forfeited $62 per month for six months. Another army private caught with $30 worth of black-market goods received the stiff sentence of six months confinement to hard labor, reduction in grade, and forfeiture of $42 per month for six months.[27]

Officers, too, were convicted of black-market offenses. The army First Logistical Command, based at Long Binh, offers several examples from 1966. A general court-martial convicted 1st Lt. John Mella on four counts of illegal currency transactions (plus three specifications of larceny by embezzlement), sentencing Mella to dismissal (dishonorable discharge), two years at hard labor, and a fine of $3,000. The convening authority suspended the hard labor sentence. Another soldier, 2nd Lt. Russell Heston, was convicted by a general court-martial on two counts of currency violations and sentenced to dismissal, one year at hard labor, and total forfeitures. The convening authority again suspended the hard labor portion of the sentence. A general court-martial convicted Capt. James Rogers on two specifications of illegal currency transactions, giving Rogers a dishonorable discharge.[28]

One of the earliest and most infamous court-martial cases involving U.S. service members in black-market activities ended the career of the so-called American Mayor of Saigon.[29] For most of 1964 and 1965, navy captain Archie Kuntze was the chief of Headquarters Support Activity, Saigon, which made him perhaps the most influential American in the South Vietnamese capital.

Through his small empire, Kuntze could allegedly fulfill just about any request, be it for food, hotel rooms, luxury items, women, medical attention for unmentionable conditions, and even firefighters to put out your fire. All of this he did in addition to his apparently superb job of getting military supplies off of cargo planes and ships to wherever they needed to go in the field.

Kuntze was a consummate operator, and he fell into a rather flagrant live-in relationship with a Chinese woman named Jannie Suen, who was every bit his equal. Kuntze had oversight of liquor procurement for all U.S. military clubs in South Vietnam. Suen easily found employment with one of Saigon's largest liquor distributors to facilitate contracts. Through under-the-table deals, Kuntze could import just about anything into Vietnam. Suen's father ran a tailor's shop and could not get scarce cloth and other materials to continue his well-established business. Heavy import duties precluded legal means for importing cloth from the United States or Hong Kong. Kuntze, however, had no such limitations and legally could bring items into the country without paying import duties. Suen's father suddenly received large bolts of cloth, duty free.

Vietnamese and U.S. investigators had always kept a loose eye on Kuntze and his liquor and import activities, but by the end of 1965 they were growing more attentive. In January 1966, Vietnamese police seized a shipment of cloth delivered to Suen's apartment that had just arrived via air from Bangkok. With no proof of duty, Suen was arrested, which quickly led investigators to Kuntze. Kuntze's bank account showed glaring gaps and far too much cash flow for a navy captain. More than $16,000 had moved in and out of his bank account in a short time. Kuntze tried to explain away the movement of money through winnings at the dice table, the sale of a set of golf clubs, and several thousand dollars worth of clothes and jewelry purchased for Suen.

Navy investigators charged Kuntze with allegedly misusing government funds and conduct unbecoming an officer (a married serviceman living with an unmarried female). Kuntze was ordered to stand trial at a general court-martial at Treasure Island, California, in November 1966. Capt. Dan Flynn, a bright and able naval legal officer, served as his defense counsel. Flynn filed a motion to relocate the trial to Vietnam, where the eighteen charges had occurred, so that he could be given a "fair" opportunity to prepare Kuntze's case. The prosecution, represented by Capt. Joseph Ross, countered that the trial had been moved to California because Saigon was hot and full of reporters and that Kuntze stood a much better chance of getting a fair trial at Treasure Island than in Saigon. The motion was denied.

Testimony against Kuntze was thin. Several witnesses said that Kuntze had given them hundreds of dollars in cash to make trips to Bangkok and Hong Kong to buy clothes, cloth, jewelry, and other luxury items, but they all had flaws in their stories. Others testified how Kuntze had orchestrated illegal currency exchanges, yet these too fell into holes in cross-examination. Army general John D. Crowley, Kuntze's boss in Saigon, testified that Kuntze did an impossible job for U.S. military forces in Vietnam in handling the enormous tonnage of supplies that poured into Saigon. Rear Admiral Jack P. Monroe, commander of U.S. Naval Forces, Philippines, echoed Crowley's sentiments and was shocked at the allegations against Kuntze.

The evidence that Kuntze had misused government funds and property for profit could have been weakened somewhat by Suen's testimony. Flynn speculated that Suen knew that the bolts of cloth were hers and that the large cash flow had been from her to pay for the cloth. In the most mysterious twist of this case, Suen had disappeared from the Saigon jail to which Vietnamese police had taken her back in January 1966. Navy investigators could not locate her.

Hundreds of thousands of dollars had legally and illegally flowed through Kuntze's hands. At one point, a witness testified, Kuntze had over $23 million stashed in an icebox! Yet all the court-martial could convict him of was minor offenses related to behavior unbecoming an officer. For letting Suen use a government car, for living with her out of wedlock, and for abusing his position to import cloth for Suen's father, Kuntze, a veteran of Guadalcanal, Bougainville, Korea, and Vietnam, received an official reprimand and the loss of 100 points on the Navy promotion list. Speculation suggested that civilian and military interference from high above put the lid on the Kuntze case because his activities could have implicated some general officers, but little evidence supports this. The case highlights the waste and mismanagement during the early years of U.S. involvement that would come to characterize the war in Vietnam.

Another case clearly implicated upper levels of command and received much more public attention than the Army would have liked. This famous corruption scandal centered on a gang of army NCOs known as the Augsburg group.[30] The Augsburg group came to Vietnam hoping to control military clubs and to make a profit from the black market. Unlike many Americans who were sucked in by the temptation of illicit profit after they arrived in Vietnam, these men had fallen into a pattern of bad habits long before. In the end, despite making short-term fortunes, most of their careers would be ruined, and an air of conspiracy that reached the Pentagon would expose to the U.S. public the depth of corruption within U.S. forces in Vietnam.

The Augsburg group consisted of NCOs William O. Wooldridge, Navarez Hatcher, William Higdon, Seymour Lazar, Theodore Bass, William Bagby, and John Nelson. With the Twenty-fourth Division in Germany in the early 1960s, these men found in each other a liking for illegal profit. With the help of a civilian businessman named Ron W. Alcorn, the Augsburg group quickly gained control of the open-mess system on army posts in Germany. This included arranging food and liquor distribution contracts, furnishings, and the most lucrative part of their game, slot machines. Wooldridge was the sergeant major for the division and as the ranking NCO had available a wide range of readily exploitable powers and resources. Army investigators had been tipped off to the group's illegal activities, which included payoffs for service contracts, accepting gifts from contractors, and skimming proceeds from club slot machines. Investigators, however, hit roadblocks set up by the group. Officers on the various posts suddenly lost records or could not recall certain allegations or incidents. Those who considered cooperating with investigators received threatening phone calls and erred on the side of caution to reconsider their stories.

Alcorn had written a letter in 1963 to the deputy commander of the Twenty-fourth Division, admitting to accepting bribes from and giving bribes to Wooldridge and other NCOs who ran the various military clubs and messes. Army CID officers were not brought in to independently investigate the allegations until mid-1965, by which time most of the principal suspects and potential witnesses had been scattered across the world and the United States at other posts. The CID file, which included Alcorn's damning letter, remained locked away at the Twenty-fourth Division headquarters in Augsburg. Nothing came of the investigation.

In the meantime Wooldridge managed to get himself appointed as the first sergeant major of the army by Chief of Staff General Harold Johnson on a strong recommendation from Gen. Creighton Abrams. Despite holding an incredibly powerful and influential position, Wooldridge was eager for more; he moved in on club operations at Fort Benning and other posts in the United States. At Fort Benning, his Twenty-fourth Division comrades Hatcher, Bagby, Bass, and Nelson were assigned to run the open mess and clubs. By 1967, CID investigators were now snooping around Fort Benning and once again the trail led to Wooldridge. But the investigation again was stymied. Investigators were denied access to the Augsburg file in Germany and were forced to remove Wooldridge from the inquiry by order of Maj. Gen. Carl Turner, then provost marshal of the army, to avoid public embarrassment for General Johnson. Wooldridge's file suddenly went missing, having been "misplaced" at some point. None of the Augsburg group at Fort Benning could be charged, and CID had been frustrated at every turn, knowing full well that they had the right suspects in their sights. Turner would continue to protect Wooldridge and others of the Augsburg group as best he could and allegedly accepted thousands of dollars in cash and gifts (namely rare and expensive antique guns) in return for his influence. Before Wooldridge went to the Pentagon as sergeant major of the army, he served as sergeant major of the First Infantry Division in Vietnam from September 1965 to July 1966. In December 1965, Sergeant Lazar was placed in charge of the club system and open mess for the First Division. Sergeant Hatcher took Lazar's place in November 1968; Hatcher in turn was replaced by one of Lazar's protégés from Augsburg and Fort Benning, Sergeant Nelson. Sgt. James P. Morrison, who also served in the club system at Augsburg, replaced Nelson in May 1969. At Long Binh, Sergeant Higdon was placed in charge of the mess and clubs in 1967. In March 1968, Sergeant Bagby took command of the club system for the Americal Division at Chu Lai. Sergeant Bass moved to Vietnam as a civilian in 1968 and worked as a contract broker representing a private company known as Maredem that supplied U.S. military clubs in Vietnam. To top it all off, Wooldridge returned to Vietnam as sergeant major for MACV in 1968 and even had the enthusiastic recommendation for the position from then army vice chief of staff Gen. Creighton Abrams. In the words of Senator Edward Gurney of Florida, "a plague of locusts descended on Vietnam" that would make organized crime of the Prohibition era look downright amateurish.

The Augsburg group took their corrupt game to a new level in Vietnam. Together they formed the Maredem Company, which brokered supplies and goods to U.S. military clubs and messes. Now the Augsburg group could use government money to buy goods from their own company to supply clubs and messes that they legally operated. In the process, they "squeezed out" several competitors that were trying to get in on the club action in Vietnam. Competitors that wanted to continue doing business with U.S. military clubs had to go through Maredem. The markup for goods sold by independent wholesalers to military clubs and messes outside of Maredem's control averaged around 30 percent; for those connected to Maredem or controlled directly by Maredem, the markup ranged from 50 percent to as high as 160 percent. Maredem was making healthy profits by controlling the mess and club system from both inside and out.

A CID investigator in Vietnam who had been involved with the original Augsburg probe first became suspicious when he read familiar names in complaints filed at MACV CID. Competitors complained to CID that the new

Maredem Company had gained a lock on supplying the clubs and mess of the Americal Division, where Sergeant Bagby served as services custodian. As CID pieced together what was going on, it found that the club and mess conspiracy extended into the black market, where the Maredem sergeants sold liquor and other goods purchased with government money for personal profit. The problem lay in finding hard evidence. It came as no surprise that MACV CID's request for the original Augsburg file was denied, and records in Vietnam, such as receipts and account books, disappeared, were destroyed, or were so expertly doctored that no discrepancies could be found.

Then leads began pointing to general officers. Brig. Gen. Earl Cole had been the USARV deputy chief of staff for personnel and administration in Vietnam and had overall supervision of the PX, mess, and club systems. He had appointed most of the Augsburg group to their convenient posts in Vietnam. CID inquiries began connecting General Cole with the scandal. Maj. Clement St. Martin, who was the officer in charge of the Long Binh mess in 1967 and 1968, had tried to bring supply discrepancies to General Cole's attention but had been repeatedly snubbed. St. Martin finally took his concerns to CID, where he was well received. General Cole was questioned but denied any wrongdoing. At an earlier dedication ceremony for a new club at Long Binh attended by Sergeant Major of the Army Wooldridge and Army Chief of Staff General Johnson, Maj. St. Martin had confronted Wooldridge with allegations of conspiracy among Wooldridge, Cole, and the others. Wooldridge had calmly and coolly told the major to stop "snooping around" or else he would get "hurt." Not soon after, in frustration St. Martin accused General Cole in front of other officers (including another general officer), alleging that Cole was involved in mess system corruption and black-market activities. Cole, familiar with the allegations and investigations, denied all.

Nonetheless, the investigation had ruffled enough feathers to warrant congressional attention. By October 1969, Wooldridge, Higdon, Lazar, and Hatcher had been ordered to appear before the Senate Committee on Government Operations. By this time, all had rotated out of Vietnam and were serving at stateside posts or had left the army. All took their Fifth Amendment right and refused to answer any questions. Wooldridge did, however, offer the press his shock and denial at accusations of any wrongdoing; the *Washington Daily News* believed him, depicting Wooldridge as a true U.S. hero who had a wife, kids, and a small home and was living on a meager monthly salary.

As late as the spring of 1971, testimony continued in an attempt to uncover and prove all the scams and corruption orchestrated by the Augsburg group,

General Cole, and others associated with mess and club systems. As a result of the congressional inquiry, the army made charges against several of the principal players in federal courts. Having been forced into action, the army did not want another cover-up scandal like My Lai on its hands. In February 1970, the Federal District Court for the Central District of California indicted Wooldridge, Higdon, Lazar, Hatcher, Bass, and Bagby on twenty-one counts of conspiracy to defraud the United States, false and fraudulent claim against the United States, bribery of public officials, and concealment of material fact. All except one were convicted and paid fines or served prison terms. Higdon was court-martialed while serving at Redstone Arsenal. He was convicted in June 1971, given a dishonorable discharge, and fined $25,000. General Cole was forced to retire at the rank of colonel. General Turner was also forced to retire and in federal court pleaded guilty to accepting bribes; he served a three-year prison sentence. Wooldridge's strongest supporter, General Abrams, was "stunned" by the whole thing and felt a "strong sense of betrayal" that his sergeant major had been the brains behind the operation. It took years for the army NCO corps to recover from the damage done to their service by the Augsburg group.

If the Augsburg case shows how deep and widespread corruption could be, the case of the Christmas cards is one of the best examples of how ludicrous the fraud committed in Vietnam could be.[31] The case involved 1.5 million Christmas cards sold to U.S. military messes and clubs in 1968 by R and R Supply Company, operated by a husband-and-wife team named Evans (who also had connections to the Prysumeen Account). The company's alleged scam was relatively simple. They purchased 1.5 million Christmas cards in packages of six from Japan Publications Company in Tokyo for $75,000, or five cents per card. R and R then took orders from various messes and clubs in Vietnam for the cards. For example, the 101st Airborne Division ordered 90,000, the Ninth Infantry ordered 144,000, and so forth. A fake invoice increased the number of cards ordered by each unit and exempted the shipments from customs duties and inspections. The 101st Airborne Division now had 450,000 on order instead of its actual order of 90,000. The air force NCO mess at Binh Hoa had not ordered any cards but was listed in the fake invoice for 36,000. Club managers on the take signed for the excess cards, although they did not receive them. The excess, some 700,000 Christmas cards, was placed in storage in a house near Tan Son Nhut.

The United Service Organizations (USO) almost messed up the entire scheme. R and R bought the cards for 5¢ each and sold them to the clubs for

20¢ each; the clubs in turn sold them to the troops for 25¢ apiece. The USO attempted to contract with the same Japanese card company to buy 180,000 cards at 12¢ each, but R and R convinced the firm to cancel the order based upon the fact that R and R had purchased such a huge order and claimed, fraudulently, that it had an exclusive right to sell Christmas cards to U.S. messes and clubs in Vietnam. The USO should have been able to buy and sell the cards to servicemen for 5¢ apiece. Instead, R and R was able to make a 300 percent profit with minimal effort and expense. The excess Christmas cards were sold to other clubs and even to Vietnamese street vendors. Nothing happened to the club managers who signed for cards they did not receive and no charges were brought against R and R despite its connection to this and other allegedly illegal activities.

The military justice system tried to do something about these problems, and so too did the American Embassy in Saigon, with help from judge advocates. In an attempt to clean up the black market and its associated corruption, Ambassador Ellsworth Bunker appointed embassy staff and MACV judge advocates to the IAC in August 1967. Within the month, the IAC had recommended more strict controls over U.S. contractors (again, many violators were civilian) and PX privileges. It also suggested increasing U.S. monetary and moral support for the South Vietnamese government's efforts, which were negligible at best, to attack these problems.[32]

By 1969, the IAC included representatives from USAID in Vietnam, and by 1970 the IAC met jointly with its new counterpart, the Vietnamese IAC. The Vietnamese IAC included the minister of finance, the director general of customs, the director general of exchange at the National Bank of Vietnam, and the chief of the Vietnamese Fraud Repression Service. The two IACs reached a high level of cooperation, often attempting to coordinate stakeouts and raids of suspected black-market areas and sharing evidence in prosecutions. Meaningful results were mixed, however, partly owing to corruption among Vietnamese officials, particularly the police.[33]

Robert H. Parker, chairman of the IAC (and director of USAID in Vietnam from 1967 to 1969) testified before the Senate Committee on Government Operations in November 1969. Parker outlined several obstacles the Americans and Vietnamese faced in their fight against the black market. In his view, the black market, a "racket" of hundreds of millions of dollars, undermined "what we are trying to achieve in Vietnam." It gave "aid and comfort to the enemy" and created an "atmosphere of illegality and fraud, immorality and cynicism" in the cities and villages of South Vietnam. These activities subverted U.S. and

Vietnamese efforts to "establish economic stability" in the war-ravaged coun-try, thus undermining the counterinsurgency and nation-building effort.[34]

Parker described illegal money changing, money order fraud, blank check fraud, and other currency violations, all of which he attributed to the black market. In some cases this fraud extended well beyond Vietnam, involving banks in India, Hong Kong, and even New York City. He was quick to note the cultural problems involved in suppressing the black market. Churches and temples provided occasional fronts for illegal currency rackets and other illicit businesses. To Vietnamese officials, raiding such houses of worship was a sen-sitive proposition in light of their experience in violating Buddhist temples during 1963. One such raid, however, did net more than $13,000 in U.S. money orders and more than $70,000 in cash.[35]

Parker's explanation of the role of U.S. civilians in these activities contained what seems to have amounted to an institutional arrogance. The Saigon embassy and other U.S. agencies often employed U.S. civilians in "temporary" short-term capacities. Because of the interim nature of their employment, Parker claimed that they distinguished themselves less in "esprit de corps and dedication to duty" than did their longer-term co-workers. The temporary workers, according to Parker, had no qualms about pursuing a "quick profit" here and there. The knowledge that the worst penalty would probably involve termination of em-ployment and deportation to the United States made the temptation to commit such crimes too tempting. Parker claimed that those with long-term commit-ments to U.S. policy would stay the course and keep out of trouble, which events in Vietnam over the years had shown was a specious proposition at best.[36]

The U.S. soldier, according to Parker, had much more to lose than his or her civilian counterpart. Court-martial sentences for black-market activities and currency violations were much more severe than potential consequences for U.S. civilians. Parker described how AWOL soldiers frequently became drawn into the black market by seeking refuge in the cities, where they could blend in with the multitudes. The price of refuge often meant working in the black market by participating in either stealing or selling goods or by acting as mid-dlemen in illegal currency exchanges. The more they participated, the deeper they were pulled into this underground world. Parker detailed the experience of one such AWOL soldier wishing to return to his unit who made contact with IAC judge advocates investigating black-market activities. His Vietnam-ese friends unmasked him as an informant, and he was eliminated (in this par-ticular case, a battle-axe "cracked his skull one night"). The previously men-tioned case of the Khe Sanh marines corresponds to Parker's observations.[37]

Despite setbacks and disappointing results, the IAC and U.S. judge advocates across South Vietnam continued to combat currency violations and black-market activities through a variety of means. The IAC advised the U.S. government to terminate contracts with U.S. companies supporting U.S. forces in Vietnam for repeat violations or if an excessive number of employees were convicted in Vietnamese courts. It directed the MACV judge advocate's office to put in place stricter currency and exchange procedures and policies. With IAC cooperation, MACV implemented its preferred use of directives, which explained to service members the dangers and repercussions of participating in such illicit schemes, and judge advocates gave lectures to troops to hammer the point home.

Part of the problem with the cooperative effort to attack currency fraud and black-market activity was inconsistency and misplaced effort. Robert Starr, legal adviser to the American Embassy in Saigon and a member of the IAC, argued that the South Vietnamese government's "prestige in the eyes of both the U.S. and the Vietnamese public could be substantially enhanced if it took more effective steps to curb black market operations." He offered no solutions, only blame. Vietnamese police tended to raid small operators and street vendors, avoiding the ringleaders. He cited a "special ten-day drive" in Saigon against suspected violators in November 1969, staged by forty teams of Vietnamese national police. The operation yielded unimpressive results. The teams arrested over 250 minor operators but missed larger, more important targets. The overall effort did not convey the "impression of a serious attempt to come to grips with the big operators." Although his evaluation was accurate, it also ignored the U.S. side of the problem.[38]

Lack of cooperation and the persistence of corruption regularly plagued efforts to get a grip on the problem. The failure of the Vietnamese government, the American Embassy, and MACV to resolve restitution of confiscated MPCs and American dollars in a timely manner provides a good example. Vietnamese raids on black-market moneychangers netted hundreds of thousands of U.S. dollars and literally tons of MPC scrip. The Department of Defense had maintained that MPCs were technically worthless in unauthorized hands. The reality was, however, that in the unauthorized hands of black marketeers, MPCs had immense value. The House Committee on Government Operations strongly recommended that MACV force the Vietnamese government to return confiscated MPCs. It was plainly evident to investigators that Vietnamese government and police officials were using confiscated MPCs to make money on the black market. Vietnamese government officials responded to the rather weak requests from MACV with the position that if MPC script were technically worthless in unauthorized hands, it should not matter that the government kept it.

In the case of U.S. dollars, the Vietnamese government had firm legal ground to retain its policy of keeping the money. As legal tender entitled to the bearer, the U.S. government did not legally own the confiscated currency just because it was the issuer. Thus, the Vietnamese government claimed it could legally and rightfully maintain possession of confiscated U.S. dollars. Vietnamese government officials confidentially told the American Embassy that they would not consider returning any scrip or dollars unless the United States paid a "premium" for its return. This compounded the issue, as the United States had long been aware that official figures from the Vietnamese government on confiscated currency did not reflect currency and MPC scrip taken by customs agents and police who kept the money instead of turning it in. With no reward or "premium" for turning in confiscated money, Vietnamese agents reckoned they might as well keep it for themselves and try to make some money off of it on the black market. In the end, MACV and the American Embassy in Saigon decided to let the issue lie despite strong urgings from Congress to resolve the matter with the Vietnamese government.[39]

Despite the corruption, the Vietnamese government did occasionally make nominal efforts to clean up its act. The Vietnamese constitution of 1967 established an inspector general–like office called the General Censorate, which was to investigate illegal activities among Vietnamese military and government agencies and officials. During its first year of operation, 1968–1969, the General Censorate investigated more than 2,000 black-market and currency fraud violations. Of the more than 2,000 individuals implicated in these cases, only 12 were prosecuted in court, 10 dismissed from office, and 20 demoted or transferred to other agencies. Thirty-eight Vietnamese military personnel also received punishment. The American Embassy's evaluation of the General Censorate concluded that "venal and corrupt officials in the [South Vietnamese government], military and civilian, are not in any grave danger of being caught and punished, at least not as a result of findings and recommendations made by the Investigations and Control Committee of the Censorate."[40] Thomas E. Naughton, the assistant director of USAID in Vietnam, also attributed the General Censorate's "doubtful prestige" to the fact that its "very existence" was "alien to the cultural, economic, and political climate in which it must work." He compared it to a "troop of Boy Scouts at a jamboree encampment in the midst of Sodom or Gomorrah." He urged the United States to give stronger support to the General Censorate, including additional legal support from U.S. military lawyers.[41]

In a war already known as a "television" war and one where the role of public support was certainly a visible factor, the U.S. and Vietnamese IACs focused some of their effort toward taking advantage of the television medium. The U.S. IAC proposed issuing press releases about black-market arrests. The Vietnamese suggested televising an award ceremony commending a customs investigator for spoiling a large black-market shipment. Ambassador Samuel D. Berger liked the idea, recommending further that the Vietnamese might establish a regular television show to explain how the South Vietnamese government was fighting illegal activities of the black market.[42] At the time this idea must have made some sense to the IAC, although in retrospect a television campaign escapes logic. In rural South Vietnam, television sets were mostly in the hands of district chiefs as prized possessions. Besides, few Vietnamese could have identified with what they saw on television—smart-looking Vietnamese men and women in front of fantastic studio sets. They might as well have been on the moon.[43]

According to MACV commander Gen. William Westmoreland, by 1969 black-market crimes and currency violations "literally went out of control," far beyond the ability of the military justice system to suppress the problem. By 1971, even as U.S. forces and U.S. civilian personnel left Vietnam in increasing numbers, U.S. involvement in these illegal activities continued at a steady pace. The "crisis of discipline" in the armed forces in Vietnam during these years certainly involved illicit activities.[44]

Once the United States left the country in force in 1973, corruption exploded, virtually paralyzing the South Vietnamese military and government, a situation that in turn shattered the already low morale of the Vietnamese people. With decreasing U.S. oversight of the battle against the black market and the increasing failure of the Vietnamese government's efforts to deal with corruption, these illicit activities thrived right through the North Vietnamese victory in 1975 and even beyond. A 1974 study conducted by one of South Vietnamese president Thieu's advisers claimed that forty of sixty senior officers investigated in the South Vietnamese army were involved in illegal activities. Another study found massive corruption among South Vietnamese military units, which sold weapons, embezzled money, practiced extortion, and even filed false pay slips for "ghost" soldiers who never existed. Government officials and private entrepreneurs intensified smuggling operations, profiteering, and other illicit schemes. The common saying in Saigon was, "The house leaks from the roof on down," implying that corruption started at the top levels of government and worked its way down to the common people on the street.[45]

The black market and currency manipulation worked against building economic stability and discouraged faith in legal processes in South Vietnam, despite the efforts of U.S. military justice, Pentagon directives, embassy initiatives, and congressional urgings. Even though MPC exchange rates were revised to better compete with black-market rates in 1970, the problem of currency manipulation continued. In 1971, the army even tried to issue credit cards for use in clubs and messes to reduce the amount of cash both in MPC and dollars available in Vietnam. PXs worldwide were ordered to stop stocking "unessential" items on their shelves. In an unprecedented step, the army created the Army Criminal Investigation Command in 1971 to better coordinate the increasingly worldwide scope of investigations, as the experience in Vietnam clearly indicated that corruption and black-market activities extended well beyond a specific theater of war.

As for corruption surrounding military mess and club services and associated black-market activities, Congress stepped in and forced the military to take action through a variety of legislative acts and Pentagon directives. For example, the Financial Record-Keeping and Currency and Foreign Transactions Reporting Act of 1970 made it more difficult to transfer funds from U.S. banks to foreign banks with secret account numbers and false names. Legislation also established an assistant secretary–level civilian inspector general in the Department of Defense to lead investigations of illicit activities in all of the services. A similar position was also created in the State Department to look into misuse of foreign-aid funds. From the military end, MACV banned slot machines from all U.S. posts and bases in Vietnam in 1971, which probably proved too little, too late as deescalation picked up steam in 1971 and 1972. The air force banned slot machines from all of its installations worldwide. The army created a new mess and club operations manual, instituted new command structures that tied club and mess operations directly to the post commander, and prohibited so-called mobile club operating teams, such as the Augsburg sergeants had utilized in Germany, Fort Benning, and Vietnam. The Defense Department initiated a massive study of control mechanisms for all nonappropriated fund activities worldwide in March 1971. All of the services created career tracks in management and finance and established independent review procedures for PXs, post offices, clubs, and messes.

Of course, Congress wanted the Defense Department to do more, including a ban on slot machines from all military bases and posts; improved contract and vendor bid oversight for suppliers to PXs, clubs, and messes; and the adoption of a code of ethics for any entity doing business with any of the military services. This last recommendation gives the impression that Congress supposed that outside influences brought corruption to the U.S. military rather than the other way around. Finally, Congress recommended to the army that it abolish the position of sergeant major of the army. It seems that because of the disastrous first one, Sergeant Major Wooldridge, the rank had proved an embarrassment. The army refused and maintains the position despite other scandals associated with the top NCO.[46]

According to the final USAID report, Vietnam's corruption was "pervasive," "inordinate" in amount, and involved "fantastically large amounts" of cash. Not all Vietnamese, of course, were corrupt, but enough were involved in illegal activities to make it a problem of immense proportions. It reached the lowest levels of government and society as well as the very highest—the depth and breadth of corruption were simply beyond control. In the end, corruption was too entrenched and U.S. investigators and military lawyers spread too thin to make this piece of the counterinsurgency program work. Apologists for corruption in Vietnam tried to wish it away by claiming this was simply the "Asian way" of doing things and that the "grease-the-wheel" premise was acceptable so long as it did not harm the economy.[47]

The problem with this attitude was that it directly conflicted with the goals of counterinsurgency and that greasing-the-wheel was indeed doing considerable harm to the economy and was counter to the rule of law. The United States had unwittingly created and fed the atmosphere of corruption in South Vietnam. The final USAID report admitted as much, stating with surprising clarity: "The decision to protect the people from runaway inflation led to import levels in excess of economic need, with a consequent distortion of economic priorities and damage to the country's social structure and moral fabric. Most of all, it involved the creation of an artificial economy almost entirely dependent on U.S. aid and, of course, vulnerable to withdrawal of that aid."[48]

By 1970, U.S. economic advisers sensed that the failure to establish a working free-market economy in Vietnam had placed the United States in the expensive position of having to support the Vietnamese economy with massive aid, up to $700 million annually, for years. By 1973, corruption and the U.S. withdrawal precluded such an eventuality. Aid decreased, inflation skyrocketed, and corruption continued. Moreover, as the problem found its way into U.S. newspapers and television news stories, Congress began questioning whether or not their constituents' tax dollars were being thrown into a bot-tomless pit. Just as General Westmoreland had earlier sought light at the end of the tunnel, so too did Congress intently listen for a reassuring sound that would indicate the bottom of the pit. Yet, Congress stubbornly kept throwing money down the pit until the end in 1975.[49]

The widespread U.S. and Vietnamese involvement in currency manipula-tion, the black market, and other corruption in Vietnam speak volumes about the U.S. experience in this conflict. It certainly spread the message that democ-racy and free-market capitalism could provide ample opportunity to pursue one's happiness, whatever one's respect for the rule of law. Despite immense effort, including that of military lawyers, military justice was unable to abate this debilitating problem.

CHAPTER EIGHT
STILL IN THE VANGUARD

One of the last trials related to Vietnam began in March 1980.[1] It was a bizarre case—one that seemed a peculiar but appropriate capstone for the U.S. experience in Vietnam. Viet Cong near Cam Hai had captured Marine Corps private Robert R. Garwood in September 1965. In December of that year, the Viet Cong released Garwood, who then did something astonishing to most Americans—he joined the National Liberation Front (NLF), also known as the Viet Cong, and took a Vietnamese name. Garwood had been subjected to intensive "reeducation" sessions during his captivity, which had apparently worked. He wrote propaganda, delivered speeches via loudspeaker near Marine Corps camps, and helped interrogate, guard, and "bring over" U.S. prisoners. The NLF provided him with identification, uniform, weapons, and freedom of movement and in 1968 made Garwood an officer. Garwood was a traitor and had taken up arms against the United States.

On more than a few occasions, Marine Corps units encountered a Caucasian in firefights with NLF forces. They guessed it was probably Garwood, since Garwood had signed his name to propaganda leaflets and was listed as a deserter in enemy hands. After 1970, Garwood dropped from sight but was assumed to be alive. In 1979, Garwood surfaced in Hanoi, where he made contact with a Finnish businessman who helped arrange to have him flown to Bangkok. Awaiting him there were the press, a Marine Corps security detail, and Capt. Joseph Composto, who had been assigned to offer Garwood legal advice if he so requested. The Marine Corps, still cognizant of the army's experience with the My Lai trials, wanted to make sure everything was done by the book with Garwood.

Garwood was charged with aiding the enemy (Article 104) and misconduct as a prisoner (Article 105) as well as desertion. The maximum sentence was death, but the case was tried as noncapital. Garwood released Captain Composto and accepted Capt. Lewis R. Olshin as his appointed military counsel. He also accepted the services of a civilian trial lawyer, Dermot G. Foley of New York. Later in the trial, a former army judge advocate, John Lowe, took over as the lead defense attorney. The defense team never really jelled, failing to agree on a defense strategy for Garwood. Foley quit. Vaughn Taylor, also a former army judge advocate, joined the team. The team then agreed that Garwood's mental competency would be their defense strategy.

Capts. Werner Hellmer and Teresa J. Wright served as trial counsel for the Garwood court-martial. It was Hellmer's first general court-martial. Col. Robert E. Switzer served as military judge for the trial, held at Camp Lejeune. A five-member panel heard the case and would decide Garwood's fate. The prosecution took eleven days to present its case. Nine former prisoners of war testified against Garwood. The defense took a month to present its case that Garwood's mental capabilities had been affected by his captivity and therefore he could not be held responsible for his actions. The panel found otherwise, convicting Garwood of communication with the enemy and assaulting a prisoner of war. Garwood's sentence included reduction in rank, total forfeiture of pay, and a dishonorable discharge. There would be no confinement. Garwood's defense team appealed, citing errors committed by Colonel Switzer during the trial. While the trial was in progress, Switzer had given interviews to CBS in which he criticized the defense strategy. But the Court of Military Appeals, though troubled with Switzer's behavior with the press, did not believe that his actions had prejudiced the court members; the court upheld the conviction. Garwood was the only U.S. serviceman convicted of such acts while with the enemy. As historian Gary Solis notes in his detailed description of the case, "Robert R. Garwood *was* the enemy."[2]

The Garwood trial served as a vivid reminder that concerns about military justice and disillusion with Vietnam lingered well after the war had ended for the United States. The criticisms hurled at the military justice system at first tended to focus on the shortcomings of the prosecution of war crimes. Professional papers from the service schools called for a revision of the Uniform Code of Military Justice to include special war crimes provisions, including listing specific offenses and punishments. The reasoning was that if such provisions were in the Uniform Code of Military Justice, then the troops would pay more attention in training sessions and thus be less likely to commit such acts.[3]

Suggested reforms of the military justice system, including extending jurisdiction over discharged servicemen to the federal court system, arose from allegations of various offenses in Vietnam. As it stood in the Vietnam era, a soldier who committed a crime while in service but was subsequently discharged without being charged was no longer under the jurisdiction of the Uniform Code of Military Justice. The only way charges could be brought was if somehow the person was again under the jurisdiction of the military justice system. Strong arguments grew out of the Vietnam experience to conjoin the jurisdiction of military courts and the federal court system. So long as federal courts respected the same rights the individual had when under military jurisdiction, including the statute of limitations, and the table of punishments was the same, then due process would be preserved and perhaps the age-old problem of command influence could be alleviated. Such a proposal would cover the gap in jurisdiction between the Uniform Code of Military Justice and U.S. obligations to international agreements, in particular the Hague and Geneva Conventions. Senator Sam Ervin Jr. offered such legislation in 1971. Ervin's bill provided for federal court jurisdiction over discharged soldiers who committed crimes while in service. What killed the bill constitutionally was that it would apply to offenses committed before its enactment. The Constitution clearly prohibits such ex post facto laws that place the individual and the rights of the individual at jeopardy.[4]

Command influence also came under the public microscope. Legal scholars and military lawyers sought a solution to the problem of command influence in trials, a concern that was and indeed still is timeless because of the very nature of military justice. One of the more recurrent criticisms was that the convening authority picked the court members. A solution to this problem of judicial fairness was to have jurors chosen by someone not connected with the convening authority or its command.[5] The severest critics boldly recommended that the military jury be the only thing retained from the entire military justice system, but only if the military members came from commands "totally disconnected" from that of the accused and were chosen by lottery instead of being picked by the commander.[6]

Reform efforts began before the war had ended for the United States in 1973. The 1972 Task Force on Military Justice focused on the dilemma of maintaining discipline while ensuring rights expected in a democratic society. As racial and civil strife had obviously reached the U.S. military at home and overseas, adjustments had to be made to meet these challenges to military discipline. Military justice was the center circle that held the three concentric circles of democratic society, the military, and military justice together in a functional relationship. The task force recommended that more minority lawyers be recruited into judge advocate ranks and that better military justice training be given to enlisted members of the services to alleviate misconceptions and lack of understanding of rights and responsibilities under the Uniform Code of Military Justice. In regard to military justice practice, the task force strongly recommended that court members be chosen at random and without the influence of the convening authority, hoping to remove the "aura of unfairness that surrounds the military court-martial."[7]

Supporters claimed that the system functioned adequately, and not surprisingly some of these voices came from the ranks of military lawyers. Robert S. Pydasheff and William K. Suter argued that concerns about command influence were unfounded, as the code actually protected the rights of the accused in much the same way as these rights found protection in the Constitution and the federal court system. These safeguards were important, according to Pydasheff and Suter, so that the system could maintain the "confidence of the bar" and the public. But if the bar misunderstood the military justice system based upon "highly inaccurate and misleading generalizations," then how could the public have faith in it? This certainly seemed the case after Vietnam. Pydasheff and Suter pointed to the guaranteed right to qualified counsel, the Article 31 statement of accused rights and warning against self-incrimination, broad protections of the Article 32 investigative process, and liberal rules on search and seizure, all of which gave the accused fairly substantial protections in comparison to the civilian judicial process. The military justice system indeed "deserved respect which any system of justice requires to function with maximum efficiency."[8]

Likewise, command responsibility, highlighted by the failure of anyone above Calley to be convicted in the My Lai trials, drew the ire of some of the thinking public. Command responsibility doctrine holds that a superior officer is criminally responsible and liable for atrocities committed by those under his command if he had knowledge or good reason to know that those under his command were about to commit or had committed such acts, and he failed to prevent these acts and/or failed to investigate, report, and punish the perpetrators. Command responsibility continues to be a very sticky problem. Hays Parks, an expert on war crimes and international criminal law, argued for more clearly defined degree of intent and criminal responsibility in both domestic and international law to erase the vagueness that allowed commanders to escape responsibility for the actions of their subordinates. A commander has a "duty to utilize all means available to . . . know of and prevent the occurrence of war crimes within his command. In particular, he cannot shun or ignore the obvious and plead ignorance as a defense in an effort to escape liability." To hold commanders responsible, prosecutors must show "actual knowledge" or the "means of knowledge" of the crimes committed under their command. Both, as seen in the My Lai cases, are difficult to prove beyond reasonable doubt. Still, it is imperative that commanders be held liable because, as Parks stated, "The duty is well established, the responsibility is well defined."[9]

More recently, University of Iowa law professor Mark J. Osiel pointed out the "myriad of problems—moral, conceptual, and practical" that plague what seems like straightforward legal sense to hold commanders culpable for war crimes committed by their subordinates, à la Barker (if he had not been killed), Medina, and Calley. There is the very natural hesitancy for intermediate-level commanders to investigate and prosecute subordinate commanders for atrocities committed under their watch because it draws jeopardizing attention to those commanders' actions regarding the allegations in question. Moreover, "contrived ignorance" on the part of commanders to distance themselves from subordinate acts complicates enforcing command responsibility. According to Oseil, command responsibility is essential and must be enforced, even to the point that "mere negligence" is culpable. The threat of punishment should, and hopefully would, motivate a commander to "take all reasonable measures to prevent war crimes" by those under his command. An officer, by being an officer and being in command, has placed himself in a position of responsibility for preventing war crimes and protecting his subordinates from being placed in positions of risk. On today's modern battlefield, communications and other technology have made it possible for a commander to be in constant contact with his troops in the field, making ignorance of subordinate criminal acts less a possibility than ever before in the history of warfare.[10]

Current U.S. policy has tried to keep war crimes committed by U.S. forces an insular issue, as the United States continues to distance itself from the International Criminal Court and other international jurisdictions. If the United States were to be friendlier toward these jurisdictions, especially those involving violations of the laws of war, then perhaps U.S. use of force abroad might have more legitimacy. One way to accomplish this would be to incorporate international standards for war crimes prosecution, in particular those relating to command responsibility, into the Uniform Code of Military Justice. This could serve as a deterrent, which it is to be hoped would result in fewer violations of accepted laws of war by U.S. forces. The international community might look more favorably on U.S. use of force knowing that the United States was at least open to conforming to international courts. The counterargument, of course, is that the United States already has set in place due process to deal with such acts. The War Crimes Act of 1996 was certainly a step in the right direction, extending federal court jurisdiction over any member of the armed forces or U.S. national who commits a violation of the laws of war as defined in the act.[11]

A much broader issue after Vietnam concerned whether the Uniform Code of Military Justice could work effectively under extended combat conditions. Command influence, the inability to maintain discipline through deterrence, lengthy investigations and trials, the "cumbersomeness" of paperwork and exhaustive staff-hours, and the fact that due process had become a fetish had perhaps made the Uniform Code of Military Justice unworkable in combat. For forces in the field and on the high seas, the system had become "exceedingly expensive, complicated, and slow moving" in achieving its original intent. Some talked of abolishing "extrinsic" rights of the accused, eliminating administrative discharges as punishment, and "streamlining" the overall system for combat conditions.[12] Military and civilian lawyers alike weighed in on the issue.

In a 1973 address to the Army Judge Advocate General's School, Yale University law professor Joseph Bishop stressed the importance of the "swift, certain, and severe" disciplinary doctrine of military justice. The more civilianized military justice becomes, Bishop maintained, the more likely it will become "neither swift nor certain." For Bishop, perhaps one of the more constructive critics of military justice, the system proved it could function in peacetime and wartime. After all, "courts-martial did not sit in foxholes in any of our recent wars." The recent experience in Vietnam and the large force structure that looked likely to be in place in the near future, however, made it less likely that military justice would get any "simpler."[13] He recommended that the trend toward a permanent independent judiciary continue and encouraged the inclusion of more civilian judges in courts-martial and on the courts of military review. The bad conduct discharge should be abolished, and the number of courts able to give dishonorable discharges should be limited, because the difference between a bad conduct discharge and a dishonorable discharge was actually rather minimal. He also suggested that the general articles, Articles 133 and 134, be repealed and replaced by more specific articles that encompassed violations under the United States Penal Code. Bishop also wanted to abolish military jurisdiction over reservists not on active duty and make decisions of the Court of Military Appeals appealable to the United States Supreme Court via petition for certiorari, just as in state supreme courts and federal district courts.[14]

MACV commander and later army chief of staff Gen. William Westmoreland and Gen. George S. Prugh, MACV legal adviser from 1964 to 1966 and later judge advocate general of the army, coauthored an extensive critique of military justice in combat. Their findings were not positive. Punishment, they concluded, often "lacks meaningful deterrent power." Moreover, the legitimate attention given to due process had endangered the "ability of the forces to achieve their mission." For commanders, the shift in balance toward the one had weakened their power to ensure the other. Recognizing that such was the dilemma for military justice in a democratic society, Westmoreland and Prugh nonetheless warned that the system could not function as intended "in times of military stress." Written in response to several bills pending before Congress in 1980 that would further civilianize and weaken the "swift, certain and severe" standard of military justice, Westmoreland and Prugh blamed the courts, in particular the Court of Military Appeals, for moving the Uniform Code of Military Justice from its original purpose. The civilianization of the code was doing more harm than good, and Congress would have to steer the code back by statute. Civilianized military justice was all well and good in peacetime, and the code certainly performed well in that function. In war, however, the code did not "adequately accomplish the main purpose of preserving discipline expected of it when discipline is most sorely tested." In times of war, the code should be fair and honor the traditional judicial standards that Americans expected, but, according to Westmoreland and Prugh, some "discretion" had to be allowed. For example, the right to a competent attorney does not have to include transporting a civilian attorney "half way around the world" to represent a soldier in combat. Testimony before a sworn magistrate, including cross-examination, should be admissible in a military court if witnesses are unavailable because of discharge or rotation. The jurisdiction issue had to be resolved so that Americans who committed "serious offenses" could not "escape accountability." Separation from service should not be taken as immunity for crimes committed while in service. Westmoreland and Prugh included draft legislation in the article to make these adjustments, but Congress did not act on their recommendations.[15]

A 1983 study by the army judge advocate general offered similar solutions to the same concerns. Like Westmoreland's and Prugh's suggestions, the primary one was that the Uniform Code of Military Justice could not function effectively in a "general war." The system had become slow and cumbersome, and practical and logistical problems hindered the "swift, certain, and severe" purpose of military justice in wartime. The report recommended eliminating limitations on jurisdiction over offenses committed in prior service, shortening pretrial and posttrial procedures and reviews, allowing convicted soldiers to waive mandatory appeals, and authorizing video and audiotape records of trials and depositions instead of the old transcription system. It was hoped that these alterations to procedure and practice would speed up what had become very slow trials, especially general courts-martial.[16] These recommendations likewise fell on deaf ears. Congress seemed intent on keeping military justice more akin to the civilian form in the Military Justice Act of 1983, including granting military personnel the right to submit habeas corpus petitions to the United States Supreme Court, thus making the Supreme Court the final arbiter of the military justice system.[17]

Also in 1983, Earle F. Lasseter and James B. Thwing, both of the Staff Judge Advocate's Office at the Army Infantry Center, recommended much more drastic changes to the Uniform Code of Military Justice in an article in the *American Bar Association Journal*. The problem, as they put it, was that "there is concern whether the present system of military justice can be administered effectively during conflict. Many lawyers in the armed forces believe that a changed tradition of military justice, which no longer combines military law with military necessity, has caused a decline in discipline during peacetime and threatens real problems for its proper administration during conflict."[18]

Lasseter and Thwing noted that since the 1968 revision of the Uniform Code of Military Justice, the officer corps no longer fully understood the military justice system as they had before the revision. This lack of understanding and knowledge made commanders tentative and hesitant and thus less likely to effectively deal with discipline problems and serious criminal acts. Fearful of being accused of command influence, commanders had also relied too heavily on their staff judge advocates to resolve "quasi-legal problems" that were "appropriately" resolved by the commander. The "traditional roles that bound the commander to the soldier and the soldier to the commander" had been seriously eroded.[19]

Reliance on so-called expedient remedies, primarily the use of discharges to get rid of troublemakers, had also weakened the disciplinary effectiveness of military justice, as had the "perceived need" to civilianize the system. The inflexibility of the military justice system concerned Lasseter and Thwing most. During conflict, the system had proven inflexible despite its "expansive mood." To remedy these issues, Lasseter and Thwing recommended a separate code and *Manual for Courts-Martial* for combat use, with clear direction as to when combat conditions applied. In combat conditions, Article 15 punishments had to be streamlined to make them more immediately effective, as was the original intent of nonjudicial punishment. Courts-martial as well should be streamlined, allowing for only general courts-martial and special courts-martial without authority to give a punitive discharge. In both instances, the accused should have the right to be represented by qualified military, not civilian, counsel, and these trials should take place before a military judge rather than a panel of court members. Furthermore, they suggested that the Article 32 investigation be replaced by a "referral hearing" in which the government would have to establish jurisdiction and probable cause and together with the convening authority would have to agree that trial was indeed necessary.

To perform their duties in time of war, military lawyers and judges would have to accept some procedural and organizational changes. First, the army would have to implement its Army Legal Services Agency organizational model, which would coordinate appellate judiciary, field judiciary, and field trial and defense counsel, and would have to add a field trial advocate division in time of war. This organization would be responsible for the "technical" side of conducting investigations, preferring charges, and referring cases for trial to commanders. The advantage of such a system in combat is that it would remove the "technical decision making and processing of criminal matters" from command control. Second, as part of their staff structure, commanders should have so-called command judge advocates who would advise on military discipline, military affairs and administrative law, and the law of war. These lawyers would have to be well trained in the "peculiarities" of units in the field under combat conditions to be able to advise commanders effectively. Lasseter and Thwing believed such changes to the military justice system could make the system more effective in combat conditions without "sacrificing the bundle of rights" that ensure due process. What they had recommended certainly pushed the envelope of sacrificing some of those rights.[20]

An Army War College paper countered Lasseter and Thwing's apparent relegation of defense counsel in time of war. Theodore B. Borek, an army judge advocate, realized that in time of war qualified defense counsel is perhaps more necessary than under any other circumstances. Those subject to Article 15s in time of war should have access to proper representation and be able to be tried by court-martial if so requested. Combat circumstances should not, according to Borek, lessen due process.[21]

Military lawyers who served in Vietnam assessed the Uniform Code of Military Justice and the other duties they performed there. Many expressed the same concerns noted above, whereas others found the system functional and adequate. Much like the overall U.S. military experience in Vietnam, military justice suffered from the failure of leadership. The officer corps, "bloated in number and poorer in quality," deteriorated because of shortcomings in personnel, promotion, and rotation policies. Deficiencies in combat leadership, perhaps most of all, hurt the U.S. effort. Military justice suffered in kind, as permissiveness and failure to administer harsh discipline harmed unit cohesiveness and the military's ability to maintain order in rear as well as combat areas. As an army judge advocate, Capt. Norman G. Cooper, put it in 1973, "only leadership and adequate training can prevent another My Lai."[22]

A staff judge advocate for the Second Brigade of the Twenty-fifth Infantry Division, Capt. David Kull, noted the additional burdens placed upon judge advocates in the 1968 code revision that made already increasingly long investigations and trials even longer.[23] Maj. Curtis Olson, staff judge advocate of the First Marine Aircraft Wing, also lamented the civilianizing of the military justice system, in particular the delays and requests of defense counsel, which made trials last longer and hurt the disciplinary purpose of military justice. Olson said the code was indeed flawed, but the military legal community in Vietnam had made it work as well as they could.[24] Marine Corps colonel (later brigadier general) Duane Faw, III MAF legal officer, took a more pessimistic position. Faw considered that the code had failed miserably, as too much expediency and leeway resulted in too many cases not getting to trial and thus too many guilty marines going unpunished, which failed the disciplinary needs of the marines in Vietnam.[25]

Air force captain Loren H. Rosson Jr. disagreed. As a special court-martial judge at Bien Hoa with the Thirty-fifth Combat Support Squadron, Rosson felt that many military offenses could have easily been dealt with through Article 15s to ease the burden on trial judges. Yet, Rosson believed in the system and the rights it afforded the accused. In his words, "being in a war zone does not justify throwing out common sense or fair treatment. Neither does it mean that every infraction of the military rules and regulations warrants a court-martial."[26] Army captain David Bengston, staff judge advocate for the 199th Infantry, heavily criticized the negative impact of command influence upon soldiers' "faith in the military justice system."[27] Air Force captain John Ernest Casper, who prosecuted and defended dozens of cases with the 483rd Combat Support Group at Cam Rahn Bay, recalled that the attitude in Vietnam was "twisted" in the sense that everyone thought that since everyone else was doing it, it must be acceptable: "That viewpoint was very mischievous because it obliterated the difference between right and wrong. Thus, sleeping on post in a war zone became only an Article 15 offense." As for the Uniform Code of Military Justice, Casper felt it was "ineffective." The "value assumptions" that made up the code "either did not exist in Vietnam or did not seem very relevant in the context of the Vietnam experience of our personnel."[28]

Marine Corps lieutenant Clarke C. Barnes, a military lawyer with the Third Marine Division in Vietnam and later a trial judge for the Marine Corps, "absolutely" believed that the code worked. Barnes considered procedural delays, be they from defense requests or rocket attacks, "just another inconvenience that would pass; justice was dispensed in spite of the situation and if a trial took a few minutes longer it simply meant everyone was a few minutes closer to going home." Barnes claimed that the most important value from his experience in Vietnam was "the camaraderie, the team work, the urgency of it all . . . it perhaps made us more self-assured."[29]

Capt. John William Mayer, who ran the legal office for the 377th Combat Support Group at Tan Son Nhut, was impressed with the ability of people to get things done and the latitude that military lawyers were given to do their jobs. Returning to civilian practice and public service as a deputy district attorney, Mayer had a tough time adjusting to the eight-hour workday, five days a week after putting in twelve to fourteen hours a day, every day. He found himself frustrated with the hours other people kept when he would rather take care of something immediately rather than later.[30] Regardless of how they felt about the effectiveness of the code and other duties they performed, lawyers who served in Vietnam almost universally came away with an invaluable experience that prepared them well for continued military legal service or civilian practice.

Recent assessments of military justice and military law activities in Vietnam point to the positive. Frederic Borch, in his superb histories of judge advocates in combat since Vietnam, praised military lawyers in Vietnam for willingly taking on tasks that circumstances necessitated, from trial to claims to contracts to education. They had done unconventional things to make the system work in Vietnam. Borch is correct to refer to these advocates as "trailblazers." The "metamorphosis" of the roles military lawyers would play in U.S. combat actions after Vietnam was born of the varied legal experience of the Vietnam War.[31]

Gary D. Solis, author of the exceptional official Marine Corps history of military law in Vietnam and the intriguing recounting of the Son Thang trials, rightfully suggested that although the Korean War occurred just as the Uniform Code of Military Justice came into being, Vietnam was the first real combat test of the system. Thousands of courts-martial were tried, thus confirming that the system could "work." As for the Marine Corps lawyers themselves, Solis noted that although their exposure to combat danger was less than what the average marine infantryman faced, the "possibility of death was constant" for Marine Corps lawyers as they crisscrossed the I Corps combat zone to try cases and carry out their numerous other duties. Such conditions made their experience in Vietnam far different from that of their predecessors in other wars. Many military lawyers were not prepared, nor were they experienced enough to do what they had to do in Vietnam. They were not given the proper facilities, support, equipment, and hours, all of which, according to Solis, "hobbled not only the lawyers, but justice." As for the code itself, Solis maintained that it was an "excellent system" that the military would "make do with" whatever the circumstances.[32] Solis related perhaps the best quote on the Uniform Code of Military Justice from the Vietnam War by Marine Corps brigadier general Charles Cushman, an assistant judge advocate general of the navy. In response to being asked if the code would be effective in future conflicts, Cushman replied, "Would it work? Of course it would work. It would work with major flaws and major difficulties and major delays, but . . . you would make it work."[33] Arguably, that is what military lawyers have been doing ever since Vietnam.

Combat operations since Vietnam have involved similar issues and added new concerns but also solutions. Operation Urgent Fury in Grenada in 1983 found only a couple of judge advocates on the ground during hostilities. Military lawyers were swamped with the suddenness of the operation. With no preinvasion warning to the troops involved, few had taken care of personal legal affairs, such as wills and other family matters, and as a consequence were trying to resolve these affairs on Grenada. Military lawyers had not been included in operational planning and thus had to provide legal advice to commanders on issues ranging from prisoners of war to interpretation of *The Law of Land Warfare*. Restrictive rules of engagement needed deciphering, claims were processed in much the same way as in Vietnam, and directives had to be issued to prohibit collection of "war trophies" and to inform soldiers in the field of proper treatment of prisoners of war and other detainees captured during the operation. The shortcomings in Operation Urgent Fury from a military justice and military law perspective highlighted a need to establish norms for "operational law."[34]

In 1989, many of these issues had at least been addressed just in time for Operation Just Cause in Panama. This time, unlike Vietnam and Grenada, military lawyers had participated in drafting rules of engagement, had reviewed operational plans for possible international law and law of war problems, and had managed to provide soldiers legal advice before deployment. One judge advocate, Lt. Col. James J. Smith, staff judge advocate of the Eighty-second

Airborne Division, became the first military lawyer to make a combat para-chute jump, and within an hour of being on the ground he was at work inter-preting the law of war for commanders. Smith quickly and correctly advised that captured enemy equipment could be used by friendly forces and that enemy troops using a temple as fortification could be fired upon despite the cultural significance of the building. Claims, prisoners of war, treatment of foreign diplomats, and a court-martial for unpremeditated murder high-lighted the Panama military justice experience. Operational law had proven a success, and lawyers had become essential to a combat command staff.[35]

The fruition of these efforts and lessons would come in the Gulf War. The several months of Desert Shield followed by the few weeks of Desert Storm had military lawyers at the forefront. Contracts, claims, jurisdiction, legal ad-vice to service personnel, the added discipline issue of the alcohol ban, rules of engagement and law of war training, and a myriad of other issues kept these lawyers busy, just as they had in Vietnam. The major difference here, however, was that military lawyers were more deeply involved in providing legal advice to war planners. The operational law concept had really taken hold. Courts-martial were tried—the First Armored Division held three general courts-martial, one special court-martial, and six summary courts-martial and pro-cessed more than 100 Article 15s from December 1990 to April 1991. One soldier was convicted of intentionally inflicting injury on himself (a shot in the foot with an M-16) to avoid hazardous duty. He was sentenced to two years confinement, total forfeiture, and a bad conduct discharge. The conviction came just before the ground war began, sending a clear signal to the First Ar-mored that discipline would be enforced. Trials rather swiftly dealt with con-scientious objectors, disobeying an order from a superior officer, and muti-nous behavior (in this case a member of the Louisiana National Guard). Civilian contractors, however, once again avoided punishment for a variety of alleged offenses because of the lack of a declaration of war and the failure of the Saudi and Kuwaiti governments to prosecute them. War crimes also arose, but in this case it was whether or not to try Iraqi military and political leaders for so-called crimes against humanity.[36]

Although taking place in a radically different context, U.S. military opera-tions in Haiti in 1994 and 1995 also represented a major step forward for the operational law concept. The Center for Law and Military Operations at the Army Judge Advocate General's School noted many improvements in organi-zation and implementation of the many roles played by judge advocates dur-ing the Haitian intervention. Judge advocates from all services participated in operational planning, including writing rules of engagement and general orders, setting procedures for foreign claims, and outlining processes for seizing property. Judge advocates accompanied U.S. forces into Haiti, a mostly unopposed intervention, and set up shop for claims, criminal investigation, legal assistance to U.S. personnel, and operational advice for commanders. The conditions were less than ideal, as described by the Tenth Mountain Division's staff judge advocate: "There is a[n] ... impact on legal operations when, for the first three weeks of the operation, everybody (lawyers included) are eating nothing but MREs, fighting for scarce water supplies, scrounging for a place to sleep, not having electricity, digging slit trenches, wearing full battle dress (flak vests, Kevlar, and locked and loaded weapons), and otherwise concerned with survival while trying to also provide legal services."[37]

In Haiti, judge advocates were heavily involved in nation-building operations that focused on establishing order and restoring the authority of the legitimate government. As in Vietnam, respect for the rule of law was a primary objective. Judge advocates also coordinated civic action efforts to assist the Haitian people, including authorization of medical supplies, food relief, and construction of infrastructure. Military justice played its traditional and necessary role, but training and professionalism continued to pay dividends, as only six courts-martial convened in Haiti. Granted, other courts-martial occurred at home stations and commanders issued hundreds of nonjudicial punishments, but the low level of military crimes in Haiti, according to the Center for Law and Military Operations report, resulted from the system's working as a deterrent. One area of concern with courts-martial, however, was convening authority. Task force commanders in Haiti could only convene courts-martial with the approval of the Secretary of Defense. To streamline and solidify chain of command, the report strongly recommended giving task force commanders convening authority.[38]

The report also stressed the importance of being prepared to conduct courts-martial and provide legal assistance to U.S. military personnel. Despite the difficult conditions of a military campaign, conducting courts-martial in a dignified, organized manner with as much public exposure as possible served deterrence, preserved soldiers' faith in due process of military justice, and showed local peoples the virtues of due process and respect for the rule of law. Legal assistance to deploying forces again received attention, as the report encouraged judge advocates to be better prepared to offer advice on wills, taxes, and other legal matters in the rush of deployment. Legal questions from commanders regarding war trophies, PX privileges, investigations, claims, contracts, and other issues all required advice from military lawyers. In addition to commending preparation procedures already in place, the report reminded judge advocates to fill their footlockers with forms, manuals, and whatever else they might need to do their jobs, just as Capt. Harrison Braxton had done when he left for Vietnam in 1963. The growing use of technology also found its way into the report, warning that in future operations lawyers should make sure that all laptop computers, software, and compact disc–read-only memory (CD-ROM) reference material were compatible across the services.[39]

Operations in the Balkans from 1995 to 1998 also challenged military justice and military law. Perhaps nowhere was establishing respect for the rule of law as critical as in Bosnia. To bring order from disorder and rebuild capable institutions to maintain and administer justice that the public and the various warring factions would abide by and respect was a formidable task.[40] Judge advocates in the Balkans had to interpret at least four different status-of-forces agreements and various treaties between U.S. and coalition forces and had to write and interpret rules of engagement for young U.S. soldiers serving in the midst of three battle-hardened armies, all in addition to claims, contracts, legal assistance, and military justice duties common for any operation.

The Center for Law and Military Operations report on judge advocate activities in the Balkans urged planners to continue using judge advocates in preoperational planning and recommended that all judge advocates deployed in such operations be given intensive briefing to heighten their operational and situational awareness once on the ground. Regarding military justice, the report cited the continuing problem of jurisdiction and convening authority and recommended that jurisdiction policy and convening authority issues be clarified and established before deployment. As in Haiti, the most common crimes in the Balkans requiring military justice attention were military crimes, such as disobedience, sleeping on post, and violations of general orders. Very few courts-martial occurred in Bosnia, according to the report, again testifying to the disciplined nature of U.S. military forces. As in Vietnam, judge advocates in the Balkans needed transport and clerical support and needed to be flexible and practical in dealing with unexpected problems. The report noted how well judge advocates performed under difficult conditions and applauded that ability to be flexible and practical. This seems to be the great tradition of judge advocate performance—flexibility and practicality are key characteristics that make judge advocates successful in their roles in combat and noncombat deployments.[41]

The war on terror has brought U.S. military lawyers back into the difficult task of nation-building, complicated by the ill-defined legal definitions of "detainees" and torture. In Afghanistan, military lawyers provided guidance for establishing a military justice system in the new Afghan National Army, much as they had done years earlier in South Vietnam. In Operation Iraqi Freedom and the subsequent occupation of Iraq, military lawyers have been called upon to investigate, prosecute, and defend a range of violations of the Uniform Code of Military Justice, including murder, rape (in several of these cases the victims have been fellow soldiers, perhaps reflecting the new gender mix of U.S. combat arms), abuse and even murder of prisoners of war and detainees, and desertion. Civilian lawyers, too, have participated in trials involving U.S. military personnel in Iraq. Holding courts-martial at a unit's home station versus on location is becoming the norm, reflecting the increasing acceptance of this practice since the first Gulf War. The legal status of captured enemy combatants continues to be a controversial legal and political question. Operational law remains an important role for military lawyers, as they are now firmly part of operational planning, writing and interpreting rules of engagement, and giving on-the-ground advice to commanders. In both Iraq and Afghanistan, military lawyers have also dealt with contracts and claims and have provided legal assistance to U.S. forces, much as they did in Vietnam.[42]

Establishing the rule of law in Iraq has been especially critical to the success of U.S. policy there. Conflict between Western and Islamic conceptions of rule of law complicates the situation, just as similar differences between U.S. and Asian ideals did in Vietnam. Maintaining order, reestablishing civil and criminal courts, and providing a foundation from which the Iraqi people can build faith in justice, all after decades of authoritarian rule followed by a U.S. invasion and occupation, is at the very least an overwhelming task. Even creating sustainable security through U.S.-trained Iraqi police forces has met with halting success because of the intense insurgency. Establishing the rule of law has arguably not occurred as of 2006, although the combat phase of Operation Iraqi Freedom has ended. Perhaps the greatest test in firmly grounding the rule of law in postwar Iraq will be the trial of ousted Iraqi dictator Saddam Hussein for war crimes and crimes against humanity and the establishment of a legitimate Iraqi government. As an Iraqi court hears Hussein's case, U.S. policymakers hope the Iraqi people, as well as the world, will see that Western, democratic concepts of justice and due process can be established in countries that have no such tradition. Only the future will tell.[43]

Status-of-forces agreements and jurisdiction remain thorny legal and diplo-matic issues. The status-of-forces agreement with Saudi Arabia has recently been under fire from the Saudi government, and agreements with Uzbekistan, Pakistan, and other nations serving as staging areas for operations in Afghani-stan apparently were not complete until well after operations commenced. Status-of-forces agreements in Japan and South Korea come under fire from the Japanese and South Korean public only in high-profile cases, such as rape or death. In South Korea, the unfortunate deaths of two girls who were run over by a U.S. troop carrier on maneuvers sparked protests in Seoul. The two soldiers driving the vehicle were acquitted in a court-martial, which had juris-diction according to the status-of-forces agreement. The verdict, however, an-gered the South Korean public; as a result, both U.S. and South Korean author-ities have agreed to review the status-of-forces agreement between the two countries. South Korea would now like to exercise jurisdiction over U.S. troops charged with offenses against South Koreans while on duty.[44]

Congress tried to resolve the jurisdictional problem once and for all with the passage of the Military Extraterritorial Jurisdiction Act in 2000, which is facing its first real test in Operation Iraqi Freedom. Under the act, U.S. citi-zens accompanying the armed forces or working under contract with the armed forces, including spouses and employees of civilian contractors, can be arrested by military police, charged, and tried in federal court if the Uniform Code of Military Justice does not take primary jurisdiction. The offense must be committed on foreign soil and be the equivalent of a felony punishable by at least a year imprisonment under federal statute. With over 30,000 contrac-tors with U.S. military forces in Iraq and some high-profile criminal allega-tions against contractors or their employees, the Military Extraterritorial Ju-risdiction Act may plug the jurisdictional hole that plagued the United States in Vietnam. The one loophole would be for offenses that do not equate a fel-ony under federal law. Instead of being proactive, as the lessons-learned stud-ies from military operations in the 1990s recommended, however, the De-fense Department did not have in place guidelines for implementing the Military Extraterritorial Jurisdiction Act until 2004. Even then, there seemed to be a disconnect between the Defense Department and the Justice Depart-ment—reminiscent of the spat between the Defense Department and the State Department over jurisdiction waivers in Vietnam—on how to put the act into practice.[45]

Consider as well the U.S. government's opposition to the International Criminal Court, especially with regard to war crimes and jurisdiction.

Although the State Department claims that the International Criminal Court treaty fails to provide protection against politically motivated abuse of due process, the real issue lies in the potential surrender of jurisdiction over U.S. military personnel accused of criminal acts while serving abroad.[46] With U.S. forces serving across the globe and so many humanitarian or regional conflict interventions possible, U.S. soldiers are certainly potential targets of the International Criminal Court. The United States has attempted to modify the treaty to include "opt-out" clauses for certain crimes and add a complex jurisdictional approval process that would require the approval of both the state where the offense was committed and the state of the nationality of the accused. U.S. objections to the International Criminal Court focus on the "indefensible overreach of jurisdiction" the court would have over signatories and nonparty states alike.[47]

Congress and the U.S. public continue to be content with the progressive civilianization of military justice. The system can never be fully civilian because of its purpose, but perhaps such is life for military justice in a democratic society. As the world becomes more complex and yet smaller because of the diverse manifestations of globalization, the U.S. military will have to further rely upon a well-trained and experienced judge advocate general's corps to do all of the things it did in Vietnam and now much more. It is indeed fortunate that as U.S. military operations change to react to new challenges and threats, military lawyers and civilian academics who study military law continue to discuss and debate the direction in which military justice and the duties and activities of military lawyers should evolve.[48]

In Southeast Asia, fighting an insurgency under limiting circumstances while trying to build legitimate government and order out of a corrupt regime proved an awesome challenge that was not confined to U.S. military might and political will. These circumstances also mightily challenged the U.S. military justice system and the lawyers charged with carrying out both the system and their numerous other duties and functions. Under these restrictive conditions in Vietnam, the system and its lawyers performed admirably well. And what of the legacy that U.S. military justice and other military law activities left on Vietnam? Gen. George S. Prugh's official army history of MACV legal duties in Vietnam, written after the U.S. war but while the South Vietnamese government still existed, hoped that the experience had left the Vietnamese with an appreciation of "American law and respect for the potential of law in the conduct of affairs of a free and civilized people."[49] Perhaps it did, but thirty years of communist authoritarian rule since then may have dimmed whatever positive memories the Vietnamese people had of U.S.-style justice and rule of law.

William G. Eckhardt, leader of the My Lai prosecution team at Fort McPherson and later professor of law at the University of Missouri at Kansas City Law School, outlined what for him were the key components of modern U.S. military doctrine in an article on the My Lai trials. These included civilian control of the military; respect for the rule of law, including the law of war; and respect for the rights of soldiers as individuals. These same components of military doctrine, Eckhardt suggested, are also among the key components to democratization, which include respect for the rule of law and individual rights.[50] If the military justice experience in Vietnam, and that of the military lawyers who practiced there, teaches nothing else, it certainly offers proof that use of force and subsequent nation-building cannot succeed without these components prominently and effectively implemented by the "boots on the ground"—that is, by military lawyers and the system they serve and represent.[51] This, to be sure, was one of the objectives of U.S. military justice in Vietnam, and one that may yet be realized in Iraq, Afghanistan, and wherever else U.S. military justice and military lawyers are in the vanguard, so long as democratic nation-building remains the espoused policy of the United States.

NOTES

ABBREVIATIONS

AD	Advisory Division
AF	Air Force
AFIN	Air Force Input
AO	Administrative Office
CG	Commanding General
CH	Corona Harvest
CMH	United States Army Center for Military History, Washington, D.C.
COMNAVFOR	Commander, Naval Forces, Vietnam
COMUSMACV	Commander, United States Military Assistance Command, Vietnam
CY	Current Year
FMF PAC	Fleet Marine Force, Pacific
GCM	General Court-Martial
GVN	Government of (South) Vietnam
HQ	Headquarters
III MAF	III Marine Amphibious Force
IV CTZ	Fourth Corps Zone
JA	Judge Advocate
JAG	Judge Advocate General
LBN	Long Binh
LMDC	Lawyers' Military Defense Committee
MACCZ IV GA	Military Assistance Command Corps Zone 4 General Administration
MACJ03	Military Assistance Command Assistant Chief of Staff for Operations
MACJA	Military Assistance Command Judge Advocate
MACV	Military Assistance Command, Vietnam
MCHC	Marine Corps Historical Center
MJVN Files	Author's personal research files on military justice in Vietnam, containing letters and questionnaires from veteran JAG officers
PACAF	Pacific Air Forces
RG 319 RAS	Record Group 319 Records of the Army Staff, United States National Archives and Records Administration, College Park, Maryland
RG 472 USFSEA	Record Group 472 Records of U.S. Forces in Southeast Asia, United States National Archives and Records Administration, College Park, Maryland
RVN	Republic of Vietnam
SJA	Staff Judge Advocate
SOP	Standard Operating Procedure
SPCM	Special Court-Martial
USACV	United States Army Support Command, Vietnam
USAF	United States Air Force

USAFHRA	United States Air Force Historical Research Agency, Maxwell Air Force Base, Alabama
USARV	United States Army, Republic of Vietnam
USARYIS	United States Army, Ryukyu Islands
USCMA	United States Court of Military Appeals
USMAC	United States Military Assistance Command
USMACV	United States Military Assistance Command, Vietnam
USNARA	United States National Archives and Records Administration, College Park, Maryland
VNIT	Vietnam Interview Tape Collection, United States Army Center of Military History

PREFACE

1. George S. Prugh, *Law at War: Vietnam 1964–1973* (Washington, D.C.: Department of the Army, 1975), 15–26.

2. D. Michael Shafer, *Deadly Paradigms: The Failure of U.S. Counterinsurgency Policy* (Princeton, N.J.: Princeton University Press, 1988), 115–119; Jeffrey Record, *The Wrong War: Why We Lost in Vietnam* (Annapolis, Md.: Naval Institute Press, 1998), 122–140.

CHAPTER 1. A NEW CODE FOR A DIFFERENT KIND OF WAR

1. The British "Rules and Articles" are quoted in full in William Winthrop, *Military Law and Precedents*, 2nd ed. (Washington, D.C.: Government Printing Office, 1920), App. VII.

2. Jonathan Lurie, *Arming Military Justice,* Vol. 1: *The Origins of the United States Court of Military Appeals, 1775–1950* (Princeton, N.J.: Princeton University Press, 1992), 3.

3. Jay Siegel, *Origins of the United States Navy Judge Advocate General's Corps: A History of Legal Administration in the United States Navy, 1775–1967* (Washington, D.C.: Government Printing Office, 1998), 22; Gerald F. Crump, "A History of the Structure of Military Justice in the United States, 1775–1920," *Air Force Law Review* 16, 4 (Winter 1974): 43–45.

4. United States Army, Judge Advocate General Corps, *The Army Lawyer: A History of the Judge Advocate General Corps, 1775–1975* (Buffalo, N.Y.: William S. Hein, 1993), 10–14 [hereafter *Army Lawyer*]; Maurer Maurer, "Military Justice under General Washington," *Military Affairs* 28 (Spring 1964): 8–16; Lurie, *Arming Military Justice,* 1: 5.

5. Lurie, *Arming Military Justice,* 1: 5–6.

6. Ibid., 1: 8–10.

7. Siegel, *Origins of the United States Navy Judge Advocate General's Corps,* 64–68.

8. Crump, "A History of the Structure of Military Justice," 49.

9. Siegel, *Origins of the United States Navy Judge Advocate General's Corps,* 75–88.

10. Crump, "A History of the Structure of Military Justice," 50–51; Siegel, *Origins of the United States Navy Judge Advocate General's Corps,* 105–108.

11. Siegel, *Origins of the United States Navy Judge Advocate General's Corps*, 108–119; James E. Valle, *Rocks and Shoals: Order and Discipline in the Old Navy, 1800–1861* (Annapolis, Md.: Naval Institute Press, 1980), 56.

12. *Army Lawyer*, 49–52.

13. Crump, "A History of the Structure of Military Justice," 51.

14. Quoted in Edward F. Sherman, "Justice in the Military," in James Finn, ed., *Conscience and Command: Justice and Discipline in the Military* (New York: Random House, 1971), 23–24.

15. United States Army, *A Manual for Courts-Martial, Courts of Inquiry and Retiring Boards, and Other Procedure under Military Law* (Washington, D.C.: Government Printing Office, 1916).

16. Robert O. Rollman, "Of Crimes, Courts-Martial, and Punishment: A Short History of Military Justice," *United States Air Force JAG Law Review* 11, 2 (Spring 1969): 218–219; *Army Lawyer*, 107–112.

17. United States Navy, *Forms of Procedure for General and Summary Courts-Martial, Courts of Inquiry, Investigations, Naval and Marine Examining and Retiring Boards, Etc., Etc.* (Washington, D.C.: Government Printing Office, 1896).

18. Siegel, *Origins of the United States Navy Judge Advocate General's Corps*, 239–242, 277–286.

19. *Army Lawyer*, 116.

20. Lurie, *Arming Military Justice*, 1: 128.

21. William T. Generous Jr., *Swords and Scales: The Development of the Uniform Code of Military Justice* (Port Washington, N.Y.: Kennikat Press, 1973), 5; *Army Lawyer*, 113–120, 125–127.

22. Sherman, "Justice in the Military," 24–25; *Army Lawyer*, 128–135.

23. See United States Congress, Senate, Committee on Military Affairs, *Hearings on Trials by Court-Martial before the Senate Committee on Military Affairs*, 65th Cong., 3rd sess. (Washington, D.C.: Government Printing Office, 1919), and United States Congress, Senate, Committee on Military Affairs, *Hearings on the Establishment of Military Justice before a Subcommittee of the Senate Committee on Military Affairs*, 66th Cong., 1st sess. (Washington, D.C.: Government Printing Office, 1919); *Army Lawyer*, 128–138. Lurie described the Ansell-Crowder dispute in detail in *Arming Military Justice*, 1: 46–126.

24. Rollman, "Of Crimes, Courts-Martial, and Punishment," 219–220; *Army Lawyer*, 136–138.

25. Siegel, *Origins of the Navy Judge Advocate General's Corps*, 298–299, 205–306, 310–316.

26. Generous, *Swords and Scales*, 13.

27. *Army Lawyer*, 159–160.

28. Sherman, "Justice in the Military," 25–26; Generous, *Swords and Scales*, 14.

29. United States Department of War, *Report of the Committee on Military Justice* (Washington, D.C.: Government Printing Office, 1947); Luther C. West, "A History of Command Influence on the Military Judicial System," *UCLA Law Review* 18 (1970–1971): 73–78; Lurie, *Arming Military Justice*, 1: 137–139.

30. United States Navy, "Report of the Ballantine Board to the Secretary of the Navy" (Department of the Navy, April 1946); Lurie, *Arming Military Justice*, 1: 131–132; Siegel, *Origins of the Navy Judge Advocate General's Corps*, 442–457.

31. United States Navy, "Report and Recommendations to the Secretary of the Navy [on the *Articles of the Government of the Navy* and Courts-Martial Procedure]" (Department of the Navy, November 21, 1945); Siegel, *Origins of the Navy Judge Advocate General's Corps*, 463–465; Lurie, *Arming Military Justice*, 1: 132–134.

32. Siegel, *Origins of the Navy Judge Advocate General's Corps*, 466–479; Lurie, *Arming Military Justice*, 1: 132–134.

33. *Army Lawyer*, 96–97.

34. Siegel, *Origins of the Navy Judge Advocate General's Corps*, 481–490.

35. *Army Lawyer*, 198–199; Lurie, *Arming Military Justice*, 1: 150–174, 209–232; West, "A History of Command Influence in the Military," 78–79.

36. West, "A History of Command Influence in the Military," 77–86; Lurie, *Arming Military Justice*, 1: 233–254.

37. The Uniform Code of Military Justice is codified as Title 10, *United States Code,* by act of Congress in 1956.

38. United States Department of Defense, *Manual for Courts-Martial, United States* (Washington, D.C: Government Printing Office, 1951).

39. *Army Lawyer*, 203–209. The Military Justice Act of 1983 provided for review of cases from the Military Court of Appeals by the Supreme Court, which makes the Supreme Court technically the final arbiter. See Lurie, *Arming Military Justice*, for a complete history of the Court of Military Appeals.

40. *Army Lawyer*, 209–211. See, for example, the description of the Gilbert case (210–211). Gilbert, an officer, was convicted and sentenced to death for misbehavior before the enemy. The board of review found insufficient evidence to support the death sentence. The army judge advocate general recommended commuting Gilbert's sentence to dismissal and thirty years imprisonment at hard labor, which President Truman accepted. The case was used as a benchmark for similar offenses, thus allowing the judge advocate general through the review process to mitigate excessive sentences from courts-martial in the field in Korea.

41. Ibid., 214–217.

42. See McElroy v. United States, 359 U.S. 904; 79 S. Ct. 580 (1959) and Toth v. Quarles, 350 U.S. 11 (1955).

43. Siegel, *Origins of the Navy Judge Advocate General's Corps*, 509–511.

44. Ibid., App. H, A87–A92.

45. *Army Lawyer*, 236–237.

46. See Miranda v. Arizona, 384 U.S. 436 (1966) and Mapp v. Ohio 367 U.S. 643 (1961).

47. Sam Ervin Jr., "The Military Justice Act of 1968," *Military Law Review* 45 (July 1969): 77–79.

48. Joseph E. Ross, "The Military Justice Act of 1968: Historical Background," *JAG Journal* (May–June 1969): 125–127.

49. Ervin, "The Military Justice Act of 1968," 78–82; Ross, "The Military Justice Act of 1968," 127–128.

50. Ervin, "The Military Justice Act of 1968," 83–84.

51. Edward F. Sherman, "The Civilianization of Military Law," *Maine Law Review* 22 (1970): 88–103.

CHAPTER 2. LAWYERS IN THE VANGUARD

1. H. Harrison Braxton Jr., letter to the author, February 19, 1998, MJVN Files. This citation also refers to the next ten paragraphs.

2. George S. Prugh, *Law at War: Vietnam 1964–1973* (Washington, D.C.: Department of the Army, 1975), 3–14.

3. James M. Granger to Lt. Col. Gary D. Solis, June 1, 1988, *Marines in Military Law* research files, USNARA; W. Hays Parks to Lt. Col. Gary D. Solis, December 22, 1988, ibid.; Clarke C. Barnes to Lt. Col. Gary D. Solis, December 10, 1986, ibid. This citation also refers to the next four paragraphs.

4. Discipline and Criminal Law, Vietnam Monograph, Box 3, RG 319 RAS; Gary D. Solis, *Trial by Fire: Marines and Military Law in Vietnam* (Washington, D.C.: Marine Corps History and Museums Division, 1989), 102.

5. Discipline and Criminal Law, Vietnam Monograph, Box 3, RG 319 RAS.

6. Ibid.

7. Christian Appy, *Working Class War: American Combat Soldiers and Vietnam* (Chapel Hill: University of North Carolina Press, 1993), 22–28.

8. Ibid., 31–33; Guenter Lewy, *America in Vietnam* (New York: Oxford University Press, 1978), 160.

9. United States Congress, Senate, Committee on Appropriations, *Department of Defense Appropriations for Fiscal Year 1970: Hearings before the Subcommittee of the Committee on Appropriations, Part 3,* 91st Cong., 1st sess. (Washington, D.C.: Government Printing Office, 1969), 299, 355–356; United States Congress, House of Representatives, Committee on Appropriations, *Department of Defense Appropriations of 1972: Hearings before a Subcommittee of the Committee on Appropriations, Part 9,* 92nd Cong., 1st sess. (Washington, D.C.: Government Printing Office, 1971), 578.

10. Lewy, *America in Vietnam,* 154–155.

11. United States Congress, House of Representatives, Committee on Appropriations, *Department of Defense Appropriations of 1972,* 608.

12. MACCZ-IV-GA Instruction in the Military Justice Act of 1968 in the IV CTZ, July 24, 1969, HQ MACV SJA AO, Box 5, File 401-02, Court Martial Administration Files, RG 472 USFSEA; Discipline and Criminal Law, Vietnam Monograph, Box 3, RG 319 RAS; Staff Judge Advocate Military Justice Conference, May 24, 1969, Long Binh, HQ MACV SJA AO General Records, Box 5, File 401-02, Military Justice Conference, May 24, 1969, RG 472 USFSEA; Solis, *Trial by Fire,* 102.

13. Staff Judge Advocate, COMNAVFOR, to Commander, U.S. Naval Support Activity, Saigon, April 21, 1969, HQ MACV Naval Advisory Group, JA Office General Records, Box 2, File 201-09A, Law Center 1969, RG 472 USFSEA.

14. A Judge Advocate General Activity Input to Project Corona Harvest on Legal Support of U.S. Air Operations in Southeast Asia, January 1, 1965– March 31, 1968, Revised April 22, 1970, CH 0214963, 81–83, USAFHRA.

15. Robert D. Heinl Jr., "The Collapse of the Armed Forces," *Armed Forces Journal* (June 7, 1971): 32–33.

16. William P. Homans Jr., Lawyers Military Defense Committee, to General Creighton W. Abrams, Commanding General, MACV, September 2, 1970, SJA General Records, Box 2, File 410-02, LMDC General, RG 472 USFSEA; "Civilian Lawyers to Aid Viet GIs—Free,"

Stars and Stripes (September 7, 1970), photocopy in Box 2, File 410-02, LMDC General, RG 472 USFSEA.

17. Maj. Gen. W. G. Donovan, Chief of Staff, MACV, to William P. Homans Jr., September 9, 1970, SJA General Records, Box 2, File 410-02, LMDC General, RG 472 USFSEA.

18. Ibid.; release form for LMDC lawyer David F. Addlestone, December 3, 1970, SJA General Records, Box 2, File 410-02, LMDC General, RG 472 USFSEA.

19. Memorandum, United Press International (UPI) Press Release of March 9, 1972, MACV SJA AO General Records, Box 5, File 401-08, Alleged Conspiracy, RG 472 USFSEA. LMDC lawyers pressured the army to release seven of the soldiers in question because the army had no evidence to hold them. Two of the ten were in the drug rehabilitation facility at Long Binh stockade, and one had already rotated back to the United States. The ten allegedly offered a $500 reward for the killing of their company commander. The seven were released from Long Binh after a UPI story on the case. All charges were dropped, although the file implies that at least a few of the soldiers were discharged for other reasons.

20. Prugh, *Law at War*, 82; Frederic L. Borch, *Judge Advocates in Vietnam: Army Lawyers in Southeast Asia, 1959–1975* (Fort Leavenworth, Kans.: United States Army Command and General Staff College Press, 2004), 40.

21. "Claims Administration," Vietnam Monograph, Box 3, RG 319 RAS.

22. Ibid.; Borch, *Judge Advocates in Vietnam*, 57.

23. MACJA Historical Report, 3rd Quarter CY 67, MACV MACJ03 Military History Branch Histories, Background Files, Box 81, File 206-02 1/5-2-3B, MACJA Historical Summaries (1967), RG 472 USFSEA.

24. Prugh, *Law at War*, 83–84.

25. Study of Foreign Claims Operations in Vietnam, January 1, 1972, HQ MACV SJA, Advisory Division General Records, Box 21, File 403-11, Foreign Claims Files (1972), RG 472 USFSEA.

26. Ibid.

27. Military Justice Activities Report, March 17, 1967, MACV MACJ03 Military History Branch Histories, Background Files, Box 81, File 206-02 1/5-2-3B, MACJA Historical Summaries (1967), RG 472 USFSEA; Borch, *Judge Advocates in Vietnam*, 57.

28. Study of Foreign Claims Operations in Vietnam, January 1, 1972, HQ MACV SJA, Advisory Division General Records, Box 21, File 403-11, Foreign Claims Files (1972), RG 472 USFSEA.

29. Naval Advisory Group General Records, Judge Advocate Office, Box 3, File 201-09A, Foreign Claims (1970), RG 472 USFSEA. This citation also refers to the next four paragraphs.

30. Mai Ban-PCF 97 Collision, January 24, 1969, Naval Advisory Group JA Office, General Records, Box 2, File 201-09A, RG 472 USFSEA. This citation also refers to the next paragraph.

31. Foreign Claims (1970), Naval Advisory Group JA Office, General Records, Box 3, File 201-09A, RG 472 USFSEA. This citation also refers to the next paragraph.

32. Naval Advisory Group General Records, Judge Advocate Office, Box 3, File 201-09A, Foreign Claims (1970), RG 472 USFSEA.

33. Study of Foreign Claims Operations in Vietnam, January 1, 1972, HQ MACV SJA Advisory Division, General Records, Box 21, File 403-11, Foreign Claims Files (1972), RG 472 USFSEA.

34. Monthly Claims Report, MAJ JA, June 9, 1966, MACV MAJ03 Military History Background Files, Box 53, File 206-02/13-20, SJA Monthly Historical Summaries (1966), RG 472 USFSEA.

35. "Claims Administration," Vietnam Monograph, Box 3, RG 319 RAS.

36. Morrison v. United States, U.S.D.C., M.D. Ga., Civil No. 822 (1970), in Morrison Case, HQ MACV SJA Administrative Office General Records, Box 2, File 401-02, Coordination—Claims, RG 472 USFSEA; Borch, *Judge Advocates in Vietnam*, 56–57. See Foster v. United States, 120 Ct. Cl. 93, 98 F. Supp. 34 (1951), *cert. denied* 343 U.S. 919 (1952).

37. "Claims Administration," Vietnam Monograph, Box 3, RG 319 RAS.

38. Borch, *Judge Advocates in Vietnam*, 92–93.

39. Prugh, *Law at War*, 84; PACAF JAG Evaluation, CH0008100, May 5, 1969, USAFHRA.

40. Solatia Payments, January 2, 1971, HQ MACV SJA Advisory Division, General Records, Box 5, File 403-11, RG 472 USFSEA.

41. Transfer of Responsibility for Solatia Program in Vietnam, March 12, 1969, HQ MACV SJA Advisory Division, General Records, Box 5, File 402-01, RG 472 USFSEA.

42. Solatia Payment Procedures, August 25, 1968, HQ MACV SJA Advisory Division, General Records, Box 5, File 402-01, RG 472 USFSEA; Solatia Procedures, March 1, 1972, HQ MACV SJA Advisory Division, General Records, Box 14, File 403-11, RG 472 USFSEA; Borch, *Judge Advocates in Vietnam*, 40.

43. Joseph A. Bohrer, letter to the author, February 9, 1998, MJVN Files. This citation also refers to the next paragraph and extract.

44. Case File: Solatia Payment to Nguyen Van Hon, HQ MACV SJA Advisory Division, General Records, Box 14, File 403-11, RG 472 USFSEA. This citation also refers to the next seven paragraphs.

CHAPTER 3. JURISDICTION FOR U.S. MILITARY AND CIVILIAN PERSONNEL IN VIETNAM

1. In the Uniform Code of Military Justice, "time of war" is used to expand jurisdiction over civilians "serving with or accompanying a force in the field" (Article 2 [10]); to initiate different statutes of limitations (Article 43 [e] and [f]); and to enforce more severe punishments, including the death penalty, for offenses considered critical during war, such as improper use of countersign, misconduct as a prisoner of war, espionage, and misbehavior as a sentinel (Articles 85 [c], 90 [2], 101, 105, 106, and 113). See William C. Westmoreland and George S. Prugh, "Judges in Command: The Judicialized Uniform Code of Military Justice in Combat," *Harvard Journal of Law and Public Policy* 3 (1980): 4n5.

2. George F. Westerman, "Military Justice in the Republic of Vietnam," *Military Law Review* 31 (January 1966): 157–158.

3. Richard A. Hunt, *Pacification: The American Struggle for Vietnam's Hearts and Minds* (Boulder, Colo.: Westview Press, 1995), 2–3, 131, 276–277.

4. Francis FitzGerald, *Fire in the Lake: The Vietnamese and the Americans in Vietnam* (New York: Vintage Books, 1989), 435–441; Gary R. Hess, *Vietnam and the United States: Origins and Legacy of War*, rev. ed. (New York: Twayne Publishers, 1998), 99–100.

5. "Multilateral Mutual Defense Assistance in Indochina, December 23, 1950," in *United States Treaties and Other International Agreements, Vol. 3, Part 2, 1952* (Washington, D.C.: Government Printing Office, 1954), 275–362.

6. Legal Status of Visiting Forces in Vietnam, draft, Box 3, Vietnam Monograph, RG 319 RAS.

7. For example, in 1966 USARV reported 127 "serious" incidents (rape, homicide, attempted homicide, aggravated assault, and so on) allegedly committed by U.S. military personnel against Vietnamese. The number rose to 246 in 1967. Courts-martial of black-market and currency violations, which often involved Vietnamese, increased from 35 in 1966 to 64 in 1967 for all services. SJA Monthly Historical Summaries (1966), MACV MACJ03 Military History Background Files, Box 53, File 206-02/13-20, RG 472 USFSEA; Historical Summaries (1967), MACV MACJ03 Military History Branch Histories, Background Files, Box 81, File 206-02 1/5-2-3B, RG 472 USFSEA.

8. MACV SJA GCM Jurisdiction, January 24, 1965, HQ MACV SJA Administrative Office, Box 5, File 401-07, Jurisdiction, RG 472 USFSEA.

9. General Court-Martial Jurisdiction, January 22, 1965, HQ MACV SJA Administrative Office, Box 5, File 401-07, Jurisdiction, RG 472 USFSEA.

10. U.S. v. Sweeny, CMA 17355 (1964).

11. MACV JA General Court-Martial Jurisdiction, MACV SJA, October 1, 1964, HQ MACV SJA Administrative Office, Box 5, File 401-07, Jurisdiction, RG 472 USFSEA.

12. Effects of General Court-Martial Jurisdiction on Discipline within Army Component, USMACV, no date, HQ MACV SJA Administrative Office, Box 5, File 401-07, Jurisdiction, RG 472 USFSEA.

13. Ibid.

14. Memorandum for the Chief of Staff, General Court-Martial Jurisdiction for COM USMACV, October 5, 1964, HQ MACV SJA Administrative Office, Box 5, File 401-07, RG 472 USFSEA.

15. Injection of Additional Legal Personnel into Vietnam, HQ MACV SJA Administrative Office, Box 5, File 401-07, Jurisdiction, RG 472 USFSEA; Additional Administrative Personnel Other than Legal Personnel Required if General Court Martial Authority Granted to CG USASCV, HQ MACV SJA Administrative Office, Box 5, File 401-07, RG 472 USFSEA.

16. Additional Administrative Personnel Other than Legal Personnel Required if General Court Martial Authority Granted to CG USASCV, HQ MACV SJA Administrative Office, Box 5, File 401-07, RG 472 USFSEA.

17. Department of State to Embassy, Saigon, No. 661, September 14, 1964, HQ MACV SJA Administrative Office, Box 5, File 401-07, Jurisdiction, RG 472 USFSEA.

18. MACV SJA General Courts-Martial Jurisdiction, January 24, 1965, HQ MACV SJA Administrative Office, Box 5, File 401-07, Jurisdiction, RG 472 USFSEA.

19. CG USARYIS to CG USA MACV, February 6, 1965, HQ MACV SJA Administrative Office, Box 5, File 401-07, Jurisdiction, RG 472 USFSEA.

20. George S. Prugh, *Law at War: Vietnam, 1964–1973* (Washington, D.C.: Department of the Army, 1975), 98–102.

21. American Embassy, Saigon, to the Department of State, Draft Status of Forces Agreement Presented to MACV by the Vietnamese Joint General Staff, April 20, 1967, CH0008106, USAFHRA.

22. Ibid.

23. Ibid.

24. A Judge Advocate General Activity Input to Project Corona Harvest on Legal Support of U.S. Air Operations in Southeast Asia, January 1, 1965–March 31, 1968, USAFHRA, 34.

25. Maj. Gen. C. W. Eifler, First Logistical Command, determined that a "time of war" existed and therefore exercised summary court-martial jurisdiction over the merchant seaman under Article 2 (10). MACV JA Court-Martial Jurisdiction over Civilians, December 8, 1966, MACV SJA Advisory Division, General Records, Box 3, File 402-01, Civilian Jurisdiction, RG 472 USFSEA.

26. American Ambassador, Saigon, to Department of State, AFIN 65492, November 14, 1966, CH0007679, USAFHRA.

27. See McElroy v. Guagliardo, 361 U.S. 281 (1960).

28. Exercise of Court-Martial Jurisdiction over Civilians Accompanying the Air Force in Vietnam, November 1966, CH0007680, USAFHRA.

29. The Eliza, Bas v. Tingey, 4 Dallas 37, 1 L.Ed. 731 (1801), cited in JAGJ 1966/8791 Court-Martial Jurisdiction of Contractor and Other Civilian Employees of the Armed Forces in Vietnam, MACV SJA Advisory Division, General Records, Box 3, File 402-01, Civilian Jurisdiction, RG 472 USFSEA.

30. Hamilton v. McClaughry, 136 F 445 (1905), cited in ibid.

31. U.S. v. Bancroft, 3 USCMA 3, 11 CMR 3, cited in ibid.

32. Ordinance No. 01/UBLDQG of June 24, 1965, Promulgating the State of War throughout the Republic of Vietnam, MACV SJA Advisory Division, General Records, Box 3, File 402-01, Civilian Jurisdiction, RG 472 USFSEA.

33. Executive Order 11216, Designation of Vietnam and Waters Adjacent Thereto as a Combat Zone for the Purposes of Section 112 of the Internal Revenue Code of 1954, April 24, 1965, MACV SJA Advisory Division, General Records, Box 3, File 402-01, Civilian Jurisdiction, RG 472 USFSEA.

34. MACJA Court-Martial Jurisdiction over Civilians, January 9, 1967, MACV SJA Advisory Division, General Records, Box 3, File 402-01, Civilian Jurisdiction, RG 472 USFSEA.

35. Exercise of Court-Martial Jurisdiction over Civilians Accompanying the Air Force in Vietnam, March 1967, CH007676, USAFHRA.

36. Secretary of Defense to COMUSMACV, AFIN 62988 (March 10, 1967), Corona Harvest 1968, Document CH007403, USAFHRA; COMUSMACV to CG USARV, AFIN 1615 (March 16, 1967), CH007677, USAFHRA.

37. United States Congress, House of Representatives, Committee on the Judiciary, *Report of the Special Subcommittee on the Application of the Uniform Code of Military Justice to American Civilians in the Republic of Vietnam*, 90th Cong., 1st sess., June 1967 (Washington, D.C.: Government Printing Office, 1967).

38. Joint MACV/Embassy Message, Saigon 11226, November 17, 1967, CH007688, USAFHRA.

39. Ibid.

40. Ibid.

41. Memorandum for Deputy Secretary of Defense, Joint Chiefs of Staff, and Assistant Secretary of Defense, December 15, 1967, CH007691, USAFHRA.

42. Draft telegram, Department of State to American Embassy, Saigon, No. 11226, December 20, 1967, CH007687, USAFHRA.

43. Memorandum for Paul Warnke, Assistant Secretary of Defense, December 21, 1967, CH007686, USAFHRA.

44. Paul Warnke to Leonard Meeker, January 2, 1968, CH007685, USAFHRA.

45. Secretary of State to the Ambassador in Saigon, No. 118329, February 21, 1968, CH007689, USAFHRA.

46. CG III MAF to RUMSMA/COMUSMACV, AFIN 54839, August 28, 1967, CH007682, USAFHRA.

47. Memorandum for the Secretary of the Navy, December 21, 1967, CH007683, USAFHRA; A Judge Advocate General Activity Input to Project Corona Harvest on Legal Support of U.S. Air Operations in Southeast Asia, January 1, 1965–March 31, 1968, 68–69; Gary D. Solis, *Trial by Fire: Marines and Military Law in Vietnam* (Washington, D.C.: Marine Corps History and Museums Division, 1989), 99–103.

48. O'Callahan v. Parker, 395 U.S. 258 (1969); Dorothy Shaffter, *"War" and the Military Courts: Judicial Interpretation of Its Meaning* (Smithtown, N.Y.: Exposition Press, 1988), 93–94; Westmoreland and Prugh, "Judges in Command," 17.

49. Latney v. Ignatius, 416 F2d 821 (CA DC Cir., 1969); Shaffter, *"War" and the Military Courts*, 93–94; Solis, *Trial By Fire*, 167–168.

50. U.S. v. Averette, 19 USCMA 363, 41 CMR 363 (1971); Shaffter, *"War" and the Military Courts*, 105–109; Solis, *Trial by Fire*, 169; Prugh, *Law at War*, 109–110; Westmoreland and Prugh, "Judges in Command," 4n5.

51. U.S. v. Anderson, 17 USMCA 588, 38 CMR 386 (1958); Shaffter, *"War" and Military Courts*, 104; Westmoreland and Prugh, "Judges in Command," 4n5.

52. MACJA Memorandum—Administrative Action upon Reports of Criminal Activity by Civilians in Vietnam, July 29, 1969, Box 3, Vietnam Monograph, RG 319 RAS; MACV Staff Memorandum 190-1, May 8, 1969, MACV MACJ03 Military History Branch Histories, Background Files, Box 260, Discipline, Law, Order—General (1971), RG 472 USFSEA; Memorandum for Laurence J. Pickering, Mission Coordinator, American Embassy, Vietnam, May 29, 1970, RG 472 USFSEA; CG USARV LBN RVN to Army Commands, Apprehension, Custody and Trial of U.S. Civilians, May 2, 1970, RG 472 USFSEA.

53. General Court-Martial Order Number 23, November 23, 1969, HQ I Field Force Vietnam, Military Justice Division, Appellate CM, Box 1, File 404-02, RG 472 USFSEA.

54. Robinson O. Everett and Laurent R. Hourcle, "Crime without Punishment: Ex-Servicemen, Civilian Employees, and Dependents," *United States Air Force Judge Advocate General Law Review* 13, 3 (Summer 1971): 195–196.

55. Robinson O. Everett, "*O'Callahan v. Parker:* Milestone or Millstone in Military Justice?" *Duke Law Journal* 1969, 5 (October 1969): 853–896.

CHAPTER 4. DISCIPLINE, MILITARY CRIMES, AND COURTS-MARTIAL

1. Guenter Lewy, *America in Vietnam* (New York: Oxford, 1978), 153–162; Richard A. Gabriel and Paul L. Savage, *Crisis in Command: Mismanagement in the Army* (New York: Hill and Wang, 1978), 8–28; Robert D. Heinl Jr., "The Collapse of the Armed Forces," *Armed Forces Journal* (June 7, 1971): 30–38; Cincinnatus, *Self-Destruction: The Disintegration and Decay of the United States Army during the Vietnam Era* (New York: W. W. Norton, 1981), 150–155.

2. See Don Carlos Rowe and Rick Berg, *The Vietnam War and American Culture* (New York: Columbia University Press, 1991).

3. Lewy, *America in Vietnam*, 152, 160; United States Congress, House of Representatives, Committee on Appropriations, *Department of Defense Appropriations for 1972, Hearings before a Subcommittee of the Committee on Appropriations, Part 9*, 92nd Cong., 1st sess. (Washington, D.C.: Government Printing Office, 1971), 584–585 [hereafter *Defense Appropriations for 1972*].

4. Earle F. Lasseter and James B. Thwing, "Military Justice in Time of War," *American Bar Association Journal* 68 (May 1983): 566–569; Thomas J. Fiscus, "Defending Military Justice: Suspect Rights," *The Inspector General Brief* 55, 3 (May–June 2003), 17; Joseph M. Brophy questionnaire, January 13, 1998, MJVN Files.

5. Staff Judge Advocate Military Justice Conference, May 24, 1969, Long Binh Post, RVN, HQ MACV SJA AD, General Records, Box 5, File 401-02, Military Justice Conference, May 24, 1969, RG 472 USFSEA; Staff Judge Advocate Conference, USARV, September 2, 1971, VNIT-968, CMH; Model Plans and New Concepts for the U.S. Army Judiciary in USARV, April 12, 1971, Box 14, File 402-08, MACV SJA U.S. Army Judiciary Circuit in USARV (1971), RG 472 USFSEA; Administrative SOP, 17th Judicial Circuit, Box 14, File 402-08, MACV SJA U.S. Army Judiciary Circuit in USARV (1971), RG 472 USFSEA.

6. General Court-Martial Docket, USARV, 1969, Appellate Court-Martial Records, USARV, Box 2, File 404-06, Court-Martial Locator Files, 1969, RG 472 USFSEA.

7. USARV Morale Indicators, January 1972, HQ MACV SJA Advisory Division General Records, Box 16, File 401-08, RG 472 USFSEA.

8. Military Justice Activities Reports, February–December, 1969, Appellate Court-Martial Records, USARV, Box 2, File 404-07 Court-Martial Statistical Files, Military Justice Division (1969), RG 472 USFSEA.

9. Heinl, "The Collapse of the Armed Forces," 35; Lewy, *America in Vietnam*, 157. Once a soldier is AWOL for more than thirty days, then he or she is administratively considered a deserter.

10. Lewy, *America in Vietnam*, 157; Christian Appy, *Working Class War: American Combat Soldiers and Vietnam* (Chapel Hill: University of North Carolina Press, 1993), 95; United States Congress, House of Representatives, Committee on Appropriations, *Department of Defense Appropriations for 1970, Hearings, Part 1 Military Personnel*, 91st Cong., 1st sess. (Washington, D.C.: Government Printing Office, 1969), 63.

11. T. J. Hanifen to Laurence G. Pickering, Memorandum—U.S. Forces Absentees, March 17, 1970, MACV MACJ 02 Military History Branch Histories, Background Files, Box 260, Discipline, Law, Order—General (1971), RG 472 USFSEA.

12. Lewy, *America in Vietnam*, 157; United States Congress, Senate, Committee on Armed Services, *Military Deserters, Hearings, 1968*, 90th Cong., 1st sess. (Washington, D.C.: Government Printing Office, 1968), 15–17 [hereafter *Military Deserters*]; quote is from Heinl, "The Collapse of the Armed Forces," 35–36.

13. *Military Deserters*, 8, 65–66; Deputy Assistant Secretary of Defense to Acting Secretary of the Navy, February 23, 1968, CH0007673, USAFHRA.

14. *Military Deserters, Hearings*, 69–70.

15. Ibid., 71.

16. Ibid.

17. Ibid., 72; Richard A. Gabriel, "Professionalism versus Managerialism in Vietnam," *Air University Review* 32, 2 (January–February 1981): 83–84.

18. D. B. Bell and T. J. Houston, *The Vietnam Era Deserter: Characteristics of Unconvicted Army Deserters Participating in the Presidential Clemency Program* (Arlington, Va.: U.S. Army Research Institute for the Behavioral and Social Sciences, 1976), 20; Benjamin H. Barnette Jr., "USAF AWOL and Desertion: Some Reasons Why" (Air Force Air Command and Staff College professional studies paper, U.S. Air Force Air University, Maxwell Air Force Base, Ala., 1972), 35–41; Lewy, *America in Vietnam*, 158; Appy, *Working Class War*, 111–112.

19. *Vietnam—Chronicle of a War*, videocassette, CBS News Collectors Series (New York, CBS, 1991).

20. Hearings results cited in Gabriel and Savage, *Crisis in Command*, 45; Heinl, "The Collapse of the Armed Forces," 31; Lewy, *America in Vietnam*, 156–157; Gabriel, "Professionalism versus Managerialism in Vietnam," 79–80; Appy, *Working Class War*, 245–246; W. Hays Parks, "Statistics versus Actuality in Vietnam," *Air University Review* 32, 4 (May–June 1981): 85, 87.

21. U.S. v. Williams, 17 USCMA 358, 38 CMR 156 (1968), in Michael I. Spak and Donald F. Spak, *Cases and Materials on Military Justice* (Chicago: Harcourt Brace Jovanovich, 1976), 242–244.

22. Appy, *Working Class War*, 246; Jerome Kroll, "Racial Patterns of Military Crimes in Vietnam," *Psychiatry* 39 (February 1976): 51–64.

23. Lewy, *America in Vietnam*, 155–156; Thomas C. Bond, "The Why of Fragging," *American Journal of Psychiatry* 133, 11 (November 1976): 1328–1329. Bond's study was also reprinted as "Fragging: A Study," *Army* (April 1977): 45–47.

24. Bond, "The Why of Fragging," 1329–1331.

25. *Defense Appropriations for 1972*, 585; Lewy, *America in Vietnam*, 156.

26. Staff Judge Advocate, U.S. Naval Support Activity, Saigon, to Force Judge Advocate, U.S. Naval Forces, Vietnam, June 7, 1971, HQ MACV Naval Advisory Group, JA Office General Records, Box 9, File 201-09A, Criminal Activity 1972, RG 472 USFSEA; Third Marine Division Program to Eliminate Acts of Violence (1969), Third Marine Violence Indices, MCHC; Gary D. Solis, *Trial by Fire: Marines and Military Law* (Washington, D.C.: Marine Corps History and Museums Division, 1989), 110–111, 168–169.

27. Solis, *Trial by Fire*, 110–111, 168–169; Third Marine Division Program to Eliminate Acts of Violence (1969), Third Marine Violence Indices, MCHC.

28. Solis, *Trial by Fire*, 169–170.

29. U.S. v. McInnis, CM 422137, USCMA 23450 (1970), in Military Justice Division, Appellate Courts-Martial, Box 1, File 404-02, RG 472 USFSEA. This citation also refers to the next five paragraphs.

30. General Court-Martial Order No. 2, April 14, 1972, HQ MACV SJA Advisory Division General Records, Box 17, File 402-08, Requests for Court Martial Orders, RG 472 USFSEA.

31. UPI Press Release, Saigon, March 9, 1972, HQ MACV SJA AO General Records, Box 5, File 401-08, Alleged Conspiracy, RG 472 USFSEA; Memorandum: UPI Press Release of March 9, 1972, March 10, 1972, RG 472 USFSEA.

32. U.S. Army Disciplinary Actions, RVN, Box 3, Vietnam Monograph, RG 319 RAS.

33. Waldemar Solf, "A Response to Telford Taylor's *Nuremberg and Vietnam: An American Tragedy*," *Akron Law Review* 5, 1 (Winter 1972): 66–67; Harry Kalven and Hans Zeisel, *The American Jury* (Boston: Little, Brown, 1966), 495; Erwin Knoll and Judith Nies

McFadden, eds., *War Crimes and the American Conscience* (New York: Holt, Rinehart and Winston, 1970), 182–195; Lewy, *America in Vietnam*, 343.

34. Kroll, "Racial Patterns of Military Crimes in Vietnam," 51–64.

35. Ibid.

36. Ann Mathews, "Army JAG's Search for Justice," *Vietnam*, December 1998, 30–36. This citation also refers to the next four paragraphs.

CHAPTER 5. VIOLATIONS OF THE LAWS OF WAR

1. United States Army, *The Law of Land Warfare*, Field Manual 27–10 (Washington, D.C.: Government Printing Office, 1956); Ernest Van Der Haag, "U. S. Crimes in Vietnam," *Nation* 23, 41 (October 22, 1971): 1174; William L. Nash, "The Laws of War: A Military View," *Ethics and International Affairs* 16, 1 (2002): 14–15. For a thorough discussion of the evolution of laws of war and how laws of war compare to U.S. democratic principles, see Anthony E. Hartle, *Moral Issues in Military Decision Making*, 2nd ed., revised (Lawrence: University Press of Kansas, 2004), 101–131.

2. United States Army, *The Law of Land Warfare*, 505 (d), 507(b). The Uniform Code of Military Justice provides for trying personnel under its jurisdiction for violations of the law of war under Articles 18 and 21.

3. Uniform Code of Military Justice, Article 90.

4. Ibid., Article 92.

5. Ibid.

6. United States Army, *A Manual for Courts-Martial, Courts of Inquiry, and Retiring Boards, and Other Procedures under Military Law* (Washington, D.C.: Government Printing Office, 1916), Rule 916.

7. United States Army, *The Law of Land Warfare*, 509(a).

8. Mark J. Osiel, *Obeying Orders: Atrocity, Military Discipline and the Law of War* (London: Transaction Publishers, 1999), 125–127.

9. Tom Bailey, "Judgment on the Firing Line," *Soldiers* 28, 8 (August 1971): 5.

10. MACV Dir 27–5, "War Crimes and Other Prohibited Acts," November 2, 1967, Box 3, Vietnam Monograph Notes/Material, RG 319 RAS.

11. MACV Dir 20–4, "Inspections and Investigations: War Crimes," May 18, 1968, Box 3, Vietnam Monograph Notes/Material, RG319 RAS.

12. "The Peers Report," in Joseph Goldstein, Burke Marshall, and Jack Schwartz, *The My Lai Massacre and Its Cover-up: Beyond the Reach of Law? The Peers Report with a Supplement and Introductory Essay on the Limits of Law* (New York: Free Press, 1976), 44–47; Michal R. Belknap, *The Vietnam War on Trial: The My Lai Massacre and the Court-Martial of Lieutenant Calley* (Lawrence: University Press of Kansas, 2002), 59–78.

13. "The Peers Report," 48–56; Belknap, *The Vietnam War on Trial*, 79–97.

14. A copy of this letter is in "The Peers Report," 34–37.

15. Belknap, *The Vietnam War on Trial*, 101–110.

16. See Toth v. Quarles (1955), United States Supreme Court.

17. "The Peers Report," 207–231, 320–345.

18. Michael Bilton and Kevin Sim, *Four Hours in My Lai* (New York: Penguin, 1993), 325–326.

19. Ibid., 239; Belknap, *The Vietnam War on Trial*, 223–225.

20. Bilton and Sim, *Four Hours in My Lai*, 329–330; Belknap, *The Vietnam War on Trial*, 225–227.

21. Bilton and Sim, *Four Hours in My Lai*, 330; Belknap, *The Vietnam War on Trial*, 225–227.

22. William H. Hammond, *Reporting Vietnam: Media and Military at War* (Lawrence: University Press of Kansas, 1998), 187–200.

23. Bilton and Sim, *Four Hours in My Lai*, 331; Belknap, *The Vietnam War on Trial*, 146–149.

24. Bilton and Sim, *Four Hours in My Lai*, 332–336; Belknap, *The Vietnam War on Trial*, 152–185.

25. Belknap, *The Vietnam War on Trial,* 183–186.

26. Quoted in U.S. v. Calley, 46 CMR 1131 (ACMR 1973), in Joseph Goldstein, Burke Marshall, and Jack Schwartz, *The My Lai Massacre and Its Cover-up: Beyond the Reach of Law? The Peers Report with a Supplement and Introductory Essay on the Limits of Law* (New York: Free Press, 1976), 516–517.

27. Belknap, *The Vietnam War on Trial*, 186–190.

28. U.S. v. Calley, 22 USCMA 534, 48 CMR 19 (1973), in Michael I. Spak and Donald F. Spak, *Cases and Materials on Military Justice* (Chicago: Harcourt Brace Jovanovich, 1976), 247–252; Belknap, *The Vietnam War on Trial*, 235–254; Bilton and Sim, *Four Hours in My Lai*, 353–357.

29. Bilton and Sim, *Four Hours in My Lai*, 347–349; Belknap, *The·Vietnam War on Trial*, 228–232.

30. Bilton and Sim, *Four Hours in My Lai*, 349–351.

31. Gary D. Solis, *Trial by Fire: Marines and Military Law* (Washington, D.C.: Marine Corps History and Museums Division, 1989), 174–175.

32. Gary D. Solis, *Son Thang: An American War Crime* (Annapolis, Md.: Naval Institute Press, 1997), 25–29; Solis, *Trial by Fire*, 175.

33. Solis, *Son Thang*, 30–31.

34. Solis, *Trial by Fire*, 176–177; Solis, *Son Thang*, 45–60.

35. Solis, *Trial by Fire*, 178–179; Solis, *Son Thang*, 60–61, 66–69.

36. Solis, *Trial by Fire*, 180–181; Solis, *Son Thang*, 79–84.

37. Solis, *Trial by Fire*, 182–183; Solis, *Son Thang*, 84–98.

38. Solis, *Trial by Fire*, 183–184; Solis, *Son Thang*, 128–212.

39. Solis, *Son Thang,* 212–224.

40. Solis, *Trial by Fire*, 186; Solis, *Son Thang*, 225–239.

41. Solis, *Trial by Fire*, 187–189; Solis, *Son Thang*, 240–293.

42. Randy Herrod, *Blue's Bastards: A True Story of Valor under Fire* (Washington, D.C.: Regnery Gateway, 1989).

43. Solis, *Son Thang*, 118–119.

44. Ibid., 189–190.

45. For literature and scholarship on the Winter Soldier movement, see, for example, Vietnam Veterans against the War, *The Winter Soldier Investigation: An Inquiry into American War Crimes* (Boston: Beacon Press, March 1972); Richard Stacewicz, *Winter Soldiers: An Oral History of the Vietnam Veterans against the War* (New York: Twayne Publishers, 1997); Andrew Hunt, *The Turning: A History of Vietnam Veterans against the War* (New York: New York University Press, 2001); Donald Jackson, "Confessions of the Winter Soldiers," *Life* 71,

2, July 9, 1971, 22–27; "Hard Times: Testimony of Vietnam Veterans Given before the National Committee for a Citizens' Commission of Inquiry on U.S. Crimes in Vietnam," *Ramparts Magazine* 9 (February 1971): 12–18.

46. "Guilty Minority," *Time,* January 5, 1968, 31–32.

47. "Military Law: Two Sides of Atrocity," *Time,* July 14, 1967, 38.

48. "The Mere Gook Rule," *Newsweek,* April 13, 1970, 30.

49. "The Case of Lieutenant Duffy," *The Nation* 210, 14 (April 13, 1970): 419–420.

50. Poolaw Case File, MCHC. This citation also refers to the next four paragraphs.

51. CG III MAF to CG FMFPAC, December 7, 1969, Poolaw Case File, MCHC.

52. Frederic L. Borch, *Judge Advocates in Vietnam: Army Lawyers in Southeast Asia, 1959–1975* (Fort Leavenworth, Kans.: United States Army Command and Staff College Press, 2004), 34–35.

53. Osiel, *Obeying Orders,* 221–230; Anthony E. Hartle, "Atrocities in War: Dirty Hands and Noncombatants," *Social Research* 69, 4 (Winter 2002): 967.

54. Solis, *Son Thang,* 292–293, 334; Robinson O. Everett, "Did Military Justice Fail or Prevail?" *Michigan Law Review* 96, 6 (May 1998): 1421–1434.

CHAPTER 6. THE DRUG PROBLEM

1. Alfred W. McCoy, *The Politics of Heroin in Southeast Asia* (New York: Harper and Row, 1972), 58–63.

2. Ibid., 64.

3. Neil L. Jamieson, *Understanding Vietnam* (Berkeley: University of California Press, 1993), 62–63; Mark W. McLeod and Nguyen Thi Dieu, *Culture and Customs of Vietnam* (Westport, Conn.: Greenwood Press, 2001), 13–31.

4. McCoy, *The Politics of Heroin in Southeast Asia,* 74–85.

5. Donald Lancaster, *The Emancipation of French Indochina* (New York: Oxford University Press, 1961), 121.

6. William O. Walker, *Opium and Foreign Policy: The Anglo-American Search for Order in Asia, 1912–1954* (Chapel Hill: University of North Carolina Press, 1991), 160–217; Jonathan Marshall, "Opium, Tungsten, and the Search for National Security, 1940–1952," in William O. Walker, ed., *Drug Control Police: Essays in Historical and Comparative Perspective* (University Park: Pennsylvania State University Press, 1991), 89; Jonathan Marshall, *Drug Wars: Corruption, Counterinsurgency, and Covert Operations in the Third World* (Forestville, Calif.: Cohan and Cohan Publishers, 1991), 38–39.

7. McCoy, *The Politics of Heroin in Southeast Asia,* 159–207.

8. Walter J. Sheldon, *Tigers in the Rice: The Story of Vietnam from Ancient Past to Uncertain Future* (London: Cromwell-Collier Press, 1969), 110–111.

9. McCoy, *The Politics of Heroin in Southeast Asia,* 158–159.

10. D. R. SarDesai, *Vietnam: Trials and Tribulations of a Nation* (Long Beach, Calif.: Long Beach Publications, 1988), 118–119.

11. Richard Kunnes, *The American Heroin Empire: Power, Profits, and Politics* (New York: Dodd and Meade, 1972), 23–25, 149–157; Marshall, *Drug Wars,* 55–60.

12. Availability and cost of marijuana cigarettes from "Command Statements, U.S. Naval Forces, Vietnam, January 8, 1971" in United States Congress, House of Representatives,

Committee on Armed Services, *Hearings by Special Subcommittee on Alleged Drug Abuse in the Armed Services*, 91st Cong., 2nd sess. (Washington, D.C: Government Printing Office, 1971), 1783 [hereafter *Alleged Drug Abuse in the Armed Services*]; Jerry W. Adcock, "Marihuana and the United States Military in Vietnam," United States Air Force Air Command and Staff College research study (U.S. Air Force Air University, Maxwell Air Force Base, Ala., 1971), 13–19; Christian Appy, *Working Class War: American Combat Soldiers and Vietnam* (Chapel Hill: University of North Carolina Press, 1993), 140–141. Availability and cost of heroin from Kunnes, *The American Heroin Empire*, 149. Possibility of volunteering to go to Vietnam because of availability of drugs from Clifton D. Bryant, *Khaki-Collar Crime: Deviant Behavior in the Military Context* (New York: Free Press, 1979), 182–187.

13. "Statement of Frank Bartimo, Assistant General Counsel of Manpower and Reserve Affairs, Department of Defense, Attachment Six," in *Alleged Drug Abuse in the Armed Services*, 1281, 1287–1289; Morris D. Stanton, "Drug Use in Vietnam: A Survey among Army Personnel in the Two Northern Corps," in *Alleged Drug Abuse in the Armed Services*, 2147.

14. "Statement of Robert T. Kelley, Assistant Secretary of Defense," in United States Congress, Senate, Committee on Military Affairs, Subcommittee on Alcoholism and Narcotics, *Military Drug Abuse, 1971: Hearings*, 92nd Cong., 1st sess. (Washington, D.C: Government Printing Office, 1971), 160–166 [hereafter *Military Drug Abuse, 1971*]; Kunnes, *The American Heroin Empire*, 150; McCoy, *The Politics of Heroin*, 149–222.

15. Kunnes, *The American Heroin Empire*, 154–155.

16. Oral History Interview, Major Francis Fishburn, Chief of Plans and Policies Division, Drug Abuse Branch, USARV, VNIT–943, CMH.

17. "Statement of Frank Bartimo, Assistant General Counsel of Manpower and Reserve Affairs, Department of Defense, Attachment Two," in *Alleged Drug Abuse in the Armed Services*, 1291–1295.

18. Kunnes, *The American Heroin Empire*, 156–159.

19. "The World Heroin Problem: Report of the Special Study Mission," in *Military Drug Abuse, 1971*, 69–71.

20. "II Field Force Briefing," in *Alleged Drug Abuse in the Armed Services*, 1849–1859.

21. "1st Air Cavalry Division Briefing, January 10, 1971," in *Alleged Drug Abuse in the Armed Services*, 1859–1888.

22. "23rd (Americal) Division Briefing, January 11, 1971," in *Alleged Drug Abuse in the Armed Services*, 1888–1911.

23. "Command Statements, U.S. Naval Forces, Vietnam, January 8, 1971," *Alleged Drug Abuse in the Armed Services*, 1781–1798. This citation also refers to the next paragraph.

24. "7th Air Force Briefing on Drug Prevention Program, January 8, 1971," in *Alleged Drug Abuse in the Armed Services*, 1799–1806. This citation also refers to the next paragraph.

25. "Marine Drug Abuse Briefing, 3rd Marine Division," in *Alleged Drug Abuse in the Armed Services*, 1176–1179.

26. Gary D. Solis, *Trial by Fire: Marines and Military Law* (Washington, D.C.: Marine Corps History and Museums Division, 1989), 170–171; "III Marine Amphibious Force and 1st Marine Division, January 11, 1971," in *Alleged Drug Abuse in the Armed Services*, 1911–1919.

27. Special Court-Martial Order Number 7, May 21, 1968, MACV-SJA Daniels SPCM 1968, HQ MACV SJA AD General Records, Box 5, File 402-08, Legal Assistance Operations Files, RG 472 USFSEA.

28. Salerno and Mitchell CID Investigation File, February–April 1968, HQ MACV SJA AD General Records, Box 5, File 402-08, Legal Assistance Operations Files, RG 472 USF-SEA. This citation also refers to the next three paragraphs.

29. SPCM 7537, U.S. v. Heggie (1972), United States Army Court of Military Review, Appellate Court-Martial Records USARV, Box 7, File 404-02, RG 472 USFSEA. This citation also refers to the next three paragraphs.

30. USARV, U.S. v. Simonaro (1969), Appellate Court Martial, Military Justice Division, Box 1, File 404-02, RG 472 USFSEA.

31. Harold A. Teeter, letter to the author, February 22, 1998, MJVN Files; Michael D. Peyton, letter to the author, January 13, 1998, MJVN Files; Robert D. Heinl Jr., "The Collapse of the Armed Forces," *Armed Forces Journal* (June 7, 1971): 31. This citation also refers to the next six paragraphs.

32. John William Mayer, letter to the author, January 21, 1998, MJVN Files.

33. W. T. Allison II, interview with author, MJVN Files.

34. Michael D. Peyton, letter to the author, January 13, 1998, MJVN Files.

35. Heinl, "The Collapse of the Armed Forces," 34–35; Lewis Sorley, *A Better War: The Unexamined Victories and Final Tragedy of America's Last Years in Vietnam* (New York: Harcourt, 1999), 281–301.

36. Seminar with Vietnam Ministry of Culture officials, Hanoi, July 10, 2000, during Council for International Education Exchange Faculty Development Seminar, Vietnam, July 8–18, 2000, attended by the author; McLeod and Nguyen, *Culture and Customs of Vietnam*, 131; SarDesai, *Vietnam: Trials and Tribulations*, 176.

CHAPTER 7. THE BLACK MARKET, CURRENCY MANIPULATION, AND CORRUPTION

1. Andrew F. Krepinevich Jr., *The Army and Vietnam* (Baltimore, Md.: Johns Hopkins University Press, 1986), 65–69; George C. Herring, "'Peoples Quite Apart': Americans, South Vietnamese, and the War in Vietnam," *Diplomatic History* 14, 1 (Winter 1990): 9–10.

2. William J. Lederer, "Our Own Worst Enemy," *Saturday Evening Post* 241, 11, June 1, 1968, 36–42; Frank McCullough, "For Profiteers, What a Lovely War," *Life* 67, August 1, 1969, 46–49; Don Luce and John Sommer, *Viet Nam: The Unheard Voices* (Ithaca, N.Y.: Cornell University Press, 1969), 187–188.

3. Clifton D. Bryant, *Khaki-Collar Crime: Deviant Behavior in the Military Context* (New York: Free Press, 1979), 86.

4. United States Agency for International Development [hereafter USAID], Office of Vietnam Affairs, *United States Economic Assistance to South Vietnam, 1954–1975: Terminal Report* (Washington, D.C: United States Agency for International Development, 1975), E–6 (pagination for this report is for the copy borrowed through interlibrary loan from Cornell University Library).

5. Gabriel Kolko, *Anatomy of a War: Vietnam, the United States, and the Modern Historical Experience* (New York: Pantheon Books, 1985), 224–225; Frances FitzGerald, *Fire in the Lake: The Vietnamese and the Americans in Vietnam* (New York: Vintage Books, 1989), 434–440; Stanley Karnow, *Vietnam: A History*, revised and updated edition (New York: Penguin

Books, 1991), 450–460; William C. Westmoreland, *A Soldier Reports* (New York: Da Capo Press, 1989), 284–285.

6. Joseph Buttinger, *Vietnam: A Dragon Embattled*, vol. 2 (New York: Frederick A. Praeger, 1967), 776–779; Walter J. Sheldon, *Tigers in the Rice: The Story of Vietnam from Ancient Past to Uncertain Future* (London: Cromwell-Collier Press, 1969), 110–111. Subject to French colonial rule, Bao Dai was emperor of Vietnam from 1925 to 1954, when he went into exile in Paris. He died in 1997.

7. USAID, *United States Economic Assistance to South Vietnam*, B3–B4. As an example of how this program worked, the CIP covered a $392 million shortfall in the South Vietnamese government's $537 million budget in 1956 through this revenue-sharing arrangement.

8. George C. Herring, *America's Longest War: The United States and Vietnam, 1950–1975*, 3rd ed. (New York: McGraw-Hill, 1996), 65; Robert D. Shulzinger, *A Time for War: The United States and Vietnam, 1941–1975* (New York: Oxford University Press, 1997), 90; "Memorandum from the Deputy Director of the Vietnam Working Group (Heavner) to the Assistant Secretary of State for Far Eastern Affairs (Hilsman), Washington, May 9, 1963," in United States Department of State, *Foreign Relations of the United States, 1961–1963*, vol. 3: *Vietnam: January–August 1963* (Washington, D.C.: Government Printing Office, 1991), 280–282; United States Congress, House of Representatives, Committee on Government Operations, *The Commercial (Commodity) Import Program for Vietnam (Follow-up Investigation), Fifth Report*, 90th Cong., 1st sess. (Washington, D.C.: Government Printing Office, 1967), 1–2.

9. Kolko, *Anatomy of a War*, 223–224; Douglas C. Dacy, *Foreign Aid, War, and Economic Development: South Vietnam, 1955–1975* (Cambridge: Cambridge University Press, 1986), 11–12.

10. United States Congress, Senate, Committee on Government Operations, *Improper Practices, Commodity Import Program, U.S. Foreign Aid, Vietnam: Hearings before the Permanent Subcommittee on Investigations of the Committee on Government Operations*, 90th Cong., 1st sess. (Washington, D.C.: Government Printing Office, 1967), 5–17; United States Congress, House of Representatives, Committee on Government Operations, *Illicit Practices Affecting the U.S. Economic Program in Vietnam (Follow-up Investigation), Fourth Report by the Committee on Government Operations*, 90th Cong., 1st sess. (Washington, D.C.: Government Printing Office, 1967), 3–4 [hereafter *Illicit Practices*].

11. *Illicit Practices*, 5–9.

12. "Telegram from the Embassy in Vietnam to the Department of State, Saigon, October 30, 1963," in United States Department of State, *Foreign Relations of the United States, 1961–1963*, vol. 4: *Vietnam: August–December 1963* (Washington, D.C.: Government Printing Office, 1991), 482–484; United States Congress, Senate, Committee on Government Operations, *Improper Practices, Commodity Import Program, U.S. Foreign Aid, Vietnam*, 91st Cong., 1st sess. (Washington, D.C.: Government Printing Office, 1969), 1–2.

13. The Uniform Code of Military Justice does not specify black-market offenses but covers such violations in a variety of articles. Those most often applied were Article 108: Misappropriation of captured or abandoned enemy property (punishment ranged from a bad conduct discharge to five years hard labor, depending upon value of property involved); Article 109: Military property of the United States: loss, damage, destruction, or wrongful disposition (punishment ranged from bad conduct discharge to five years hard labor, depending upon value of property involved); Article 123: Forgery (punishment ranged from

dishonorable discharge to five years hard labor); and Article 134: Other offenses, including false documentation (dishonorable discharge, three years hard labor), mail fraud (dishonorable discharge, five years hard labor), and buying or selling stolen property (dishonorable discharge, six years hard labor).

14. George S. Prugh, *Law at War: Vietnam 1964–1973* (Washington, D.C.: Department of the Army, 1975), 83–84.

15. United States Congress, House of Representatives, Committee on Government Operations, *A Review of the Inequitable Monetary Rate of Exchange in Vietnam, Twenty-sixth Report*, 91st Cong., 2nd sess. (Washington, D.C.: Government Printing Office, 1970), 7 [hereafter *A Review*].

16. "Memorandum from the Chairman of the Joint Chiefs of Staff (Taylor) and the Secretary of Defense (McNamara) to the President, Washington, October 2, 1963," in United States Department of State, *Foreign Relations of the United States, 1961–1963*, 4:340–341.

17. United States Congress, Senate, Committee on Government Operations, *Fraud and Corruption in Management of Military Club Systems; Illegal Currency Manipulations Affecting South Vietnam: Hearings before the Permanent Subcommittee on Investigations of the Committee on Government Operations, Part 3*, 91st Cong., 1st sess. (Washington, D.C.: Government Printing Office, 1970), 583–584 [hereafter *Fraud and Corruption*]; *A Review*, 8. For a discussion of the black market in World War II, see Kevin Conley Ruffner, "The Black Market and Postwar Berlin: Colonel Miller and an Army Scandal," *Prologue: The Journal of the National Archives* 34, 3 (2002): 171–185.

18. *Fraud and Corruption*, 610–613.

19. In 1972, the rate actually topped 495 piasters to the dollar. Ibid., 104–106.

20. W. Hays Parks to Lt. Col. Gary D. Solis, December 22, 1988, *Marines in Military Law Research Files*, USNARA. Parks has had a fascinating legal career in military law since his tour in Vietnam. He has become an expert on law of war matters as well as war crimes investigations. He has represented the United States at law of war talks in Geneva, The Hague, and Vienna and investigated alleged Iraqi war crimes in Kuwait during the Iraqi occupation of 1990–1991. After several years as special assistant to the judge advocate general of the army for law of war matters, Parks is currently law of war chair in the Office of the General Counsel, Department of Defense. This citation also refers to the next five paragraphs.

21. *Fraud and Corruption*, 200–201.

22. "Court Martial cases against U.S. Service personnel and completed disciplinary action against civilian personnel for black market and currency violations," no date, HQ MACV SJA Advisory Division, General Records, Box 3, File 401-02, RG 472 USFSEA.

23. William C. Westmoreland and George S. Prugh, "Judges in Command: The Judicialized Uniform Code of Military Justice in Combat," *Harvard Journal of Law and Public Policy* 3 (1980): 59–60.

24. *Fraud and Corruption*, 570.

25. General Court-Martial Order Number 54, September 10, 1972, U.S. v. Walters, Appellate Review, Appellate Courts-Martial USARV, Box 20, File 404-02, RG 472 USFSEA.

26. *Fraud and Corruption*, 609–669. This citation also refers to the next two paragraphs.

27. Staff Judge Advocate Monthly Historical Summaries, June–December, 1966, MACV MACJ03 Military History Background Files, Box 53, File 202-02/13-20 (1966), RG 472 USFSEA. These data are for cases tried and do not include data for cases investigated or referred to trial, suggesting that the number of alleged violations was certainly higher.

<mark>im</mark>

28. Report of Black Market and Currency Manipulation Activities, HQ 1st Logistical Command, October 13, 1966, HQ MACV SJA Advisory Division General Records, Box 3, File 401-02, RG 472 USFSEA; Report of Black Market and Currency Manipulation Activities, the Support Troops, United States Army Vietnam, October 14, 1966, HQ MACV SJA Advisory Division, General Records, Box 3, File 401-02, RG 472 USFSEA; MACV Historical Summaries, 1967, MACV MACJ03 Military History Branch Histories, Background Files, Box 81 File 206-02, RG 472 USFSEA. Again, these data are for cases tried.

29. Joseph Di Mona, *Great Court-Martial Cases* (New York: Grosset and Dunlap, 1972), 188–220. This citation also refers to the next six paragraphs.

30. *Fraud and Corruption*, 1–68, 75–87, 280–284; Zeb B. Bradford, "With Creighton Abrams in Vietnam," *The Assembly: Magazine of the Association of Graduates of the United States Military Academy,* May/June 1998, 29–30. This citation also refers to the next nine paragraphs.

31. *Fraud and Corruption*, 669–671. This citation also refers to the next paragraph.

32. Historical Report, 3rd Quarter CY 67, MACJA Historical Summaries, 1967, MACV MACJ03 Military History Branch Histories, Background Files, Box 81, File 206-02, RG 472 USFSEA.

33. Westmoreland, *A Soldier Reports*, 43–44; Guenter Lewy, *America in Vietnam* (New York: Oxford University Press, 1978), 184–186.

34. Statement of Robert H. Parker, Chairman of the Irregular Activities Committee, American Embassy, Saigon, HQ USMAC SJA Advisory Division, General Records, Box 1, File 401-05 Irregular Activities Committee, RG 472 USFSEA.

35. Ibid.

36. Ibid.

37. Ibid.

38. Robert Starr to Samuel D. Berger, December 8, 1969, HQ USMACV SJA Advisory Division, General Records, Box 1, File 401-05 Irregular Activities Committee, RG 472 USFSEA.

39. *Illicit Practices*, 12–14.

40. The GVN General Censorate, December 16, 1969, HQ USMACV SJA Advisory Division, General Records, Box 1, File 401-05 Irregular Activities Committee, RG 472 USFSEA.

41. Ibid.

42. Minutes of the Fifth Joint Meeting of the GVN-US Committees on Irregular Practices, September 10, 1970, HQ USMACV SJA Administrative Office, General Records, Box 1, File 401-05 Coordination—Irregular Practices Committee (1970), RG 472 USFSEA.

43. Luce and Sommer, *Viet Nam: The Unheard Voices*, 271–272.

44. Westmoreland and Prugh, "Judges in Command," 60. See also Lewy, *America in Vietnam*, 153–161.

45. James H. Willbanks, *Abandoning Vietnam: How America Left and South Vietnam Lost Its War* (Lawrence: University Press of Kansas, 2004), 204–207.

46. *Fraud and Corruption*, 285–300; United States Congress, House of Representatives, Committee on Government Operations, *Vietnam and The Hidden U.S. Subsidy (Inequitable Currency Exchange Rates), Eighth Report*, 92nd Cong., 1st sess. (Washington, D.C.: Government Printing Office, 1971), 1–13.

47. USAID, *United States Economic Assistance to South Vietnam*, 234–235.

48. Ibid., 236.

49. Ibid., 237; Kolko, *Anatomy of a War*, 228–230.

CHAPTER 8. STILL IN THE VANGUARD

1. "Marines Call It Treason," *Newsweek* 97, February 16, 1971, 41; Larry Witt, "Marine Robert Garwood, the Last P.O.W. Back from Vietnam, Faces Court-Martial for Desertion," *People Weekly* 12, December 17, 1979, 50–52; Gary D. Solis, *Trial by Fire: Marines and Military Law in Vietnam* (Washington, D.C.: Marine Corps History and Museums Division, 1989), 223–230. This citation also refers to the next three paragraphs.

2. Solis, *Trial by Fire*, 230.

3. See Lt. Col. Richard T. Yery, "Trial of War Crimes under the Uniform Code of Military Justice," professional study paper (U.S. Air Force Air War College, Air University, Maxwell Air Force Base, Ala., April 1971).

4. Norman G. Cooper, "My Lai and Military Justice—To What Effect?" *Military Law Review* 59 (Winter 1973): 93–127; Edward F. Sherman, "Military Justice without Military Control," *Yale Law Journal* 82 (1973): 1398; Charles W. Corddry, "Jurisdiction to Try Discharged Servicemen for Violations of the Laws of War," *JAG Journal* 26, 1 (Fall 1971): 63–76.

5. E. M. Barker, "Command Influence: Time for a Revision?" *JAG Journal* 26, 1 (Fall 1971): 62.

6. Luther C. West, *They Call It Justice: Command Influence and the Court-Martial System* (New York: Viking Press, 1977), 286.

7. United States, Department of Defense, *Report of the Task Force on the Administration of Military Justice in the Armed Forces* (Washington, D.C.: Government Printing Office, 1972), 2:81–82; see also 1:7–23, 2:71–73.

8. Robert S. Pydasheff and William K. Suter, "Military Justice?—Definitely!" *Tulane Law Review* 49 (March 1975): 588, 602. This remains an issue today—see Christopher W. Behan, "Don't Tug Superman's Cape: In Defense of Convening Authority Selection and Appointment of Court-Martial Panel Members," *Military Law Review* 176 (June 2003): 190–308.

9. W. Hays Parks, "Command Responsibility for War Crimes," *Military Law Review* 62 (Fall 1973): 102, 103; see also 1–62, 101–104.

10. Mark J. Osiel, *Obeying Orders: Atrocity, Military Discipline and the Law of War* (London: Transaction Publishers, 1999), 192–193, 305.

11. Michael L. Smidt, "Yamashita, Medina, and Beyond: Command Responsibility in Contemporary Military Operations," *Military Law Review* 164 (June 2000): 155–234.

12. George L. Bailey, "Military Justice and Combat Readiness" (the Naval War College Center for Advanced Research, Newport, R.I., June 1978), ii–iv, 88–91.

13. Joseph W. Bishop Jr., "The Case for Military Justice," *Military Law Review* 62 (Fall 1973): 216, 222, 224.

14. Ibid., 215–224.

15. William C. Westmoreland and George S. Prugh, "Judges in Command: The Judicialized Uniform Code of Military Justice in Combat," *Harvard Journal of Law and Public Policy* 3 (1980): 6, 4, 82, 83, 84, 79–90.

16. E. A. Gates and Gary V. Casida, *Report to the Judge Advocate General by the Wartime Legislation Team* (Washington, D.C.: United States Army, 1983), 50–52.

17. William G. Eckhardt, "The Role of the Lawyer in War: Lawyering for Uncle Sam When He Draws His Sword," *Chicago Journal of International Law* 4 (Fall 2003): 435–436.

18. Earle F. Lasseter and James B. Thwing, "Military Justice in Time of War," *American Bar Association Journal* 68 (May 1983): 566.

19. Ibid., 567.

20. Ibid., 567–569.

21. Theodore B. Borek, "Legal Service during War," United States Army War College military studies program paper (Army War College, Carlisle Barracks, Pa., 1987), 52.

22. West, *They Call It Justice*, 278–279; Richard A. Gabriel and Paul L. Savage, *Crisis in Command: Mismanagement in the Army* (New York: Hill and Wang, 1978), 10–12; W. Hays Parks, "Crimes in Hostilities," *Marine Corps Gazette* 60, 16 (1976): 36; Cooper, "My Lai and Military Justice," 127.

23. Exit interview, Capt. David Kull, Second Brigade, Twenty-fifth Infantry Division, VNIT–834, CMH.

24. Lt. Col. Curtis W. Olson to Maj. W. Hays Parks, December 12, 1976, *Marines and Military Law* Research Files, USNARA.

25. Oral History Interview, Brig. Gen. Duane Faw, Oral History Office, MCHC.

26. Loren H. Rosson questionnaire, MJVN Files.

27. Exit Interview, Capt. David Bengston, 199th Infantry, VNIT-731, CMH.

28. John Ernest Casper questionnaire, MJVN Files.

29. Clarke C. Barnes questionnaire, *Marines and Military Law* Research Files, USNARA.

30. John William Mayer questionnaire, MJVN Files.

31. Frederic L. Borch, *Judge Advocates in Vietnam: Army Lawyers in Southeast Asia, 1959–1975* (Fort Leavenworth, Kans.: United States Army Command and General Staff College Press, 2004), 120–121; Frederic L. Borch, *Judge Advocates in Combat: Army Lawyers in Combat Operations from Vietnam to Haiti* (Washington, D.C.: Office of the Judge Advocate General and the United States Army Center for Military History, 2001), 51.

32. Gary D. Solis, *Son Thang: An American War Crime* (Annapolis, Md.: Naval Institute Press, 1997), 334–337.

33. Solis, *Trial by Fire*, 244.

34. Borch, *Judge Advocates in Combat*, 65–82.

35. Ibid., 95–117.

36. Ibid., 121–195; William R. Hagan, "The Judge Advocate in Desert Storm/Desert Shield," *Military Advocate* (Spring 1991): 3. See also Peter Masterton, "The Persian Gulf War Crimes Trials," *Army Lawyer* (June 1991).

37. Quoted in United States Army Center for Law and Military Operations, *Law and Military Operations in Haiti, 1994–1995: Lessons Learned for Judge Advocates* (Charlottesville, Va.: United States Army Judge Advocate General's School, 1995), 33.

38. Ibid., 106–121.

39. Ibid., 125–182.

40. Mac Warner, Mike Dziedzic, Tyler Randolph, et al., *SFOR Lessons Learned in Creating a Secure Environment with Respect for the Rule of Law: Based on a Study of Bosnia* (Washington, D.C.: United States Army, 2000), ii.

41. United States Army Center for Law and Military Operations, *Military Operations in the Balkans, 1995–1998: Lessons Learned for Judge Advocates* (Charlottesville, Va.: United States Army Judge Advocate General's School, 1998), 56–198.

42. See, for example, United States Army Center for Law and Military Operations, "Legal Support for the Afghan National Army, The Judge Advocate General's Legal Center and School," *Army Lawyer* (December 2003); "Marine Officer Is Found Guilty of Dereliction,

Alcohol Counts," San Diego *Union Tribune,* March 27, 2004; Russ Bynum, "Anti-War Soldier Charged with Desertion," Associated Press Service, March 26, 2004; "Six U.S. Military Police Charged with Abuse of 20 Iraqi Prisoners," Reuters News Service, April 16, 2004; Michael Beattie and Lisa Yonka Stevens, "An Open Debate on United States Citizens Designated as Enemy Combatants: Where Do We Go from Here?" *Maryland Law Review* 62 (2003); United States Army Center for Law and Military Operations, *Lessons Learned from Afghanistan and Iraq,* vol. 1: *Major Combat Operations, 11 September 2001–1 May 2003* (Charlottesville, Va.: United States Army Judge Advocate General's School, 2004); JoAnn Wypijewski, "Judgment Days: Lessons from the Abu Ghraib Courts-Martial," *Harper's,* February 2006, 39–50.

43. Robert Perito, *Establishing the Rule of Law in Iraq,* special report 104 (Washington, D.C.: United States Institute of Peace, 2003), 1–16.

44. Khang Hyun-Sung, "Thousands Join Anti-US Protests in South Korea," *South China Morning Post,* December 15, 2003, 1, 7, 10.

45. See, for example, the excellent paper by Richard G. Schenck on the increasing use of contractors in combat operations; this report was written before the 2003 Iraq war, in which tens of thousands of contractors have been used in Operation Iraqi Freedom and in the subsequent rebuilding tasks: Richard G. Schenck, "Contractors: A Strategic Asset or Achilles' Heel?" United States Army War College strategy research project, Carlisle Barracks, Pa. (April 2001). See also Joseph R. Perlak, "The Military Extraterritorial Jurisdiction Act of 2000: Implications for Contractor Personnel," *Military Law Review* 169 (2001); Chris Lombardi, "Law Curbs Contractors in Iraq," *ABA Journal E-Report* 3, 19 (May 14, 2004), http://www.abanet.org/journal/ereport/my14iraq.html; Jonathon Groner, "Untested Law Key in Iraqi Abuse Scandal," *Legal Times,* May 11, 2004; Jason Sherman, "Reining in Contractors in Iraq," *Federal Times,* May 10, 2004; Dan Eggen and Walter Pincus, "Ashcroft Says U.S. Can Prosecute Civilian Contractors for Prison Abuse," *Washington Post,* May 7, 2004; United States Department of Defense, General Counsel, "Proposed Rules: Criminal Jurisdiction over Civilians Employed by or Accompanying the Armed Forces Outside the United States, Certain Service Members, and Former Service Members," 32 CFR Part 153 *Federal Register* 69, 1 (February 2, 2004); Mark W. Bina, "Private Military Contractor Liability and Accountability after Abu Ghraib," *John Marshall Law Review* 38 (Summer 2005).

46. Pierre-Richard Prosper, Ambassador-at-Large for War Crimes Issues, "Address at the Peace Palace in The Hague" (The Hague, Netherlands, December 19, 2001), http://www.state.gov/s/wci/rm/8053.htm.

47. David J. Scheffer, "The United States and the International Criminal Court," *The American Journal of International Law* 93, 12 (1999): 20.

48. See, for example, James B. Roan and Cynthia Buxton, "The American Military Justice System in the New Millennium," *Air Force Law Review* 52 (2002); Michael F. Lohr and Steve Gallota, "Legal Support in War: The Role of Military Lawyers," *University of Chicago Journal of International Law* 4 (Fall 2003); Charles J. Dunlap Jr., "It Ain't No TV Show: JAGS and Modern Military Operations," *University of Chicago Journal of International Law* 4 (Fall 2003); and Kevin J. Barry, "A Face Lift (and Much More) for Aging Beauty: The Cox Commission Recommendations to Rejuvenate the Uniform Code of Military Justice," *Law Review of Michigan State University–Detroit College of Law* (Spring 2002).

49. George S. Prugh, *Law at War: Vietnam, 1964–1973* (Washington, D.C.: Department of the Army, 1975), 117.

50. William G. Eckhardt, "My Lai: An American Tragedy," *University of Missouri at Kansas City Law Review* 68, 671 (Summer 2000): 702–703.

51. Eckhardt, "The Role of the Lawyer in War," 444.

BIBLIOGRAPHY

Adcock, Jerry W. "Marihuana and the United States Military in Vietnam." United States Air Force Air Command and Staff College research study. U.S. Air Force Air University, Maxwell Air Force Base, Ala., 1971.

Allport, Dorothy V. *Bibliography on Military Justice and Military Law*. Washington, D.C.: United States Court of Military Appeals, 1960.

Appy, Christian. *Working Class War: American Combat Soldiers and Vietnam*. Chapel Hill: University of North Carolina Press, 1993.

Bailey, George L. "Military Justice and Combat Readiness." The Naval War College Center for Advanced Research, Newport, R.I., 1978.

Bailey, Tom. "Judgment on the Firing Line." *Soldiers* 28, 8 (August 1971): 5–8.

Baird, Jay W., ed. *From Nuremberg to My Lai*. Lexington, Mass.: D. C. Heath, 1972.

Barker, E. M. "Command Influence: Time for a Revision?" *JAG Journal* 26, 1 (Fall 1971): 47–62.

Barnette, Benjamin H., Jr. "USAF AWOL and Desertion: Some Reasons Why." United States Air Force Air Command and Staff College professional studies paper. U.S. Air Force Air University, Maxwell Air Force Base, Ala., 1972.

Barry, Kevin J. "A Face Lift (and Much More) for Aging Beauty: The Cox Commission Recommendations to Rejuvenate the Uniform Code of Military Justice." *Law Review of Michigan State University–Detroit College of Law* (Spring 2002): 57–125.

Beattie, Michael, and Lisa Yonka Stevens. "An Open Debate on United States Citizens Designated as Enemy Combatants: Where Do We Go from Here?" *Maryland Law Review* 62 (2003): 975–1027.

Behan, Christopher W. "Don't Tug Superman's Cape: In Defense of Convening Authority Selection and Appointment of Court-Martial Panel Members." *Military Law Review* 176 (June 2003): 190–308.

Belknap, Michal R. *The Vietnam War on Trial: The My Lai Massacre and the Court-Martial of Lieutenant Calley*. Lawrence: University Press of Kansas, 2002.

Bell, D. B., and T. J. Houston. *The Vietnam Era Deserter: Characteristics of Unconvicted Army Deserters Participating in the Presidential Clemency Program*. Arlington, Va.: U.S. Army Research Institute for the Behavioral and Social Sciences, 1976.

Bilton, Michael, and Kevin Sim. *Four Hours in My Lai*. New York: Penguin, 1993.

Bina, Mark W. "Private Military Contractor Liability and Accountability after Abu Ghraib." *John Marshall Law Review* 38 (Summer 2005): 1237–1263.

Bishop, Joseph W., Jr. "The Case for Military Justice." *Military Law Review* 62 (Fall 1973): 215–224.

———. "The Quality of Military Justice." *New York Times Magazine*, February 22, 1970: 15–20.

Bond, Thomas C. "The Why of Fragging." *American Journal of Psychiatry* 133, 11 (November 1976): 1328–1331.

Borch, Frederic L. *Judge Advocates in Combat: Army Lawyers in Combat Operations from Vietnam to Haiti.* Washington, D.C.: Office of the Judge Advocate General and the United States Army Center for Military History, 2001.

———. *Judge Advocates in Vietnam: Army Lawyers in Southeast Asia, 1959–1975.* Fort Leavenworth, Kans.: United States Army Command and General Staff College Press, 2004.

Borek, Theodore B. "Legal Service during War." United States Army War College military studies program paper. Army War College, Carlisle Barracks, Pa., 1987.

Bradford, Zeb B. "With Creighton Abrams in Vietnam." *The Assembly: Magazine of the Association of Graduates of the United States Military Academy* (May/June 1998): 27–32.

Bryant, Clifton D. *Khaki-Collar Crime: Deviant Behavior in the Military Context.* New York: Free Press, 1979.

Buttinger, Joseph. *Vietnam: A Dragon Embattled.* Vol. 2. New York: Frederick A. Praeger, 1967.

Bynum, Russ. "Anti-War Soldier Charged with Desertion." Associated Press Service (March 26, 2004).

"The Case of Lieutenant Duffy." *Nation* 210, 14, April 13, 1970, 419–420.

Cincinnatus. *Self-Destruction: The Disintegration and Decay of the United States Army during the Vietnam Era.* New York: W. W. Norton, 1981.

Clarke, Jeffrey J. *The U.S. Army in Vietnam—Advice and Support: The Final Years.* Washington, D.C.: United States Army Center for Military History, 1988.

Cooper, Norman G. "My Lai and Military Justice—To What Effect?" *Military Law Review* 59 (Winter 1973): 93–127.

Corddry, Charles W. "Jurisdiction to Try Discharged Servicemen for Violations of the Laws of War." *JAG Journal* 26, 1 (Fall 1971): 63–76.

Crouchet, Jack. *Vietnam Stories: A Judge's Memoir.* Boulder: University Press of Colorado, 1997.

Crump, Gerald F. "A History of the Structure of Military Justice in the United States, 1775–1920." *The Air Force Law Review* 16, 4 (Winter 1974): 47–68.

Currey, Cecil Barr. *Long Binh Jail: An Oral History of Vietnam's Notorious U.S. Military Prison.* Dulles, Va.: Brassey's, 1999.

Dacy, Douglas C. *Foreign Aid, War, and Economic Development: South Vietnam, 1955–1975.* Cambridge: Cambridge University Press, 1986.

Davidson, Phillip B. *Vietnam at War: The History, 1946–1975.* New York: Oxford University Press, 1988.

Di Mona, Joseph. *Great Court-Martial Cases.* New York: Grosset and Dunlap, 1972.

Dunlap, Charles J., Jr. "It Ain't No TV Show: JAGS and Modern Military Operations." *University of Chicago Journal of International Law* 4 (Fall 2003): 479–491.

Eckhardt, William G. "My Lai: An American Tragedy." *University of Missouri at Kansas City Law Review* 68 (Summer 2000): 671–703.

———. "The Role of the Lawyer in War: Lawyering for Uncle Sam When He Draws His Sword." *Chicago Journal of International Law* 4 (Fall 2003): 431–444.

Eggen, Dan, and Walter Pincus. "Ashcroft Says U.S. Can Prosecute Civilian Contractors for Prison Abuse." *Washington Post,* May 7, 2004, A18.

Ervin, Sam, Jr. "The Military Justice Act of 1968." *Military Law Review* 45 (July 1969): 77–98.

Everett, Robinson O. "Did Military Justice Fail or Prevail?" *Michigan Law Review* 96, 6 (May 1998): 1421–1434.

———. "*O'Callahan v. Parker:* Milestone or Millstone in Military Justice?" *Duke Law Journal* 1969, 5 (October 1969): 853–896.

———, and Laurent R. Hourcle. "Crime without Punishment: Ex-Servicemen, Civilian Employees, and Dependents." *United States Air Force Judge Advocate General Law Review* 13, 3 (Summer 1971): 184–223.

Finn, James, ed. *Conscience and Command: Justice and Discipline in the Military.* New York: Random House, 1971.

Fiscus, Thomas J. "Defending Military Justice: Suspect Rights." *The Inspector General Brief* 55, 3 (May–June 2003): 16–18.

FitzGerald, Frances. *Fire in the Lake: The Vietnamese and the Americans in Vietnam.* New York: Vintage Books, 1989.

Gabriel, Richard A. "Professionalism versus Managerialism in Vietnam." *Air University Review* 32, 2 (January–February 1981): 77–85.

Gabriel, Richard A., and Paul L. Savage. *Crisis in Command: Mismanagement in the Army.* New York: Hill and Wang, 1978.

Gates, E. A., and Gary V. Casida. *Report to the Judge Advocate General by the Wartime Legislation Team.* Washington, D.C.: United States Army, 1983.

Generous, William T., Jr. *Swords and Scales: The Development of the Uniform Code of Military Justice.* Port Washington, N.Y.: Kennikat Press, 1973.

Goldstein, Joseph, Burke Marshall, and Jack Schwartz. *The My Lai Massacre and Its Coverup: Beyond the Reach of Law? The Peers Report with a Supplement and Introductory Essay on the Limits of Law.* New York: Free Press, 1976.

Groner, Jonathon. "Untested Law Key in Iraqi Abuse Scandal." *Legal Times,* May 11, 2004, http://www.law.com (accessed May 19, 2004).

"Guilty Minority." *Time,* January 5, 1968: 31–32.

Hagan, William R. "The Judge Advocate in Desert Storm /Desert Shield." *Military Advocate,* Spring 1991: 1–2.

Hammond, William H. *Reporting Vietnam: Media and Military at War.* Lawrence: University Press of Kansas, 1998.

"Hard Times: Testimony of Vietnam Veterans Given before the National Committee for a Citizens' Commission of Inquiry on U.S. Crimes in Vietnam." *Ramparts Magazine* 9, February 1971, 12–18.

Hartle, Anthony E. "Atrocities in War: Dirty Hands and Noncombatants." *Social Research* 69, 4 (Winter 2002): 963–979.

———. *Moral Issues in Military Decision Making,* 2nd ed., revised. Lawrence: University Press of Kansas, 2004.

Heinl, Robert D., Jr. "The Collapse of the Armed Forces." *Armed Forces Journal,* June 7, 1971, 30–38.

Herring, George C. *America's Longest War: The United States and Vietnam, 1950–1975.* 3rd ed. New York: McGraw-Hill, 1996.

———. "'Peoples Quite Apart': Americans, South Vietnamese, and the War in Vietnam." *Diplomatic History* 14, 1 (Winter 1990): 1–23.

Herrod, Randy. *Blue's Bastards: A True Story of Valor under Fire.* Washington, D.C.: Regnery Gateway, 1989.

Hersh, Seymour. *My Lai 4: A Report on the Massacre and Its Aftermath.* New York: Random House, 1970.

Hess, Gary R. *Vietnam and the United States: Origins and Legacy of War*. Rev. ed. New York: Twayne Publishers, 1998.

Hunt, Andrew. *The Turning: A History of Vietnam Veterans against the War*. New York: New York University Press, 2001.

Hunt, Richard A. *Pacification: The American Struggle for Vietnam's Hearts and Minds*. Boulder, Colo.: Westview Press, 1995.

Jackson, Donald. "Confessions of the Winter Soldiers." *Life* 71, 2, July 9, 1971, 22–27.

Jamieson, Neil L. *Understanding Vietnam*. Berkeley: University of California Press, 1993.

Kalven, Harry, and Hans Zeisel. *The American Jury*. Boston: Little, Brown, 1966.

Karnow, Stanley. *Vietnam: A History*. Rev. and updated ed. New York: Penguin Books, 1991.

Khang, Hyun-Sung. "Thousands Join Anti-US Protests in South Korea," *South China Morning Post* (December 15, 2002): 1, 7, 10.

Knoll, Erwin, and Judith Nies McFadden, eds. *War Crimes and the American Conscience*. New York: Holt, Rinehart and Winston, 1970.

Kolko, Gabriel. *Anatomy of a War: Vietnam, the United States, and the Modern Historical Experience*. New York: Pantheon Books, 1985.

Krepinevich, Andrew F., Jr. *The Army and Vietnam*. Baltimore, Md.: Johns Hopkins University Press, 1986.

Kroll, Jerome. "Racial Patterns of Military Crimes in Vietnam." *Psychiatry* 39 (February 1976): 51–64.

Kunnes, Richard. *The American Heroin Empire: Power, Profits, and Politics*. New York: Dodd and Meade, 1972.

Lancaster, Donald. *The Emancipation of French Indochina*. New York: Oxford University Press, 1961.

Lasseter, Earle F., and James B. Thwing. "Military Justice in Time of War." *American Bar Association Journal* 68 (May 1983): 566–569.

Lederer, William J. "Our Own Worst Enemy." *Saturday Evening Post* 241, 11, June 1, 1968, 32–41.

Levy, David W. *The Debate over Vietnam*. 2nd ed. Baltimore, Md.: Johns Hopkins University Press, 1995.

Lewy, Guenter. *America in Vietnam*. New York: Oxford University Press, 1978.

Lohr, Michael F., and Steve Gallota. "Legal Support in War: The Role of Military Lawyers." *University of Chicago Journal of International Law* 4 (Fall 2003): 465–478.

Lombardi, Chris. "Law Curbs Contractors in Iraq," *ABA Journal E-Report,* May 14, 2004, http://www.abanet.org/journal/ereport/my14iraq.html (accessed May 19, 2004).

Luce, Don, and John Sommer. *Viet Nam: The Unheard Voices*. Ithaca, N.Y.: Cornell University Press, 1969.

Lurie, Jonathan. *Arming Military Justice*. 2 vols. Princeton, N.J.: Princeton University Press, 1992.

"Marine Officer Is Found Guilty of Dereliction, Alcohol Counts." San Diego *Union Tribune*, March 27, 2004, B1.

"Marines Call It Treason." *Newsweek* 97, February 16, 1971, 41.

Marshall, Jonathan. *Drug Wars: Corruption, Counterinsurgency, and Covert Operations in the Third World*. Forestville, Calif.: Cohan and Cohan Publishers, 1991.

Masterton, Peter. "The Persian Gulf War Crimes Trials." *Army Lawyer,* June 1991: 7–18.

Mathews, Ann. "Army JAG's Search for Justice." *Vietnam,* December 1998, 30–36.

Maurer, Maurer. "Military Justice under General Washington." *Military Affairs* 28 (Spring 1964): 8–16.

Mayers, Lewis. *The American Legal System: The Administration of Justice in the United States by Judicial, Administrative, Military, and Arbitral Tribunals.* Rev. ed. New York: Harper and Row, 1964.

McCoy, Alfred W. *The Politics of Heroin in Southeast Asia.* New York: Harper and Row, 1972.

McCullough, Frank. "For Profiteers, What a Lovely War." *Life* 67, August 1, 1969, 46–49.

McLeod, Mark W., and Nguyen Thi Dieu. *Culture and Customs of Vietnam.* Westport, Conn.: Greenwood Press, 2001.

"The Mere Gook Rule." *Newsweek,* April 13, 1970, 29–30.

"Military Law: Two Sides of Atrocity." *Time,* July 14, 1967, 38.

Moss, George Donelson. *Vietnam: An American Ordeal.* 4th ed. Upper Saddle River, N.J.: Prentice Hall, 2002.

Moyer, Homer E., Jr. *Justice and the Military.* Washington, D.C.: Public Law Education Institute, 1972.

———. "Procedural Rights of the Military Accused: Advantages over a Civilian Defendant." *Maine Law Review* 22 (1970): 21–56.

Nash, William L. "The Laws of War: A Military View." *Ethics and International Affairs* 16, 1 (2002): 14–17.

Olson, James S., and Randy Roberts. *My Lai: A Brief History with Documents.* Boston: Bedford Books, 1998.

Osiel, Mark J. *Obeying Orders: Atrocity, Military Discipline, and the Law of War.* London: Transaction Publishers, 1999.

Parks, W. Hays. "Command Responsibility for War Crimes." *Military Law Review* 62 (Fall 1973): 1–104.

———. "Crimes in Hostilities." *Marine Corps Gazette* 60, 16 (1976): 33–39.

———. "Statistics versus Actuality in Vietnam." *Air University Review* 32, 4 (May–June 1981): 84–88.

Perito, Robert. *Establishing the Rule of Law in Iraq.* Special Report 104. Washington, D.C.: United States Institute of Peace, 2003.

Perlak, Joseph. "The Military Extraterritorial Jurisdiction Act of 2000: Implications for Contractor Personnel." *Military Law Review* 169 (2001): 91–140.

Prugh, George S. *Law at War: Vietnam, 1964–1973.* Washington, D.C.: Department of the Army, 1975.

Pydasheff, Robert S., and William K. Suter. "Military Justice?—Definitely!" *Tulane Law Review* 49 (March 1975): 588–602.

Quinn, Robert Emmett. "Some Comparisons between Courts-Martial and Civilian Practice." *Military Law Review* 46 (October 1969): 57–77.

Record, Jeffrey. *The Wrong War: Why We Lost in Vietnam.* Annapolis, Md.: Naval Institute Press, 1998.

Roan, James B., and Cynthia Buxton. "The American Military Justice System in the New Millennium." *The Air Force Law Review* 52 (2002): 185–211.

Rollman, Robert O. "Of Crimes, Courts-Martial, and Punishment: A Short History of Military Justice." *United States Air Force JAG Law Review* 11, 2 (Spring 1969): 212–222.

Ross, Joseph E. "The Military Justice Act of 1968: Historical Background." *JAG Journal* (May–June 1969): 125–129.

Rotter, Andrew, ed. *Light at the End of the Tunnel: A Vietnam War Anthology*. Rev. ed. Wilmington, Del.: Scholarly Resources, 1999.

Rowe, Don Carlos, and Rick Berg. *The Vietnam War and American Culture*. New York: Columbia University Press, 1991.

Ruffner, Kevin Conley. "The Black Market and Postwar Berlin: Colonel Miller and an Army Scandal." *Prologue: The Journal of the National Archives* 34, 3 (2002): 170–183.

SarDesai, D. R. *Vietnam: Trials and Tribulations of a Nation*. Long Beach, Calif.: Long Beach Publications, 1988.

Scheffer, David J. "The United States and the International Criminal Court." *The American Journal of International Law* 93, 1 (1999): 12–22.

Schenck, Richard G. "Contractors: A Strategic Asset or Achilles' Heel?" United States Army War College Strategy Research Project. April 2001. Available at http://stinet.dtic.mil/oai/oai?&verb=getRecord&metadataPrefix=html&identifier=ADA391192.

Shafer, D. Michael. *Deadly Paradigms: The Failure of U.S. Counterinsurgency Policy*. Princeton, N.J.: Princeton University Press, 1988.

Shaffter, Dorothy. *"War" and the Military Courts: Judicial Interpretation of Its Meaning*. Smithtown, N.Y.: Exposition Press, 1988.

Sheldon, Walter J. *Tigers in the Rice: The Story of Vietnam from Ancient Past to Uncertain Future*. London: Cromwell-Collier Press, 1969.

Sherman, Edward F. "The Civilianization of Military Law." *Maine Law Review* 22 (1970): 3–103.

———. "Military Justice without Military Control." *Yale Law Journal* 82 (1973): 1398–1425.

Sherman, Jason. "Reining in Contractors in Iraq." *FederalTimes.com*, May 10, 2004, http://federaltimes.com/index.php?S=2897996 (accessed May 19, 2004).

Sherrill, Robert. *Military Justice Is to Justice as Military Music Is to Music*. New York: Harper and Row, 1969.

Shulzinger, Robert D. *A Time for War: The United States and Vietnam, 1941–1975*. New York: Oxford University Press, 1997.

Siegel, Jay. *Origins of the United States Navy Judge Advocate General's Corps: A History of Legal Administration in the United States Navy, 1775–1967*. Washington, D.C.: Government Printing Office, 1998.

"Six U.S. Military Police Charged with Abuse of 20 Iraqi Prisoners." Reuters News Service, April 16, 2004.

Smidt, Michael L. "Yamashita, Medina, and Beyond: Command Responsibility in Contemporary Military Operations." *Military Law Review* 164 (June 2000): 155–234.

Solf, Waldemar. "A Response to Telford Taylor's *Nuremberg and Vietnam: An American Tragedy*." *Akron Law Review* 5, 1 (Winter 1972): 43–68.

Solis, Gary D. *Son Thang: An American War Crime*. Annapolis, Md.: Naval Institute Press, 1997.

———. *Trial by Fire: Marines and Military Law in Vietnam*. Washington, D.C.: Marine Corps History and Museums Division, 1989.

Sorley, Lewis. *A Better War: The Unexamined Victories and Final Tragedy of America's Last Years in Vietnam*. New York: Harcourt, 1999.

Spak, Michael I., and Donald F. Spak. *Cases and Materials on Military Justice*. Chicago: Harcourt Brace Jovanovich, 1976.

Spector, Ronald H. *The U.S. Army in Vietnam—Advice and Support: The Early Years.* Washington, D.C.: United States Army Center for Military History, 1985.

Stacewicz, Richard. *Winter Soldiers: An Oral History of the Vietnam Veterans against the War.* New York: Twayne Publishers, 1997.

Taylor, Telford. *Nuremberg and Vietnam: An American Tragedy.* Chicago: Quadrangle Books, 1970.

United States Agency for International Development. Office of Vietnam Affairs. *United States Economic Assistance to South Vietnam, 1954–1975: Terminal Report.* Washington, D.C: United States Agency for International Development, 1975.

United States Army. *The Law of Land Warfare.* Field Manual 27–10. Washington, D.C.: Government Printing Office, 1956.

———. *A Manual for Courts-Martial, Courts of Inquiry, and Retiring Boards, and Other Procedure under Military Law.* Washington, D.C.: Government Printing Office, 1916.

United States Army. Center for Law and Military Operations. *Law and Military Operations in Haiti, 1994–1995: Lessons Learned for Judge Advocates.* Charlottesville, Va.: United States Army Judge Advocate General's School, 1995.

———. "Legal Support for the Afghan National Army, the Judge Advocate General's Legal Center and School." *Army Lawyer* (December 2003): 33–36.

———. *Lessons Learned from Afghanistan and Iraq.* Vol. 1: *Major Combat Operations, 11 September 2001–1 May 2003.* Charlottesville, Va.: United States Army Judge Advocate General's School, 2004.

———. *Military Operations in the Balkans, 1995–1998: Lessons Learned for Judge Advocates.* Charlottesville, Va.: United States Army Judge Advocate General's School, 1998.

United States Army. Judge Advocate General Corps. *The Army Lawyer: A History of the Judge Advocate General Corps, 1775–1975.* Buffalo, N.Y.: William S. Hein, 1993.

United States Congress. House of Representatives. Committee on Appropriations. *Department of Defense Appropriations for 1970, Hearings, Part 1: Military Personnel.* 91st Cong., 1st sess. Washington, D.C.: Government Printing Office, 1969.

———. *Department of Defense Appropriations of 1972: Hearings before a Subcommittee of the Committee on Appropriations, Part 9.* 92nd Cong., 1st sess. Washington, D.C.: Government Printing Office, 1971.

United States Congress. House of Representatives. Committee on Armed Services. *Hearings by Special Subcommittee on Alleged Drug Abuse in the Armed Services.* 91st Cong., 2nd sess. Washington, D.C: Government Printing Office, 1971.

United States Congress. House of Representatives. Committee on Government Operations. *The Commercial (Commodity) Import Program for Vietnam (Follow-up Investigation), Fifth Report.* 90th Cong., 1st sess. Washington, D.C.: Government Printing Office, 1967.

———. *Illicit Practices Affecting the U.S. Economic Program in Vietnam (Follow-up Investigation), Fourth Report by the Committee on Government Operations.* 90th Cong., 1st sess. Washington, D.C.: Government Printing Office, 1967.

———. *A Review of the Inequitable Monetary Rate of Exchange in Vietnam, Twenty-sixth Report.* 91st Cong., 2nd sess. Washington, D.C.: Government Printing Office, 1970.

———. *Vietnam and The Hidden U.S. Subsidy (Inequitable Currency Exchange Rates), Eighth Report.* 92nd Cong., 1st sess. Washington, D.C.: Government Printing Office, 1971.

United States Congress. House of Representatives. Committee on the Judiciary. *Report of the Special Subcommittee on Application of the Uniform Code of Military Justice to American*

Civilians in the Republic of Vietnam. 90th Cong., 1st sess. Washington, D.C.: Government Printing Office, 1967.

United States Congress. Senate. Committee on Appropriations. *Department of Defense Appropriations for Fiscal Year 1970: Hearings before the Subcommittee of the Committee on Appropriations, Part 3.* 91st Cong., 1st sess. Washington, D.C.: Government Printing Office, 1969.

United States Congress. Senate. Committee on Armed Services. *Military Deserters, Hearings.* 90th Cong., 1st sess. Washington, D.C.: Government Printing Office, 1968.

United States Congress. Senate. Committee on Government Operations. *Fraud and Corruption in Management of Military Club Systems; Illegal Currency Manipulations Affecting South Vietnam: Hearings before the Permanent Subcommittee on Investigations of the Committee on Government Operations, Part 3.* 91st Cong., 1st sess. Washington, D.C.: Government Printing Office, 1970.

———. *Improper Practices, Commodity Import Program, U.S. Foreign Aid, Vietnam.* 91st Cong., 1st sess. Washington, D.C.: Government Printing Office, 1969.

———. *Improper Practices, Commodity Import Program, U.S. Foreign Aid, Vietnam: Hearings before the Permanent Subcommittee on Investigations of the Committee on Government Operations.* 90th Cong., 1st sess. Washington, D.C.: Government Printing Office, 1967.

United States Congress. Senate. Committee on Labor and Public Welfare. Subcommittee on Alcoholism and Narcotics. *Military Drug Abuse, 1971: Hearings.* 92nd Cong., 1st sess. Washington, D.C.: Government Printing Office, 1971.

United States Congress. Senate. Committee on Military Affairs. *Hearings on the Establishment of Military Justice before a Subcommittee of the Senate Committee on Military Affairs.* 66th Cong., 1st sess. Washington, D.C.: Government Printing Office, 1919.

———. *Hearings on Trials by Court-Martial before the Senate Committee on Military Affairs.* 65th Cong., 3rd sess. Washington, D.C.: Government Printing Office, 1919.

United States Court of Military Appeals and Judge Advocate Generals of the Armed Forces. *Annual Joint Report of the U.S. Court of Military Appeals and the Judge Advocate Generals of the Armed Forces Submitted to the Committees on Armed Services of the Senate and the House of Representatives and to the Secretary of Defense and Secretary of the Treasury and the Secretaries of the Departments of the Army, Navy, and Air Force.* Various years.

United States Department of Defense. *Manual for Courts-Martial, United States.* Washington, D.C.: Government Printing Office, 1951.

———. *Manual for Courts-Martial, United States.* Washington, D.C.: Government Printing Office, 1969.

———. *Manual for Courts-Martial, United States, 2000 Edition.* Washington, D.C.: Government Printing Office, 2000.

———. *Report of the Task Force on the Administration of Military Justice in the Armed Forces.* 2 vols. Washington, D.C.: Government Printing Office, 1972.

United States Department of Defense. General Counsel. "Proposed Rules: Criminal Jurisdiction over Civilians Employed by or Accompanying the Armed Forces outside the United States, Certain Service Members, and Former Service Members." 32 CFR Part 153 *Federal Register* 69, 1 (February 2, 2004).

United States Department of War. *Report of the Committee on Military Justice.* Washington D.C.: Government Printing Office, 1947.

United States Navy. *Forms of Procedure for General and Summary Courts-Martial, Courts of Inquiry, Investigations, Naval and Marine Examining and Retiring Boards.* Washington, D.C.: Government Printing Office, 1896.

———. "Report of the Ballantine Board to the Secretary of the Navy." Department of the Navy. April 1946.

———. "Report and Recommendations to the Secretary of the Navy [on the Articles of the Government of the Navy and Courts-Martial Procedure]." Department of the Navy. November 21, 1945.

United States Treaties and Other International Agreements, Vol. 3, Part 2, 1952. Washington, D.C.: Government Printing Office, 1954.

Valle, James E. *Rocks and Shoals: Order and Discipline in the Old Navy, 1800–1861.* Annapolis, Md.: Naval Institute Press, 1980.

Van Der Haag, Ernest. "U.S. Crimes in Vietnam." *Nation* 23, 41, October 22, 1971, 1171–1176.

Vietnam—Chronicle of a War. CBS News Collector Series. New York: CBS, 1991. Video.

Vietnam Veterans against the War. *The Winter Soldier Investigation: An Inquiry into American War Crimes.* Boston: Beacon Press, 1972.

Walker, William O. *Opium and Foreign Policy: The Anglo-American Search for Order in Asia, 1912–1954.* Chapel Hill: University of North Carolina Press, 1991.

———, ed. *Drug Control Police: Essays in Historical and Comparative Perspective.* University Park: Pennsylvania State University Press, 1991.

Warner, Mac, Mike Dziedzic, Tyler Randolph, et al. *SFOR Lessons Learned in Creating a Secure Environment with Respect for the Rule of Law: Based on a Study of Bosnia.* Washington, D.C.: United States Army, 2000.

West, Luther C. "A History of Command Influence on the Military Judicial System." *UCLA Law Review* 18 (1970–1971): 1–156.

———. *They Call It Justice: Command Influence and the Court-Martial System.* New York: Viking Press, 1977.

Westerman, George F. "Military Justice in the Republic of Vietnam." *Military Law Review* 31 (January 1966): 137–158.

Westmoreland, William C. *A Soldier Reports.* New York: Da Capo Press, 1989.

———, and George S. Prugh. "Judges in Command: The Judicialized Uniform Code of Military Justice in Combat." *Harvard Journal of Law and Public Policy* 3 (1980): 1–93.

Wiener, Frederick Bernays. "Are the General Military Articles Unconstitutionally Vague?" *American Bar Association Journal* 54 (April 1968): 357–364.

Willbanks, James H. *Abandoning Vietnam: How America Left and South Vietnam Lost Its War.* Lawrence: University Press of Kansas, 2004.

Winthrop, William. *Military Law and Precedents.* 2nd ed. Washington, D.C.: Government Printing Office, 1920.

Witt, Larry. "Marine Robert Garwood, the Last P.O.W. Back from Vietnam, Faces Court-Martial for Desertion." *People Weekly* 12, December 17, 1979, 50–52.

Yery, Lt. Col. Richard T. "Trial of War Crimes under the Uniform Code of Military Justice." Professional study paper, U.S. Air Force Air War College, Air University, Maxwell Air Force Base, Ala., April 1972.

INDEX

Abrams, Creighton, 33, 156, 157, 159
Adams, John, 1, 2
Afghanistan, 183, 184
AIDS, 139
Air Force, U.S.
 AWOLs, 72, 74, 75
 courts-martial, 53
 drug abuse and, 125 (table), 128 (table),
  129 (table), 131, 138
 judge advocates, 16, 32
 slot machines and, 165
Air Force units, U.S.
 Second Air Division, 21, 22
 Seventh Air Force, 24, 26, 44–45, 131
Alcorn, Ron W., 156
Alien and Sedition Acts of 1798, 2
Allison, Tommy, 27
Ambort, Louis R., 104–5, 106–7, 109
Americal Division, 93, 94, 96
 Augsburg corruption scandal and, 157, 158
 drug problem and, 129–30
American Bar Association, 7, 11, 13
American Bar Association Journal, 175
American Embassy, Saigon
 black market and corruption and, 160, 161,
  162, 163
 jurisdiction and, 59, 60–61, 62, 64, 66
 U.S. advisers and, 21
American Legion, 19
American Mayor of Saigon, 153
amnesty programs (drug user), 125–28, 129,
 130–32
amphetamines and barbiturates, 127 (table),
 129 (table), 130
Ansell, Samuel Tilden, 7–9, 10, 11, 13
Ansell-Crowder dispute, 8
Ap Bac, battle at, 21
appellate boards of review, 20
Appy, Christian, 29, 75
Army, U.S.
 Augsburg corruption scandal and, 155–59
 AWOLs, 73–74, 75–76
 black market activities and, 153–54, 165
 courts-martial, 5–6, 10, 12–13, 53, 70

drug use and, 121–22, 124, 125 (table),
 127–29, 132–34
First Logistical Command, 153
judge advocates, 4–5, 6–7, 10, 12, 31
 See also Criminal Investigation Division
 (CID); MACV
Army Court of Military Review, 83, 87, 101,
 134
Army Criminal Investigation Command, 165
Army units, U.S.
 Americal division (Twenty-third Infantry),
  93, 94, 96, 129–30, 157, 158
 First Armored Division, 180
 First Cavalry, 71, 76, 77–78, 127, 128–29
 First Division, 110
 Eleventh Brigade, 93, 96
 Twenty-fourth Division, 156
 Twenty-fifth division, 127
 155th Assault Helicopter Company, 65
 II Field Force, 127, 128
"Articles for the Government of the Navy," 3,
 9, 12
Articles of War, U.S., 1, 2, 5–6, 12, 58
atrocities
 definition of, 90, 93
 "following orders" defense and, 91, 97–98,
  99–100, 102, 108, 110–12
 My Lai incident and, 92–103
 Son Thang incident and, 92, 103–9
Augsburg group, 155–59
Averett, Raymond, 64
AWOLs, 71–76

bad conduct discharges, 19, 20, 73, 125, 126,
 134, 173
Bagby, William, 156, 157, 158, 159
Bailey, F. Lee, 102
Baldree, Charles, 24
Balkans, 182
Ballantine, Arthur, 11
Ballantine Report, 11, 12
Bancroft, George, 3
Ban Me Thuot, 65
Bao Dai, 142

Bar Association of New York City, 19
Barker, Frank A., 93, 94
Barnes, Clarke C., 27, 178
Bartimo, Frank, 122
Bass, Theodore, 156, 157, 159
Belknap, Michal, 98
Bengston, David, 177
Berger, Samuel D., 164
Bernhardt, Michael, 102
Bin Tay, 94
Bishop, Joseph, 173
black market
    CIP and, 145
    exchange rates, 147, 148 (table)
    items sold on, 140–41
    legal cases involving, 147–55, 194n7
    opium trade and, 119
    Uniform Code of Military Justice and,
        145–46, 150, 153, 204–5n13
    U.S. campaign against, 141–42, 145–46,
        153, 160–62
    U.S. civilians and, 60, 61, 150–52, 161
    Vietnamese economy and, 140–45
    See also currency fraud
Blue Bastards (Herrod), 109
Bohrer, Joseph A., 46
Bond, Thomas C., 78–79
Bono, Sonny, 122
Borch, Frederic, 178
Borek, Theodore B., 176
Bosnia, 182
Bowling, Sergeant, 76–77
Boxer Rebellion (1900), 58
Boyd, Thomas R., 104, 105–6, 107
Bozant, Augustine, 81
Braxton, H. Harrison, Jr., 21–22, 23, 182
Brinks Hotel bombing, 42
British military regulations, 1, 2
Brown, Charles E., 106, 107, 108
Brown, Ossie, 97
Bunker, Ellsworth, 61, 160
Bushell, Gary E., 108

Calley, William, 93, 95, 97, 103
    court martial and appeal of, 98–102
Calloway, Howard, 102
Camp Red Ball, 47, 48
Cam Ranh Bay, 57
    air base at, 135–37
Casper, John Ernest, 177
Center for Law and Military Operations, 180–82

Central Intelligence Agency (CIA), drug trade
    and, 120
Chamberlain, George, 8
Chinese opium trade, 117–18, 119
Christmas card fraud case, 159–60
CID. See Criminal Investigation Division
civilianization of military justice, 5, 7–8,
    13–15, 17–18, 174, 175, 177, 185
civilian lawyers (U.S.) in Vietnam, 32–33
civilians, U.S.
    black market and currency fraud by, 60, 61,
        150–52, 161
    courts-martial of, 58, 60–61, 63–64, 65–66,
        135, 151
    drug abuse by, 135
    in Middle East wars, 180
    U.S. military jurisdiction over, 16, 50, 51,
        57, 58, 60–66, 135, 151, 184
    South Vietnamese jurisdiction over, 59, 60,
        62, 151
Civil War, U.S., 4, 71
claims and solatia program, U.S., xi, 34–49
claims program, Vietnamese, 43 48, 49
Clark, George Ramsay, 9
Clark, Ramsay, 33
Clark Air Base, 21
Code Committee, 18–19
Cole, Earl, 158, 159
combat refusals, 76–78
Combined Anti-Narcotics Enforcement Com-
    mittees, 123, 131
command influence, 11, 12, 13–14, 19, 170,
    171, 174, 175, 177
command responsibility doctrine, 171, 172
Commercial Import Program (CIP), 142, 144,
    145
Composto, Joseph, 168
Congress, U.S.
    on corruption in military, 146, 159, 165–66
    drug problem in Vietnam and, 127 (table),
        128 (table), 129 (table)
    on jurisdiction, 59–60, 184
    on military justice, 8–9, 12–14, 18–19, 175,
        185
    My Lai incident and, 95, 97
    navy and, 3, 4, 9, 13
    See also House, U.S.; Senate, U.S.
Connor, Albert O., 98, 101
Con Thien, 27
Continental Congress, U.S., 1–2
Cooper, Charles G., 105, 106–7

Cooper, Norman G., 177
corruption
    Augsburg group scandal and, 155–59
    CIP and, 144–45
    in South Vietnamese government and soci-
        ety, x, 51–52, 120, 123, 141–43, 144, 145,
        163, 164–65, 166
    U.S. attempts to combat, 164, 165–66
    See also black market; currency manipula-
        tion
Cosgriff, Bill, 149
Court of Military Appeals, 15–16, 18–19, 53,
        64, 77, 101, 169, 173, 174
courts-martial
    air force, 53
    army, 5–6, 10, 12–13, 53, 70, 71
    black market and currency cases and, 153,
        161, 194n7
    of civilians, 58, 60–61, 63–64, 65–66, 135,
        151
    drug abuse cases and, 130
    establishment of, 2, 3, 4
    general, 5, 12–13, 15, 28, 31, 53–54, 55,
        68–69, 70–71, 130, 175–76
    MACV and, 55, 60–61, 62, 66, 153
    navy, 9, 12, 53
    number of, 9, 10, 67, 70–71, 194n7
    special, 5, 12, 20, 28, 31–32, 53–54, 68, 69,
        70–71, 130, 175–76
    summary, 5, 28, 31, 57, 68, 70–71, 130
    Uniform Code of Military Justice on,
        13–14, 18–19, 54, 59
    USASCV and, 55
crime
    Marine Corps and, 85 (table), 86 (table)
    U.S., against Vietnam civilians, 84–87,
        194n7
    See also black market; currency fraud; frag-
        ging; murder; rape
Criminal Investigation Division (CID)
    Augsburg group corruption scandal and,
        156–58
    black market and, 150
    drug trafficking and, 122–23, 129, 130, 132
    My Lai incident and, 95, 97
Crowder, Enoch, 8
Crowley, John D., 155
Crowly, Leonard G., 36
currency exchange rates, 148 (table)
currency fraud (manipulation)
    amount of money involved in, 147

definition of, 146
legal cases involving, 147–53, 194n7
U.S. campaign against, 141, 153, 161–64
by U.S. civilians, 60, 61, 150–52
Cushman, Charles, 179

Da Nang
    Air Base, 132
    black market in, 141, 148, 149–50, 151
    foreign claims in, 36, 41
    Marine Corps and, 27, 63, 80
Daniel, Aubrey, 98, 99, 100, 101
Daniels, James, 132
Davis, Stewart, 88
Defense Department, U.S.
    claims and, 36, 42
    contracts, 13, 152
    on corruption in military, 165–66
    on jurisdiction, 50, 59, 60, 61, 62–63, 184
    MACV and, 24
DeGill Corporation, 152
desertion, 71–75
Desert Shield, 180
Desert Storm, 180
Diem, Ngo Dinh, 23
dishonorable discharge, 5, 73, 173
Do Van Man, 111
Donovan, William E., 49
Doyle, Brooks S., Jr., 98–99
drug use
    amnesty program and, 125–28, 129, 130–32
    anti-drug programs, 122, 128, 129, 130, 131
    army and, 121–22, 124, 125 (table), 127–29,
        132–34
    at Cam Ranh Bay Air Base, 135–37
    CIA and, 120
    Marine Corps and, 124, 125 (table), 128
        (table), 129 (table), 131–32
    navy and, 125 (table), 128 (table), 129
        (table), 130–31, 138
    at Pleiku Air Base, 135–36
    rehabilitation programs and, 125–27, 128,
        131
    trafficking and, 117–21, 122, 135–37, 138
    U.S. campaign against, 122–23, 128–29,
        130–32
    U.S. civilians and, 135
    U.S. government tolerance of, 120
    U.S. military use of, 121–22, 124, 132–34
due process
    International Criminal Court and, 185

due process *(continued)*
  military justice and, 1, 2, 7, 20, 25, 170,
    172–73, 174, 176, 181
  My Lai trials and, 101
  Vietnamese legal system and, 57
Duffy, James B., 111, 112
Duffy, La Verne J., 151
Dunbar, James, 147–50
Dynalectron Corporation, 65

East India Company, 117
Eckhardt, William G., 102, 186
Eifler, C. W., 195n25
Elleget Enterprises, 152
Elliot, J. Robert, 101–2
Enmark, William, 95
Ervin, Sam, 18, 19–20, 170
Espinoza, Carlos, 132–33
Evans, B. L., 96
Everett, Robinson O., 66
Executive Order 10149, 15

Faw, Duane, 177
Federal Tort Claims Act, 42
Felix, John, 47
Fifth Circuit Court, 102
Fillmore, Millard, 3
Financial Record-Keeping and Currency and
    Foreign Transactions Reporting Act, 165
Flynn, Dan, 154, 155
Foley, Dermot G., 168
"following orders" defense, 91, 97–98, 99–100,
    102, 108, 110–12
Ford, Atlas A., 83
foreign claims, 35, 36–49
Foreign Claims Act, 35, 43, 47–48
Forrestal, James, 13
Fort Benning, Ga., 156–57
Fort Bliss "mutiny," 7
Fort Sam Houston race riot, 7
fragging, 67, 68, 78–83
Frankfurter, Felix, 6
Fraser, Donald, 48, 49
French, opium trade and, 118–19
French-Indochina War, 119, 142
French Union, 52

Garrison, Denzil D., 108
Garwood, Robert, 168–69
Geneva Convention, 90, 92, 170

George III (England), 1
Gilbert case, 190n40
Gim Po, 46
Golden Triangle, opium in, 120
Goldstein, Abraham S., 33
Gomsrud, Lowell R., 47–49
Green, Samuel G., Jr., 104, 105, 106, 107–8,
    109
Grenada, 179
Gulf War, 180
Gurney, Edward, 157

Ha Van An, 40
Haeberle, Ronald, 96
Hague Convention, 90, 92, 170
Haiti, 180–81
Halberstam, David, 22
Halderson, Clark, 27
hard narcotics. *See* heroin
Hargrove, John J., 107–8
Hatcher, Navarez, 156, 157, 158, 159
Haugney, Edward H., 58
Headquarters Support Activity, Saigon, 153
Headquarters, U.S. Army Ryukyu Islands
    (HQUSARI), 53
Heggie, Charles, 133–34
Hellmer, Werner, 169
Henderson, Oran K., 93, 94, 96, 102–3
Hendricks, Gary A., 80–81
Hendrix, Edward W., 113–14
Herbert, F. Edward, 97
heroin, 122, 123–24, 126 (table), 128 (table),
    130, 132, 136, 137
Herrod, Randell D., 104–9
Hersh, Seymour, 96
Heston, Russell, 153
Higdon, William, 156, 157, 158, 159
Ho Chi Minh, 119
Hodges, Kenneth, 98
Holladay, John L., 94
Homans, William P. Jr., 33
House, U.S.
  Armed Service Committee, 12, 13
  Committee on Government Operations,
    162
  Military Justice Act and, 19
Howard, Kenneth, 102
Hue, black market in, 141, 145
Hussein, Saddam, 183
Hutto, Charles, 97, 98

Huynh Thi Thi, 37–38
Hynyr, Jeffrey, 132, 133

IAC. *See* Irregular Activities Committee
illegal drugs. *See* drug use
Inchin Hia Lam, 87–88
International Criminal Court, 172, 184–85
Iran, 119
Iraq, 183
Irregular Activities Committee (IAC)
    U.S., 60, 72, 160–62, 164
    Vietnamese, 160, 164

Jag Journal, 13
Japan, 184
Jaso, John, 83
Jefferson, Thomas, 1, 2
Jevne, Franz P., 106, 107
Johnson, Harold, 156, 158
Johnson, Lyndon, 58
Jones, William K., 80
Judge Advocate General's Corps (army), 12,
    31
Judge Advocate General's Schools, 16, 180
judge advocates
    army, 4–5, 6–7, 10, 12, 31
    backgrounds of, 26
    duties of, 2, 3, 4, 6–7, 10, 12, 23, 24–26, 29,
        180–82
    living and working conditions of, 22–23,
        26–28
    navy, 4, 6, 9, 10, 11–12, 13
    number of, 28, 31
jurisdiction
    black market activities and, 145–46,
        150–51
    International Criminal Court and, 185
    Military Extraterritorial Jurisdiction Act,
        184
    Pentalateral Agreement and, 52–53, 55, 56,
        59
    South Vietnamese over Americans, 50–53,
        54–57, 59, 60–62, 125, 145–46, 150–51
    Uniform Code of Military Justice and, 50,
        53, 56, 57, 58–59, 60, 62–64, 65, 66,
        169–70, 174, 184, 193n1
    U.S. military, over civilians, 50, 51, 57, 58,
        59, 60–66, 135, 150–51, 174, 193n1
    U.S. military, over military personnel, 50,
        51, 54–55, 57, 169–70

U.S./South Vietnam agreement on, 50–53,
    55–56, 57
    See also status-of-forces agreements
Justice Department, U.S., 184

Kalven, Harry, 84
Kay, Richard B., 98, 99
Kennedy, Reid W., 98, 99, 100, 102
Kerekes, Gabriel, 146
Kerwin, Walter T., 30
Khmer Serai, 87
Korean War, 15–16, 58, 71, 144, 178, 190n40
Koster, Samuel W., 94, 95, 96
Krichten, Michael S., 104, 106, 107, 108
Kroll, Jerome, 85–86
Krueger, Ralph C., 111
Kruger, John, 111
Kull, David, 177
Kuntze, Archie, 153–54, 155

Lackland Air Force Base Air Force Chaplain's
    School, 16, 22
Laird, Melvin, 48
Laos, 119
Lasseter, Earle F., 175, 176
Latimer, George, 98, 99, 100, 101
Latney, James H., 63
Latney case, 63–64, 65
Law of Land Warfare, The, 90, 91, 92,
    111–12
Lawrence, Keith B., 108
laws of war, 90–92, 114–15, 172
Lawyers' Military Defense Committee
    (LMDC), 33–34, 83–84, 192n19
Lazar, Seymour, 156, 157, 158, 159
Le Eh, 40
LeGear, Daniel H., Jr., 106
Lewy, Guenter, 84, 85 (table), 86 (table)
Life (magazine), 96
Little Black Market, 140
LMDC (Lawyers' Military Defense Commit-
    tee), 33–34, 83–84, 192n19
Lodge, Henry Cabot, 57
Long Binh
    army at, 27, 122, 153, 158
    Pioneer House rehabilitation center, 127
Lowe, John, 168
Lowry Air Force Base, 131
Luper, Robert B., 96
Lurie, Jonathan, 2

MACV (Military Assistance Command, Vietnam), 54
  anti-drug efforts of, 122–23
  assistance-in-kind fund, 43–44
  civilian attorneys and, 33–34
  claims and, 25, 43–44
  courts-martial and, 55, 60–61, 62, 66, 153
  currency fraud and, 162–63
  jurisdiction and, 53, 54, 55, 56, 59, 60–61, 64, 66
  on military justice in combat, 173–74
  number of judge advocates and, 69
  U.S. advisers and, 21, 24
  on war crimes, 92, 96
MACV Staff Judge Advocate's Division, 24–26, 33–34, 44, 53, 55, 64
Magill, Edward, 97
Mai Ban, 39
Mansfield, John, 33
Manual for Courts-Martial, 6, 11, 69, 82, 90–91, 98, 175
Manual for Courts Martial, United States (1951), 14
Manufacturers Hanover Trust Company, 151–52
Mapp v. Ohio, 18
Maredem Company, 157–58
Marengo, Anthony, 113–14
marijuana, 122, 123–24, 126, 128, 130, 132
Marijuana and Drug Suppression Council, 129
Marine Corps, U.S., 9
  AWOLs, 72–73, 75
  black market case, 147–50
  combat refusals, 76–77
  crimes against Vietnamese and, 85 (table), 86 (table)
  drug use and, 124, 125 (table), 128 (table), 129 (table), 131–32
  fragging and, 79–82
  Garwood case and, 168–69
  lawyers, 17, 178–79
  prisoner of war murder case, 112–14
  Son Thang incident and, 103–9
Marine Corps units
  First Marine Division, 26, 80, 105, 106, 114, 131
  Third Marine Division, xii–xiii, 80, 131
  Fifth Marine Regiment, 112
  Seventh Marine Division, 103
  III Marine Amphibious Force (III MAF), 24, 26, 44–45

Marshall, Burke, 33
Mathews, James, 88
Matthews, Pat, 149
Maxwell Air Force Base, 16
Mayer, John William, 178
McCarthy, John J., Jr., 87–88
McGuire, Matthew F., 11–12
McGuire committee, 11–12
McInnis, Michael, 81–82, 83
McKnight, Robert W., 96
McNamara, Robert, 29
Medina, Ernest, 93, 99, 102
Meeker, Leonard, 61, 62
Mella, John, 153
Meo, 119
"mere gook rule," 112
Merrill, Michael P., 107
Military Assistance Command, Vietnam. *See* MACV
Military Civic Action Program, 35
Military Claims Act, 35
military codes, U.S., 1. *See also* Uniform Code of Military Justice
Military Extraterritorial Jurisdiction Act, 184
Military Justice Act (1968), 19, 20, 31, 32, 69
Military Justice Act (1983), 175
military justice system
  civilianization of, 5, 7–8, 13–15, 17–18, 174, 175, 177, 185
  compared to civilian systems, 2, 4–5, 7–8, 171
  Early Republic and, 1–2
  role of, xi, 1
  See also Uniform Code of Military Justice
Miller, Donald L., 84
Miller, Richard, 108
Miranda v. Arizona, 18
Mitchell, David, 97
Mitchell, Ernie, 132, 133
Mobley, Jack, 132, 133
Monroe, Jack P., 155
Moore, Keither, 81–82
Morgan, Edmund J., 13
Morrison, Donald W., 42
Morrison, James P., 157
Moynihan, Daniel P., 29
MPCs, 146, 147, 162–63, 165
murder, 5, 78–79, 81, 83, 84, 85 (table), 86 (table), 88
  fragging as, 67, 68, 78–83
  at My Lai, 92–103
  at Son Thang, 103–9

My Khe, 94
My Lai incident, 92–97
    trials, 98–103

Nasa, John L., 111
Nation (magazine), 112
National Committee for Citizens' Commis-
    sion of Inquiry on U.S. War Crimes in
    Vietnam, 110
National Liberation Front (NLF), 168
nation building efforts by U.S., 181, 183,
    186
    in Vietnam, ix–xi, 34, 51, 55, 121, 140–45,
        151, 166–67
Naughton, Thomas E., 163
Naval Investigation Service, 114
Naval Justice School, 16
Naval Reserve Law Program, 17
NAVFORV (United States Naval Forces, Re-
    public of Vietnam, 24, 26, 44–45, 130
Navy, U.S.
    AWOLs and, 72, 74
    black market activities and, 153–55
    Congress and, 3, 4, 9, 13
    courts-martial and, 9, 12, 53
    drug abuse and, 125 (table), 128 (table),
        129 (table), 130–31
    judge advocates and, 4, 6, 9, 10, 11–12, 13
    Law Centers, 32
    legal programs, 16–17
    regulations, 1–2, 3–4, 6
Nelson, Jay, 81
Nelson, John, 156, 157
New York Lawyers' Association, 13
Ngo Dinh Diem, 23
Ngo Dinh Nhu, 23
Nguyen Duc Bu, 61
Nguyen Lan, 40
Nguyen Tuy, 40
Nguyen Van Hoc, 112
Nguyen Van Hon, 47–49
Nha Trang, 38, 39, 133
Nhu, Ngo Dinh, 23
Nixon, Richard M., 101
nonjudicial punishment
    drug use and, 128, 130
    number of, 67, 70, 71
    project 100,000 and, 30
    purpose of, 17, 68, 175
    Uniform Code of Military Justice and, 17,
        30, 68, 70, 71, 128, 130, 175

North, Oliver, 108
Nuremberg Principles, 90, 98

O'Callahan v. Parker, 63, 66
Okinawa, 53
Olshin, Lewis R., 168
Olson, Curtis, 177
Operation Cherry, 87
Operation Freeze, 80
Operation Iraqi Freedom, 183, 184
Operation Just Cause, 179–80
Operation Lotus Blossom, 137
Operation Urgent Fury, 179
opium, 117–20, 130, 138
Osiel, Mark J., 91, 172

Padden, Theodore J., 114
Pakistan, 184
Palmer, Bruce, 31
Palmer, Harry, 108
Panama, 179–80
Parker, Robert H., 160–61
Parks, Hays, 149, 150, 171, 205n20
Parson, Nels, 96
Partin, John, 98, 99
Passantino, Franklin, 110
Pawlaczyk, George, 110
Peers, William, 95
Peers Report, 96, 102
Pennie, John, 70
Pentalateral Agreement, 52–53, 55, 56, 59
Personnel Claims Act, 41–42
Pham Long, 40
Phu Bai, 150
Pick, Francis, 147
Pick's Currency Yearbook, 147
Pioneer House rehabilitation center, 127
Pleiku, 42
    air base, 135, 136
Poolaw, Robert W., 112–14
prisoners of war, treatment of, 92, 112–13
Project 100,000, 29–30
Prugh, George S., 34, 173–74, 185
Prysumeen Account, 151–52, 159
Psychiatry, 85
Pugsley, James, 39–40
Pullen, Martin, 81–82
Pydasheff, Robert S., 171

Quang Tri, 32
Qui Nhon, 31, 41, 42

Raby, Kenneth Albert, 98
racial prejudice against Vietnamese, 84–86
racial tensions, 30–31, 83–84, 85–86, 87
Rahman, 151–52
R and R Supply Company, 159–60
rape, xiii, 5, 86 (table), 93–94
rehabilitation programs (drug user), 125–27, 128
Reichenberg, Norman, 97
Revolutionary War, U.S., 1
Ridenhour, Ronald L., 95
Roberts, Jay, 95
Robinson, George R., 97
Rogers, James, 153
Ross, Joseph, 154
Rosson, Loren H., Jr., 177
Rothblatt, Henry B., 102, 111, 112
"Rules for the Regulation of the Navy of the United Colonies of North America," 1–2
Russello, Mark, 132

Saigon
    black market in, 141, 145, 148–50
    Claims Division in, 36, 37
    foreign claims in, 41–42
    navy Law Center in, 32
    See also American Embassy, Saigon
Salerno, Lawrence, 132, 133
Sarl Electronics, 152
Saudi Arabia, 184
Schwarz, Michael A., 104, 105–7, 109
Seaman, Jonathan, 96
Senate, U.S.
    Armed Forces Committee, 12
    Committee on Government Operations, 146–47, 151, 152, 158, 160
    Military Justice Act (1968) and, 20
Sherman, Edward F., 20, 33
Sherman, William Tecumseh, 5
Simonaro, Anthony, 65, 135
Skiles, J. Len, 108
Smeriglio, John, 133–34
Smith, James J., 179–80
Smith, Lawrence, 133–34
Snee, Joseph M., 19
solatia payments, xi, 34, 35, 40, 44–46, 47–49
Soldiers (magazine), 92
Solf, Waldemar, 58, 84
Solis, Gary, 79, 85 (table), 169, 178–79
Son My, 93
Son Thang incident, 92, 103–9

South Korea, 184
South Vietnam. See South Vietnamese government; Vietnam
South Vietnamese government
    claims program of, 43, 49
    corruption in, x, 51, 123, 141–43, 144, 163, 164–65, 166
    currency fraud and black market activities and, 150–51, 162–65
    General Censorate, 163–64
    jurisdiction over Americans, 50–53, 54–57, 59, 60–62, 125, 145–46, 150–51
St. Amour, Paul, 107, 108
St. Martin, Clement, 158
Star Distributing Company, 152
Starr, Robert, 162
State Department, U.S.
    on black market, 145
    on corruption in military, 165
    on jurisdiction, 50, 55, 56, 57, 59–64, 185
status-of-forces agreements, 73, 184
    between U.S. and South Vietnam, 50–51, 52, 55–56, 57, 60
Sternberg, Ben, 54
Stimson, Henry L., 6
Stipe, Gene, 108
Suen, Jannie, 154, 155
Supreme Court, U.S., 175
Suter, William K., 171
Swann, Michael, 97
Switzer, Robert E., 169

Tan Son Nhut, 21, 22, 27, 47
Task Force Barker, 93, 94
Task Force on Military Justice (1972), 170
Tate, Richard L., 80
Tax Department Store, 36, 37, 47
Taylor, Vaughn, 168
Tectonics Asia Incorporated, 152
Teeter, Harold, 136–37
Tet Offensive, 47, 49
Theer, Richard E., 105–6, 107
Thich Quang Duc, 21
Thompson, Hugh, 94, 97
Thomsen, Tom, 111
Thorn, Robert, 81, 82
Thwing, James B., 175, 176
Time (magazine), 110
Torres, Sergeant, 77
Tow, Jerry E., 83
Tower, Philip C., 80

Trockman, Howard P., 107
Truman, Harry, 14, 15, 190n40
Turner, Carl, 156–57
Turner, Howard, 112

Uniform Code of Military Justice
    AWOL and desertion and, 73–75
    black market and currency fraud and,
        145–46, 150, 153, 204–5n13
    command influence and, 13–14
    complexity of, 18
    courts-martial and, 13–14, 18–19, 54, 59
    creation of, 13–14, 15
    international standards and, 172
    Iraq and, 183
    jurisdiction and, 50, 53, 56, 57, 58–59, 60,
        62–64, 65, 66, 169–70, 174, 184, 193n1
    Korean War and, 15–16
    murder and, 78, 79
    nonjudicial punishment and, 17, 30, 68, 70,
        71, 128, 130, 175
    on obeying orders, 91, 111–12
    reform efforts for, 18–20, 169–74, 175,
        176–78
    review system of, 15–16
    revisions, 16, 17
    revisions in 1968, 18–20, 31–32, 66, 115,
        175, 177
    right to counsel and, 14, 19–20, 32–33,
        68–69, 171, 176
    supporters of, 171, 178–79
    "time of war" clause, 58, 64, 173–74, 193n1
    war crimes and, 90, 92, 93, 110, 114–16, 169
Uniform Code of Military Justice Articles
    Article 2, 57, 58–59, 60, 63–64, 65, 66,
        193n1
    Article 15, 17, 68, 70–71, 130, 175, 177
    Article 31, 69, 171
    Article 32, 14, 28, 31, 32, 69, 70, 71, 96, 99,
        106, 108, 109, 114, 171, 176
    Article 37, 13–14
    Article 38, 33
    Article 43, 64, 193n1
    Article 80, 82
    Article 85, 73, 75, 193n1
    Article 86, 73, 74, 75
    Article 90, 82, 91, 193n1
    Article 91, 77
    Article 92, 74, 91
    Article 99, 77
    Article 101, 193n1

    Article 103, 43, 193n1
    Article 104, 168
    Article 105, 168, 193n1
    Article 106, 193n1
    Article 108, 204n13
    Article 109, 204n13
    Article 113, 193n1
    Article 118, 70, 79, 114
    Article 119, 79
    Article 123, 17, 204n13
    Article 133, 173
    Article 134, 65, 74, 79, 132, 135, 173,
        205n13
United Service Organization (USO),
    159–60
United States Army, Republic of Vietnam
    (USARV), 24, 26, 31, 70, 194n7
    Claims Division, 35–37, 41, 43, 44–45,
        47–48
United States Army Support Command, Viet-
    nam (USASCV), 54, 55
United States Naval Forces, Republic of Viet-
    nam (NAVFORV), 24, 26, 44–45, 130
University of Michigan Law School, 16
University of Virginia, 16
Upshur, Abel, 3
U.S. Agency for International Development
    (USAID), 141, 143 (table), 144–45, 160,
    163, 166
U.S. aid to Vietnam, 143–45, 166–67. See also
    nation building efforts by U.S.: in Viet-
    nam
USARV. See United States Army, Republic of
    Vietnam
U.S. Military Assistance Command, Vietnam.
    See MACV
U.S. Office of Strategic Services (OSS), 120
U.S. v. Anderson, 64
U.S. v. Averette, 64, 65, 135
Uzbekistan, 184

Vanderbilt, Arthur T., 11
Van Long, 39–40
Viet Cong, 168
Vietnam
    corruption in, x, 51–52, 120, 123, 141–43,
        144, 145, 163, 164–65, 166
    economy in, 140–45, 160–61
    justice system in, ix, 51, 57, 62, 123
    See also South Vietnamese government;
        Vietnamese civilians

Vietnamese civilians
  American crimes against, 84–87, 194n7
  See also My Lai incident; Son Thang incident
Vietnamese Directorate of Military Justice, 25
Vietnamese Joint General Staff, 56
Vietnam Veterans Against the War, 109–10

Walsted, David, 111
Walters, James, 151
Wander, Bill, 110
war crimes
  "following orders" defense and, 91, 97–98, 99–100, 102, 108, 110–12
  Middle East and, 180
  My Lai incident and, 92–103
  Son Thang incident and, 92, 103–9
  Uniform Code of Military Justice and, 90, 92, 93, 110, 114–16, 169
War Crimes Act (1996), 172
"War Crimes and Other Prohibited Acts" (MACV), 92
War Department, U.S., 12
  Advisory Committee on Military Justice, 11
Warnke, Paul, 61, 62
war on terror, 183
War Veterans' Bar Association, 13
Washington, George, 1, 2

Washington Daily News, 158
Watke, Frederic, 94
Watson, John, 132, 133
Webb, James H., Jr., 109
Westmoreland, William, 61, 95, 164, 167, 173–74
Widdecke, Charles, 109
Wilkerson, Charles, 110
Williams, Captain, 108
Williams, Frank, 112–14
Williams, Joseph, 76–77
Willingham, Thomas K., 94
Wilson, William, 95
Wiltse, Isaac, 40
Winter Soldier investigation, 109–10
Wolfe, Sergeant, 76, 77
Wondolowski, Peter, 82, 111
Wooldridge, William O., 156, 157, 158, 159, 166
World War I, 5, 6, 7
World War II, 10, 71, 142
World Wide Consultants, 152
Wright, Teresa J., 169

Yorck, David, 110
Young, George H., 94, 96

Zeissel, Hans, 84